A Documentary Study of Hendrik de Man, Socialist Critic of Marxism

A Documentary Study of Hendrik de Man, Socialist Critic of Marxism

Compiled, edited, and
largely translated
by Peter Dodge

PRINCETON UNIVERSITY PRESS
PRINCETON, NEW JERSEY

Contents

A Documentary Study
of Hendrik de Man,
Socialist Critic of Marxism

Introduction

In June 1973 an International Colloquium on the Works of Hendrik de Man, sponsored by the law faculty of the University of Geneva,[1] broke the conspiracy of silence that had surrounded this Belgian socialist heretic, a figure who since his break with orthodox Marxism during World War I had been subject to the reproach addressed in earlier days to the revisionist Bernstein: "Eduard, you're a fool! One does these things, but one does not say them!"[2] But in de Man's case doctrinal heresy went far beyond revisionism to a critique of the philosophical presuppositions that Marxism shared with the utilitarian tradition of social analysis as a whole; during the interwar period his efforts at ideological regeneration of the socialist movement lost in cogency with the growing threat of annihilation from the totalitarian Right; and in the end his entire credibility, his authority, was destroyed by his participation in the *Munichois* policy of King Leopold even after the occupation of Belgium in 1940. Earlier ostracism was now followed by exile and by moral obliteration, especially by those most sympathetic to his ideas and therefore most vulnerable to guilt by association. From being regarded as a figure comparable to Marx himself, he became a nonperson, as was most strikingly demonstrated at the colloquium itself, where despite sustained efforts it was possible to attract only one participant from Germany, the country in which he had made his intel-

---

[1] "Sur l'oeuvre d'Henri de Man," Rapports au Colloque international organisé par la Faculté de droit de l'Université de Genève, les 18, 19 et 20 juin 1974, sous la présidence du professeur Ivo Rens, *Revue européenne des sciences sociales et Cahiers Vilfredo Pareto* (listed by the Library of Congress as *Cahiers Vilfredo Pareto: Revue européenne des sciences sociales*), vol. 12, no. 31, 1974; and "Sur l'oeuvre d'Henri de Man," *Actes* du Colloque international . . . , 3 vols., Faculté de droit de l'Université de Genève, 1974.

[2] Henry de Man, *Psychology of Socialism*, London: Allen & Unwin, 1928, p. 165.

lectual home for many years and where also the ideological
issues that he had so brilliantly analyzed have now found a
de Manian solution without de Man.[3] A figure whose intellectual contribution certainly ranks him among the leading
theoreticians of the socialist movement, a pioneer
sociologist of labor and industry, in his personal biography
a valiant and tragic exemplar of the traumata of the West,
he has simply disappeared from the history books. In this
volume, we hope to correct this historical omission and,
what is even more urgent, to convince the reader of the
far-ranging significance of de Man's intellectual contributions to the understanding of our world today.

Born 1885 in Antwerp to a cultivated and prosperous
family of the Flemish bourgeoisie, Hendrik de Man was
brought up in the expectation of fulfilling his father's frustrated ambition of pursuing a military career in an elite
corps. A spartan regimen, an absolute rectitude, and an
unswerving devotion to duty were to be the characteristics
by which he came to be known in the sphere of activity in
which he chose to make his career, the burgeoning socialist
movement of industrial workers, which promised to overthrow the comfortable world of capitalist prosperity in
which he had been nurtured. Indeed Emile Vandervelde,
for many years leader of both the Belgian Labor party and
the Socialist International, once remarked that "socialism is
attached to de Man just as the tonsure is to a priest,"[4] and
as the man of the cloth experiences tension in reconciling
himself to the everyday world by which he is surrounded,
so de Man, pursuing his own vocation, experienced chagrin and disappointment in reconciling himself to the
world of utilitarian calculation, political maneuver, and
material self-seeking that he encountered during the

[3] An effort by the Friedrich-Ebert-Stiftung in November 1977 to organize a conference to consider de Man in the German context likewise had to
be canceled for lack of German participants.
[4] Henri de Man, *Après Coup: Mémoires*, Brussels-Paris: Toison d'Or,
1941, p. 309.

course of his career. "Rather Prussian, a bit *scharf* for our tastes,"[5] in another of Vandervelde's characterizations, de Man was either adored or detested by his associates, and from his uneasy relationship with the movement to which he devoted his life he derived a critical appreciation of both its glories and its deficiencies, expressed in a never ending series of newspaper articles, pamphlets, essays, and books.

Certainly the site of his birth carried other implications for his outlook. By heritage he was a polyglot internationalist, though with a firm and deep-rooted identification with the Flemings—in both their golden age of the fifteenth century and their mute and downtrodden condition at the turn of the twentieth century. At ease both in Flemish and in French, the language of cultivated discourse in his homeland, he was brought up in the expectation of using English and German as well, and in the course of his life he aquired sufficient mastery of these languages through residence abroad to write with nearly equal facility in all four. But it was not only his linguistic facility that distinguished his outlook but also an appreciation of the irrefragable significance of nationality, a stubborn and irreducible fact that ill accorded with the tenets of that Marxism to which he became an early convert. As a translator at innumerable trade-union and socialist congresses in his twenties, he was virtually unique among his compeers in his cosmopolitan background, and the depth of his international experience is revealed by his later remark that he had as many homelands as languages. The ability to participate fully in the life of a variety of cultures while preserving a unique personal autonomy, and the specific combination of a Continental passion for ideological ratiocination together with his own experience of the disparate social reality of Britain and America, contributed to the distinctive perspective that he was to express in his social and socialist theory.

[5] Emile Vandervelde et al., *Le Cinquentenaire du Parti Ouvrier Belge 1885-1935*, Brussels: L'Eglantine, 1936, p. 307.

His family background was important in yet another way, for de Man exemplified the bourgeois renegade, the Oedipal rebel, who triumphantly turned the moral weapons of the paternal oppressors against the older generation by demonstrating the bourgeois origins of the socialist critique of capitalist society. As a recruit to class-based socialism, as an idealistic intellectual, he was convinced of the necessity of taking into consideration not only the existing material interests of the proletariat but also the impetus from the cultural heritage of the past in order to explain the historical emergence of the socialist movement and enable it to maintain its mission of constructing a just society. Indeed, a principal thesis that he was to expound held that, while the conventional Marxist reliance on the pursuit of proletarian self-interest to bring about the revolution and a socialist society had made sense in the conditions of mid-nineteenth-century capitalism in which it had been developed, it was disastrously incomplete both in understanding the actual historical genesis of the socialist movement and in providing guidance in the unanticipated conditions of twentieth-century capitalism. Comparative analysis would, reveal that it was only the coincidence of social and economic stratification that had made interpretation in terms of historical materialism plausible, and in fact behind the façade of the class struggle for interests was the assertion of man's human dignity, a moral demand that was the precipitate of Western history that perhaps reached its fullest expression in the bourgeois humanism of the thirteenth century. Viewed from this angle, the participation of disaffected elements from the bourgeoisie in the workers' socialist movement was to be regarded not so much as an inconvenient and mildly embarrassing appendage to an otherwise unambiguous providential instrument of history but rather as a component integral to the preservation of the potential historical mission of a class-bound movement. Moreover, this transcendence of class interests was indispensable in the contemporary world since the structure of capitalism was, contrary to expectations, not bringing about a numerical preponderance of the proletariat, and, furthermore, the implementation of a socialist society would require far, far more than the workers' conquest of power and the dislodgment of the old order. Thus the participation of extraproletarian elements in the past, present, and future of the socialist movement was, in de Man's eyes, to be exalted rather than minimized.

But the discovery of these ideological ramifications was delayed for many years, since de Man at first exhibited a convert's zeal by immolating himself in the workers' cause. His initial reaction to awareness of social injustice was to embrace philosophical anarchism, a doctrine that in its intransigence and its distrust for authority was particularly suited to a young rebel and a citizen of Belgium, with its memories of centuries of oppression by foreign-dominated government and with its primordial linguistic communities. In fact, however, it was sympathetic participation in a strike of the Antwerp dockworkers—a strike that began in economic grievances, but was converted by the Belgian Labor party into a general strike aimed at abolishing the plural vote—that led de Man to become a member of the party's Socialist Young Guard on May Day, 1902. But with regard to the issue of political action he repudiated those who, like Alexandre Millerand in France or the Bavarian wing of the German Social Democratic party, showed by their accession to office or by their support of a governmental budget their implicit legitimization of the bourgeois state; his viewpoint was rather represented by Wilhelm Liebknecht's *Kein Kompromiss, kein Wahlbündnis*,[6] in which electoral politics was recommended only to the extent that it contributed to raising the class consciousness of the proletariat. He now gave his unreserved allegiance to this radical Marxism, which by its disabused political insight, scientific plausibility, and historical inevitability legitimated his own repudiation of the bourgeois world.

[6] Berlin: Vorwärts, 1899.

His dedication to this cause and his rapid rise to a position of leadership of the Antwerp Young Guards whereby he edited the Flemish monthly youth organ, served on the Antwerp council of the socialist organizations, was a representative of the Flemish movement to the national youth organization, and contributed to the dissemination of antimilitarist tracts, which led to brushes with the law, were of course hardly applauded by his family, and it was agreed not to talk about the abrasive subject of politics at home. To his family's horror his studies, first at the University of Brussels, subsequently at the Polytechnical Institute in Ghent, suffered as a consequence of his political engagement, and when he was sacked from Ghent for participation in a demonstration occasioned by the news of "Bloody Sunday" in St. Petersburg in January 1905, it was with mutual relief that it was agreed he should depart to Leipzig, the Mecca of radical Marxism, to make his own way in the world.

The years that followed were of decisive importance in consolidating the intellectual basis with which de Man was to make his reputation. In the first place, he managed to secure a position on the leading organ of the radical left of the Social Democratic party, the *Leipziger Volkszeitung*. Not only did this position allow him to maintain a precarious existence, it catapulted him into full participation in the vigorous battles waged against revisionism, and acquainted him with luminaries of the international socialist world, such as Karl Kautsky, Rosa Luxemburg, Franz Mehring, Karl Liebknecht (with whom he collaborated in founding the Socialist Youth International), and even Trotsky. But at the same time he came to the realization that a university education could be highly relevant to a revolutionary socialist, and he was fortunate enough to study under leading German academics at the University of Leipzig, including the psychologist Wilhelm Wundt, the cultural historian Karl Lamprecht, and the economic historian Karl Bücher. He wrote his dissertation on the "Cloth Industry of Ghent in the Middle Ages," presenting a Marxist analysis that formally contradicted the schema of economic development by which Bücher had made his professional reputation—nevertheless de Man was recommended for graduation *summa cum laude*.

Following this success he spent the better part of a year in England, living a hand-to-mouth existence as a translator and occasional correspondent for the German socialist press. He had the chance to become personally acquainted with the operation of a distinctive political system, and despite his deep-set reservations he could not help but be impressed with certain aspects of the operation of bourgeois democracy. His sojourn abroad was ended in 1910 by an invitation from the rising Belgian socialist leader Emile Vandervelde to head the newly created Centrale d'Education Ouvrière, which had just been set up to provide training for the administration of the intricate and growing socialist conglomerate of mutual insurance societies, cooperatives, and trade unions that formed a counterpart to the political movement. During the next four years he threw himself into the work of the Belgian Labor party not only by providing vigorous leadership in the training of socialist cadres, but also by collaborating with the Walloon Louis de Brouckère in an attempt to win the party over to a radical-Marxist position, particularly to repudiate its current policy of electoral cooperation with the Liberals against the Catholic party. In this attempt and in his approach to his pupils as well, his effort was to keep the party and its class from the mere pursuit of interests, to transmute everyday activities into the fulfillment of the historical destiny that fell to the socialist workers' movement. Although he managed to stir up as much opposition as support, and the party remained true to its alliance with the Liberals, there certainly was momentum in the direction of a radicalization of policy, and it seemed only a matter of time, organization, and effort to bring about the Day of Revolution.

All these certainties of outlook were drastically and forever changed by the outbreak of World War I. As a convinced internationalist with years of experience in Germany, as a socialist armed with the interpretation of war as a matter of capitalistic rivalries, and as a militant who in the role of interpreter accompanied Hermann Müller and Camille Huysmans in their ill-fated mission to Paris in behalf of the Second International, de Man was overwhelmingly committed to the socialist repudiation of war; yet war came nevertheless, and to Belgium as the hapless victim of unprovoked aggression on the part of a militaristic and autocratic government. Under these bewildering circumstances he found himself a volunteer in the Belgian army, one who participated fully in the horrors of trench warfare as a common soldier and soon, as an officer, commanding a battery of mortars. But it was agonizing for him to rationalize the carnage in which he took part, especially in view of his knowledge of the humanity of those on the other side, and it required a severe reexamination of the ideological presuppositions in terms of which he had hitherto constructed his behavior. First of all, in explicit opposition to the thesis enunciated at Zimmerwald by the socialists of the neutral nations and to the position he had vigorously espoused in former days, he now came to insist upon the crucial significance of the existence of political democracy to the socialist. Without democracy, it was possible for autocratic and ruthless governments effectively to suppress and cow a strong socialist movement, as the example of the Central Powers showed; with political democracy, despite its manifold imperfections, the ultimate victory of socialism was ineluctable. Of course this argument was embarrassed by the presence of autocratic Russia on the Allied side, a fact that made the February Revolution of 1917 all the more welcome, as did Wilson's Fourteen Points; doubts as to the rightness of his course of action and the terrible sacrifice of a generation were now set at rest. As it happened, he was sent along with Vandervelde and de Brouckère on an official mission to the Kerensky government with the aim of persuading the Russians to keep in the war, and this experience was of profound significance for his ideological development. As a Belgian combatant he opposed Bolshevik "revolutionary defeatism," and his experience of the chaos of Russia and of the ruthlessness of its politics permanently disabused him of any enthusiasm for the Communist model. Directly after his Russian experience he was sent by the Belgian government to the United States for some six months, an experience that was to have an equally marked impression on him. For if the United States was disappointing to a socialist because it lacked any significant socialist movement, the reason for this anomaly was important: America's realization of social as well as political democracy. The virtual absence of class consciousness in this bastion of capitalism threw the greatest doubt on the adequacy of Marxist interpretation, although of course it was possible to argue the exceptional circumstances, and therefore the temporary nature, of the American phenomenon.

Participation in the war, then, together with the contrasting examples of Russia and the United States, drove de Man to an appreciation of both the instrumental and the integral significance of democratic organization for the attainment of socialism and cast doubt upon the cogency of his Marxist ideology. Indeed, in his reaction to Versailles, a cruel mockery of Wilsonian idealism, he invested his hopes now in the New World with which he had become familiar—but the postwar America of "normalcy," with Palmer raids, isolationist withdrawal, and political reaction proved most disappointing. He himself was the object of attack at the University of Washington, where he had been offered a position in social psychology, for his participation in the political campaign against the "Lumber Trust" and for his association of some months with the Wobblies—the Industrial Workers of the World—on an island in Puget Sound. He was glad to return to Belgium in the fall of 1920 to take up a new position as head of an Ecole Ouvrière Supérieure that was designed to prepare a workers' elite for the implementation of industrial democracy. But the Belgian Labor party was still supportive of the *revanchiste* policy of France's Poincaré, and after a series of incidents in which he felt he could not remain silent despite the party position, he once again left his native land for the Germany against which he had fought for so many years.

The next decade in de Man's life was the most fruitful, establishing him as a figure of international import in socialist and intellectual circles with the publication in 1926 of his full-scale critique of Marxism, the *Psychology of Socialism*.[7] At first he remained involved in workers' education, teaching at the Frankfurt Labor College, but in 1929 he was appointed to a newly created chair in social psychology at the University of Frankfurt. In addition to a countless series of articles and brochures he published during this period two other major studies, *Joy in Work*[8] in 1927, a pioneer study in industrial sociology, and, in early 1933, a long volume designed to be the positive statement of an ideological alternative to Marxism, *Die sozialistische Idee*.[9]

The basic problem with which he struggled was to understand the reasons, and therefore the cure, for the debacle of the socialist movement, equally visible in reformist accommodation to a decadent capitalist system in the West and in the triumph of a decadent revolutionary socialism in the Soviet Union. In both cases, he argued, a decisive portion of the blame must be assigned to the Marxist ideology by which the movements had been guided. Operating in terms of a nineteenth-century model of social reality and human behavior, this ideology had supposed that the utilitarian analysis of classical economics would suffice to

[7] London: Allen & Unwin, 1928; first published as *Zur Psychologie des Sozialismus*, Jena: Diederichs, 1926.

[8] London: Allen & Unwin, 1929; first published as *Der Kampf um die Arbeitsfreude*, Jena: Diederichs, 1927.

[9] Jena: Diederichs, 1933; the book was never translated into English.

explain the ineluctable evolution of capitalism and to guide
the postrevolutionary jump into freedom. But in fact history had its own cunning, and the evolution of capitalism
had proceeded in terms unforeseen by Marx, notably in
the failure of the proletariat to become an overwhelming
numerical mass of the population—a fact that cast into
doubt his assumption of the democratic nature of a socialist
revolution. Moreover, generalizing to the nature of human
action from essentially the European experience, Marx
had attributed class consciousness to the distribution of
economic variables. In fact, its virtual absence in the
American case demonstrated that class consciousness was
rather the consequence of the distribution of social variables, namely, the system of invidious distinction based on
ownership which had luxuriated in the European capitalism that had been superimposed on the historical estate
society. Thereby the dignity of the individual, sanctified by
both the religious and the secular traditions of the West,
was attainted, and it was thus the experience of social injustice, not the fact of economic deprivation itself, that had
led the European proletariat to exhibit the behavior that
Marx had attributed solely to the pursuit of interests. En-
couragement of the pursuit of interests would be fatal to
the vitality of the socialist movement above all because it
was evident that capitalism could supply the material needs
of the proletariat; thus it was the success rather than the
failure of capitalism that de Man most feared, for it sapped
the movement through the embourgeoisement of the proletariat, through covert reformist accommodation to the
existing order, which was only veiled by revolutionary
rhetoric.

As for the responsibility of Marxist doctrine for the im-
broglio in Russia, de Man was less explicit, largely because
he was primarily concerned with galvanizing the Western
socialist parties and felt that the Communist model was an
unlikely candidate for Western imitation. Of course the
backward and autocratic historical heritage of Russia had

set the stage for the disasters that beset that unhappy land. But even in the case of Western countries de Man was distrustful of simplistic formulas for socialization of the means of production; nationalization without the imposition of effective, local workers' control meant bureaucratization. And effective workers' control required the participation of an alert, educated, and responsible proletariat in the determination of policy. Thus the Marxist presupposition that the implementation of socialism was guaranteed by the proletarian conquest of power was most doubtful, and its insistence upon defining socialism in essentially economic terms had in fact sanctified the erection of the brutal Soviet tyranny.

Living in Weimar Germany, de Man was witness to the Nazi seizure of power. One reason that *Die sozialistische Idee* did not match the *Psychology of Socialism* in its impact on the intellectual world was that it was seized upon publication and received (an indifferent) Frénch translation only in 1935; further, the coming of the depression and the threat from the totalitarian Right created a new political atmosphere in which niceties of ideological justification appeared trivial compared to the question of which side one was on. In fact, however, the *Plan du Travail*[10] drawn up by de Man and enthusiastically adopted as a program by the Belgian Labor party at Christmas 1933 was in large part a pragmatic application of the ideological reformulation with which he had been concerned. Distinguishing his *Plan* from the conventional minimal-maximalist programmatic distinction practiced by socialists was the conception that it was indispensable to realize a complex of "structural" reforms of the economy immediately if the system as a whole was not to collapse under the impact of the depression; moreover, such a program offered the political possibility

[10] Henri de Man, rapporteur, *Le Plan du Travail*, Forty-eighth Congress of the Belgian Labor Party, Brussels, 24 and 25 December 1933; Brussels: Lucifer, 1933.

of rallying the immense majority of the population, equally the victims of monopoly capitalism. In fact the *Plan* served to revive the élan of the Labor party, of which de Man had become a leader rivaling the aging Vandervelde, and when in 1935 opportunity was offered to enter into a tripartite Government of National Renovation, which promised to reverse the disastrous deflationary policies of the previous administrations, the *Plan* was essentially sacrificed. De Man became, first, minister of public works, and then in succeeding governments during the next three years, minister of finances.

His official experience was significant for the development of his ideological outlook, for it confirmed the intense distaste that he had always exhibited for the give-and-take of political life. By temperament utterly devoted to his cause, he was intolerant of the professional politicians of any party, most of all his own, and saw in opposition to his programs only the machinations of the capitalist opponent. While the program of public works and other efforts of the successive governments were moderately successful in reducing the rate of unemployment, he felt increasingly frustrated by the reluctance of these governments to undertake structural reforms and by the financial community's extraparliamentary opposition to his policies. In the apocalyptic atmosphere of the late thirties he felt, generalizing from his own experiences, that perhaps the last opportunity for the realization of socialism was being foreclosed by capitalist manipulation of the parliamentary process, and that, hence, the operation of bourgeois democracy might now impede rather than make possible the coming of socialism. On the basis of these convictions he called for a fundamental constitutional revision that would strengthen the stability and power of the executive and give legitimate representation to various interests through the organization of a corporatist economic council.

At the same time the late thirties revived another major

and fateful issue for de Man, that of the legitimacy of warfare in an age of mass destruction. Just as he had been a
bitter-ender in World War I in order to validate his emergent faith that it was only through the victorious prosecu-
tion of the war that socialism might be attained, so now
with a pacifist commitment refired by the disastrous outcome of that conflict, he remained true to a policy of appeasement even after Munich. And this decision was to
have fearful political consequences, since he had become
titular leader of the Labor party and also remained the
only important Belgian political leader to support Leopold
II in his decision to surrender to the invading German
army. With characteristic candor and fervor he now issued
a "Manifesto"[11] in which he celebrated the cessation of the
parliamentary regime of the capitalist plutocracy and
looked forward to the achievement of socialism within a
newly united Europe. In articles in a revamped socialist
newspaper and in other publications for some months he
preached the same message, but a series of incidents demonstrated the impossibility of carrying through an autonomous policy, above all after the invasion of Russia. In November 1941 de Man effectively retired from public life
and left Belgium to lead a solitary existence in an Alpine
hut on Mont Blanc, where he devoted himself to reflection
and to writing. At the end of the war he managed to escape
to Switzerland, from where he was soon to hear of his conviction in absentia for treason by a Belgian military court,
an act that added humiliation and bitterness to the last
years of exile. Nevertheless his fulfillment in a new mar-
riage, the reworking of his autobiography, the writing of a
volume of somber reflections on the future of the world
bore witness to the continued vitality of this extraordinary
figure. In the end, he concluded that the socialist movement unavoidably participated in the decadence of the
capitalist world order, and that the best the responsible individual could do was to cultivate his own garden in the

[11] "Manifeste aux membres du P.O.B.," *Gazette de Charleroi*, 3 July 1940.

hope that something of the patrimony of the ages would be thus preserved.

De Man died in an automobile accident in 1953.

No treatment, however cursory, of this rich and variegated life can avoid the question of the extent to which the ideological innovations with which de Man was associated had in fact led to his last-minute attempt to construe Nazism in the image of socialism.[12] His ideological opponents, above all the unreconstructed Marxists, have tended to argue that his actions demonstrated the untenability of "voluntaristic socialism"; and, leaving aside the embarrassing Communist justification of the Nazi-Soviet Pact in Marxist terms, certainly it is true that the many socialists who resisted de Man's ideological innovations experienced little ambivalence in opposing Hitler. There undoubtedly were certain aspects of de Man's ideology that permitted him to rationalize a reconciliation with Nazi doctrine. In the first place, his attempts to broaden the class basis of socialism, to reach out to those outside the proletariat and to transmute the class struggle into something more than a competitive struggle for interests, certainly gave him a stand to appreciate the idea of the Volksgemeinschaft that was prohibited to his more orthodox socialist colleagues. Second, his denigration of procedural democracy, logically compatible with though not demanded by the tenets of a Marxist outlook, was of course a prominent theme in Nazi propaganda. Thirdly, there gradually emerged in de Man's thought an elitist emphasis that contrasted sharply with the more prosaic politicalism of others. In his search for means to overcome the contamination of the bourgeois world, he turned at first to an idealized proletariat, but his experience in workers' education provided him with an unsurpassed realistic if sympathetic knowledge of the lim-

[12] For a fuller treatment of this issue, see my "Voluntaristic Socialism: An Examination of the Implications of Hendrik de Man's Ideology," *International Review of Social History*, vol. 3, part 3, 1958, pp. 385-417.

ited mentality of the proletariat; alarmed by its embourgeoisement, he then turned to the presence of disinterested intellectuals as the saving grace within the party.
Although he explicitly repudiated a superior role for intellectuals within the movement,[13] as in the concluding passage of chapter 7 below, he believed political leaders
should take an active, creative role,[14] and it is not without
significance that he characterized himself as sharing the attitude toward the masses of Shakespeare's Coriolanus: "I
had rather be their servant in my way than sway with them
in theirs."[15] Yet another strand of ideological development
that is suggestive is the parallelism between his own call for
the recognition of authority, nationality, and order and
that of certain of the French neosocialists, most notably
Marcel Déat, who in fact became a notorious collaborator.

But it should be emphasized that there was, so to speak, a
conspiracy of historical circumstances that drove de Man in
the direction of what can perhaps best be described as an
uneasy acceptance of the fact of Nazi hegemony, and that
others subscribing to his ideology, such as the Belgian
équipe planiste, not burdened with the personal dilemmas
that we have described, utterly repudiated the policy he
chose in those days. Moreover, despite his provocative borrowing from a fascist vocabulary, in fact the governmental
reorganization that he urged in the late thirties was largely
modeled after the successful democratic examples of the
Anglo-American world. His glee at the collapse of the old
order soon changed into a policy of trying to make the best
of a bad job, an attempt that proved hopeless. His fateful,
disastrous decision to essay a policy of neutralism was in
fact the product of the personal experiences that had
driven him to construct his ideological innovations, rather
than being the logical consequence of the latter. Rather

[13] See his *Intellectuelen en het Socialisme*, Brussels: De Wilde Roos, n.d.
[1926].
[14] See his *Massen und Führer*, Potsdam: Alfred Protte, 1932.
[15] Henri de Man, *Cavalier seul*, Geneva: Cheval Ailé, 1948, p. 298;
"Coriolanus," II, i, 200-201.

paradoxically, we can say that the same ascetic intensity of moral convictions that brought de Man to the personal and ideological dilemmas we have indicated also brought him to the formulation of an ideological system whose most general import can perhaps be best suggested by saying that it explores the implications of the collapse of the Left's chiliastic expectations that a socialist society would come about as a corollary to the political triumph of the proletariat. We are left with an instrument that by its recognition of extraeconomic dimensions in the analysis of human action permits the adequate guidance of a socialist movement within the rules of the game of a pluralistic society— an ideology that legitimizes precisely the give-and-take of legislative politics that its author found intolerable, and which also furnishes a logically based criterion for the rejection of totalitarianisms of both Right and Left.

The implication of these conclusions is that de Man's writings are by no means of historical interest only and that it is desirable to rescue his consideration as a social thinker from the folly of the war years.[16] The continued fascination of dissident Western intellectuals with the beguiling certainties of an attenuated Marxism underscores the importance of one who, largely accepting the Marxist analysis of the operation of capitalist society, nevertheless called attention to the grave limitations of its nineteenth-century mode of analysis. And the positive implications of his voluntaristic mode of analysis are equally far-reaching, furnishing grounds for understanding the limited efficacy of that erstwhile panacea of socialism, the nationalization of the means of production; the extension of the meaning of socialism from the economic realm to an all-pervasive cultural transformation; the implementation of socialism as an immediate if partial accomplishment even within the capitalist order; and, as we have noted, the repudiation of

[16] For a fuller treatment of this issue, see my "Ideological Preconceptions and Sociology: Reflections on the Contemporary Significance of Hendrik de Man," *Sociologia Internationalis*, vol. 12, no. 1/2, 1974, pp. 5-23.

totalitarianism whatever the name in which it may speak.
De Man's observations on the class order of capitalist society, on the difficulties of establishing effective industrial
democracy, on the nature of industrial society, anticipated
conclusions that others, decades afterward, have painfully
won and triumphantly proclaimed.[17] In terms of the inherent significance of his ideas, he deserves to regain the
outstanding place in social thought he once held. It is
hoped that this volume will allow the reader to judge the
soundness of these observations.

In making the selection from the seventeen books, forty-
odd brochures, and some four hundred articles that comprise the works of Hendrik de Man, two criteria have
been foremost. The first has been to choose passages of
central and continued significance for the analysis of social
phenomena. Both as socialist and sociologist, de Man had
much to say of relevance to the world of today, with regard
not only to the philosophical issues that have just been
treated but also to their implications for application to the
institutions of the industrial order. Thus in a bureaucratized world uneasily Communist or capitalist, his
analysis of the problematics of socialization has a profound
and disturbing salience, and his insistence upon the extraeconomic dimensions of institutional reform has a relevance that is more obvious in the world of high gross national product than at the time of writing. The second
major criterion of selection has been to permit the reader
to understand the circumstances, both historical and, to a
lesser degree, personal, that led de Man to develop his
ideas and to pursue his rather spectacular career. To aid

[17] See, e.g., Anthony Giddens, whose *Class Structure of the Advanced
Societies* (New York: Barnes & Noble, 1973) extracts from a sophisticated
analysis of divergent conceptualizations of social class the conclusion that
there may be inexpugnable differences among societies in similar stages of
economic development. In another context, note the growing acknowledgment in the practice (if only sporadically in the ideology) of socialist
parties of the irrelevance of nationalization to the problems of equality
and self-determination within industrial society.

the reader's understanding, each selection has been introduced by passages that serve to identify its significance in
terms of his life and his contribution to social analysis. The
intention has been thereby to construct a volume that can
be understood in terms of its content alone—but at the
same time, it is to be hoped that the reader will be led to
make further investigations, both of the works of de Man
himself and of commentary upon his lifework. To this end
a selective bibliography is provided of both primary and
secondary material.

It should be noted that certain passages in the headnotes
below have appeared in my biographical study, *Beyond
Marxism: The Faith and Works of Hendrik de Man* (The
Hague: Nijhoff, 1966), and in "Le socialisme: du mouvement social au groupement d'intérêt," *Revue européenne des
sciences sociales et Cahiers Vilfredo Pareto*, vol. 12, no. 31,
1974, pp. 63-74.

All citations are to works by de Man, and all notes are by
the editor, unless otherwise specified. Similarly, the editor
is responsible for the translation of all the selections but
three. In the two cases where previous translations have
been used, the texts have been Americanized in spelling
and annotation has been provided. The last chapter gives
the reader an opportunity to read de Man's own English.

It is a pleasure to acknowledge the generosity of Jan de
Man and Elisa Lecocq-de Man, who have permitted me to
reproduce the texts below; as well as the willing aid of
Michel Brélaz of Geneva, secretary-general of the Association for the Study of the Works of Hendrik de Man;
Robert Abs, librarian of the Institut Emile Vandervelde of
Brussels; Frits de Jong, director of the International Institute of Social History of Amsterdam; Nathanael Greene of
Wesleyan University, who provided a thoughtful critique
to my efforts; the Central University Research Fund as well
as the library of the University of New Hampshire; and
Louis Hudon, Grover Marshall, and Marron Fort at the
same institution, whom I badgered about fine points of
translation. I have endeavored to rise above the compelling

rhythms of the original texts in putting them into English, but have not had the flexibility that de Man himself enjoyed in freely rewriting his own works in accordance with the stylistic demands implicit in each of the four languages he commanded. Hence for a work of scholarship, fidelity to the original text won over felicity of expression when imagination failed—but I trust that the contest is only occasionally visible, and that the result in general is worthy of the original author, whose mastery of expression as a scholar and as a polemicist is evident in whatever language he wrote.

University of New Hampshire
October 1978

1

The Era of Democracy

In 1907, a twenty-two-year-old postulant at the Mecca of radical Marxism in Leipzig, where he contributed to the *Leipziger Volkszeitung* and attended the university as a doctoral student, de Man still maintained his contacts with the Flemish socialist youth organization in which he had already played a significant role. The pamphlet excerpted below, a fuller version of talks that he had recently given back in Flanders, is illustrative of his pre-World War I, unreconstructed faith. A number of issues that were to play a crucial role both in the history of the socialist movement in the decades to come, and in his own later efforts to reconstitute the ideological basis of the movement, are evident in its pages. Here, however, their resolution is unself-consciously within the orthodox Marxist tradition, although with hindsight it is now possible to detect foreshadowings of the ideological innovations that de Man was to develop.

Perhaps the most fundamental issue is that of man's "voluntaristic" response to his historical circumstances; in the present text the moral and explanatory basis for the struggle of the proletariat is assumed to be self-evident from the fact of capitalist exploitation. The pursuit of interests then is identical with the struggle for self-preservation and calls for as little justification; the only problem is to direct the energies of this struggle in the historically effective, organized form of the class-conscious socialist movement. A second theme, in later works to receive far-ranging elaboration, concerns the appropriate deployment of forces until the day of revolution has arrived; here the question is disposed of through the implicit assumptions that (a) that day is not far off; (b) class struggle will have as its most notable effect the growing consciousness on the part of the proletariat of its class-bound, underdog position; and (c) nevertheless there are at least some short-term gains to be wrested from the enemy.

Third, while the bulk of the pamphlet is directed at a knowledgeable analysis of the balance of political forces within particular countries—an analysis that we have not reproduced, in line with de Man's acknowledgment that the details were only of transitory significance—the underlying assumption is that ultimately the power and numbers of the proletariat will be sufficient to bring about the conquest of power on a mass-democratic basis through exploiting the political and legal rights of the bourgeois order. Last, however—and this is the polemical basis for the whole pamphlet—the proletariat is not to be taken in by the snares of formal, bourgeois democracy, which can and will serve as a buttress and disguise for the interests of the bourgeoisie threatened by the rising proletariat rather than as an open road to the realization of socialism.

While the author makes no pretense of originality—in the preface to the pamphlet he refers the interested reader to Karl Kautsky and Anton Pannekoek for further guidance[1]—in a sense that is the point of its inclusion here, to form the baseline for the later ideological developments with which de Man is identified. Nevertheless even in this early work it is possible to note beyond the clichés of orthodox Marxism the vigor and knowledge the author brings to his analysis, the assurance and deftness of his capacity to pamphleteer, and at the same time his ability to bring an intellectual's familiarity with the European cultural heritage to bear on mundane questions of political tactics. These same qualities were to serve him well in his

---

[1] Kautsky, 1854-1938, the mentor of (German) social democracy, with whom de Man was later to break decisively; Pannekoek, 1873-1960, Dutch astronomer and socialist theoretician (dates supplied by the International Institute of Social History in Amsterdam); at this point both leaders in radical-Marxist rejection of the revisionism associated particularly with Eduard Bernstein's *Evolutionary Socialism*, first published in 1899.

later, heterodox, and original work of ideological reformulation.

HET TIJDVAK DER DEMOKRATIE[2]

The [1905] revolution in Russia with its immediate goal of a democratization of the state, the introduction of universal suffrage in Austria and Hungary, the overthrow of the Conservative government in England, the spreading and flowering of radical democracy in France, the progress of the "liberal" parties during the last Reichstag election in Germany, the fall of the Kuyper government in the Netherlands, the revival of a "democratized" liberalism in Belgium—these are the essential events in the history of the last few years that have originated and confirmed the belief of many socialists in the onset of an era of democracy in Europe, from which socialism should gradually but directly emerge. Indeed, the catchword "democracy" has become so accepted in the Belgian socialist press that day after day it is used as inseparable from, even synonymous with, socialism. However, what is meant by the term "democracy" is usually not easy to discern. To the remark of the apprentice in Goethe's *Faust*:

> But an idea is bound to the word,

Mephistopheles replies:

> Quite so! Only one shouldn't be too troubled,
> For precisely where ideas fall short,
> A word can be readily supplied.
> Using words, it is easy to dispute,
> Using words, it is easy to build up theories,
> Using words, it is easy to believe . . .

Nowadays there are indeed few words used with better effect to disguise their lack of a determinate and clear

[2] Ghent: Germinal, 1907, pp. 11-19, 86-88.

meaning than "democracy." The French political economist Le Play[3] once said: "What one strives in vain to attain
through an ever so skillful association of clearly defined
words is rendered easy with unclear expressions which, according to the outlook of those who read and understand
them, can be used in the most different, even contradictory, senses. Many words lend themselves to such use at
present, but four are particularly prone to cover up
thought: the words freedom, progress, equality, and democracy." In his frankness, the good Le Play seems not to
have noticed that these are precisely the chosen catchwords
of bourgeois democracy, the pillars of liberal ideology. All
too often the word "democracy" is uncritically taken from
the conceptual arsenal of this liberal ideology to add to our
own supply, which however has enough intellectual
weaponry not to have need of enriching itself by the acquisition of wooden swords.

Democracy as a Goal and as a Movement

But what does this word "democracy" mean?
   In the many cases where use hides a lack of a clear conceptualization, it, of course, means nothing at all.
   But insofar as there is actually a meaning, in general this
can be regarded from two points of view: as absolute and
relative, or, if one wishes, as a goal and as a movement.
   From its Greek origin, it means the same as rule of the
people. The absolute meaning then appears as a constitutional or governmental form on the basis of the realization
of political rule by free and equal citizens, in opposition to
the forms (autocracy, aristocracy, plutocracy, oligarchy,
etc.) in which this rule is exercised only by one or a few individuals. When one thinks through to the ultimate logical
implications of this "democratic principle," one can outline
with considerable assurance the political institutions that
are appropriate to democracy as a goal: a republic (swept

[3] 1806-1882.

clean from the residues of a monarchical system) with universal and equal suffrage and the utmost practicable direct legislation, with guarantees of the freedom of the individual, of thought and of publication, of assembly and of association, independent of all religious bodies, with universal and equal obligations to the military, like eligibility and accountability of all government officials, including the judiciary. There can be dispute about details, but there is no doubt that these are the general features of ideal democracy, those that are summed up under the rubric of political reforms in the Erfurt Program[4] and (although not so clearly, succinctly, or precisely) in the Program of the Belgian Labor party.[5] Social policy (labor legislation, welfare policy, etc.), as well as taxation policy, are not here treated, since in general they will be determined by economic considerations that are in themselves entirely independent of the form of government.

So much for the sketching of democracy as a goal. That in this respect it is bound up with the goal of social democracy necessarily and in the closest way as the only possible form of government for a socialist society needs no further emphasis. If, on the basis of analysis of the term "social democracy," one wishes to speak of a political and an economic principle in socialism, then one can say that the political principle is none other than democracy as a goal. But we shall later demonstrate that the realization of a fully democratic form of government is unthinkable without the realization of integral socialism.

Nevertheless, this democracy is in its nature not at all socialistic. Completely aside from the great role that democratic forms of government and ideals played in antiquity, it was not the proletariat that was the first to have made a democratic political order as its political ideal.

The bourgeoisie had done that long before.

[4] Adopted by the German Social Democratic party in 1891.
[5] The *Déclaration de Quaregnon* of 1894.

The development in medieval society of the means of production gave rise to new relations of production, new classes, new class differentiations, new class struggles. Capitalism was born, the bourgeoisie was born. But the bourgeoisie, the newest, growing class, was oppressed; it felt held down and confined by the restrictions of a political organization that was adapted to the needs and interests of other classes, which had conquered their political hegemony under other, outgrown economic conditions. This bourgeoisie was thus forced into a political class struggle in which it figured as a revolutionary class, with the goal of seizing state power in its own hands in order to institute a form of government after its own model. An ideal form of government was for them that which assured unlimited freedom of exploitation and of competition, and which guaranteed the unhindered development of capital; it was the political fulfillment of the ideas of freedom and equality—the doctrinal expression of their material life conditions so as to form the spiritual foundations of the capitalist way of production and exchange—a state without despotism, with no other bond among men than naked self-interest, as the *Communist Manifesto* has expressed it, with all the freedoms and rights of the individual which they proclaim as immortal, inalienable "rights of man": in a word, democracy. This was the political ideal of the bourgeoisie in their revolutionary struggle against feudal despotism, against aristocratic magnates, against clericalism.

By now this struggle is in most countries largely, if not completely, finished. As the ideal of a democratic form of government is nowhere fully carried out, the industrial, and especially the commercial, bourgeoisie more or less continue to fight for it. This striving of nonproletarian elements for democracy (as goal) we call the democratic movement.

Nowadays, this democratic movement does not have entirely the same mark of unity of revolutionary energy as when for the bourgeoisie it was a question of being or not being, a matter of the conquest of the most vital conditions of their existence and development. The bourgeoisie are no longer an oppressed class but have become an oppressing class. The capitalistic way of production, which has been able to develop freely thanks to the political triumph of the bourgeoisie, has formed a proletariat, in turn an exploited class, which to the degree that it becomes more conscious and more determined in its struggle for political power against all the classes that now possess this power (bourgeoisie, landowners, petty bourgeoisie, etc.), has totally changed the nature of the struggle.

In time the proletarian class struggle became the pivot and main point of all politics, and pushed all other questions into the background; or rather, shall this help or hinder social democracy? is either the only question asked or is asked before anything else, by those on both sides. Now the bourgeoisie have the proletariat use against them the laws and freedoms that they had conquered for themselves, the freedom of assembly and association, freedom of the press, universal suffrage; they are fought with the weapons that they have forged themselves, which they themselves in part still need.

Whether and to what degree they will now abandon these laws and freedoms, their democratic ideal, depends in the first place on the extent they feel threatened, on the one hand by the proletariat, on the other hand by the aristocracy and clericalism—on which side and in which struggle they have more to gain or to lose. Under the influence of psychological factors, such as the power of revolutionary traditions, religious or national loyalties, or simply through deliberate judgment, they will also divide themselves into opposing factions inclining more or less toward one of two poles of the opposition to socialism: to the tactic of outright reaction, with violation of political rights, systematic stupefaction, boundless exploitation, which in the end leads to the bloodbath; or to the tactic of bandages and ointments, of "class reconcilation" and "social peace," of reforms . . . giving rise to the illusion that one can expect from a democratic political order the abolition of all conflict of economic interests.

These are indeed the broad strokes in terms of which bourgeois policy in all the capitalistically developed countries is formed; a closer characterization, however, cannot be entertained, since the conditions that determine the attitude of nonproletarian classes and parties differ from country to country, and since, in addition, general observations, if they are not to lose their applicability, must be so loosely drawn that they can no longer explain any given phenomenon, while on the other hand, if they wish to take account of all the idiosyncracies of reality and be applicable to all exceptions, they lose in the end their general meaningfulness. Accordingly, the elaboration of the universal, that is, theory, is to be dropped, and we must attend to the level of specific phenomena. If we wish to investigate what is the role of the democratic ideal in the policies of bourgeois parties, we must observe the circumstances in each country, ascertain the movements and inclinations of classes and parties, search out their causes, and then draw up the possible general conclusions.

With a pre-cut ready-made recipe, with a formula that tries to establish the direction of the evolution of the bourgeois parties a priori, one is thus not well served. From the undeniable fact that, just as in natural phenomena reaction follows action, the growth of the socialist workers' movement then brings about a growing reactionary conviction among the ruling classes and weakens the political divisions among them, one may not conclude that all the bourgeois parties must always become more reactionary, to the point of fusion into "one reactionary mass." Whoever believes that this evolution toward reaction must take place necessarily, constantly, generally, always uniformly and in the same direction; that the bourgeoisie, just like the sun and with the same natural necessity, must move from left to right, is driven to the conclusion—in view of the triumphant advance of the democratic fraction of the bourgeoisie in Russia, France, England, Holland, Belgium, and elsewhere—that the "evolutionary law" that he has constructed is not the expression of any natural necessity, since it currently allows of more exceptions than confirmations. But from the circumstance that at a given time there are a variety of reports seeming to show an evolution toward democracy in several countries of Europe neither should one draw the general conclusion that this is the present and future path of development of bourgeois society, that we are always approaching closer to a democratic form of government, shall always more and more enjoy its laws and freedoms, eventually to arrive, without clashes, without class struggle, at a socialist society. The parallel growth of the socialist movements of the workers and of the democratic movement of a part of the bourgeoisie, as we have seen it during the last few years, notably with us in France, England, Holland and Belgium, has brought many of our party members to the conclusion that, just as both phenomena are brought about by the same, steadily working causes and are oriented by and to the same goal ("democracy," which in the end will become "socialist"), so should the progress of democracy and that of the workers' movement be similar, combined, inseparable.

Well then, this conclusion is erroneous, this conclusion is false, this conclusion is dangerous. In the first place, then, not abstract reasoning but the examination of phenomena on which judgment will rest, shall serve to convince us. We shall analyze these phenomena, seek their causes, and then see to which general conclusions they lead. . . .

The answer to the question, is the political development of the capitalist states in the direction of democracy? is of the greatest significance not only from a theoretical standpoint but also in view of its pragmatic consequences. We have seen that this general development toward democracy, which people have wanted to see in the events of foreign countries that we have described, is nothing but an illusion, a fantasy and self-deceit. Insofar as there is any general development, it goes in the opposite direction.

However, that does not mean that we must prepare ourselves for an ever increasing reduction of the rights and reforms favoring the proletariat; it only means that the bourgeoisie in general will be less ready to support those reforms whereby the power of the proletariat is increased. It would be the worst sort of pessimism to conclude that we have no immediate political improvements to expect, that we must stop and put all our hope only in the revolutionary overthrow of capitalist society.

No; political democracy—that is, a certain minimum of political rights and laws—is the absolutely indispensable condition for the success of social revolution. That is already shown by the struggle, which has demanded such a tremendous sacrifice, of the Russian proletariat to bring about that minimum of democracy that the labor movement finds as necessary to development as light itself. But the proletariat will be more and more the only force supporting all battles for democracy and must depend only on its own resources for democracy's realization. To the degree that democracy becomes more indispensable for the proletariat, it becomes more dangerous to the bourgeoisie, and as the struggle for each crumb of freedom and law becomes more difficult, closer and closer approaches that final struggle in which there will be no quarter, where the prize will be the control of political power, the very existence of capitalistic exploitation and of democracy at one and the same time.

It has already been indicated that it is impossible for democracy in a capitalist society to be a transitional form leading to a socialist order in state and society. Democracy does not lessen the class struggle—rather, it places the proletariat in a better position to carry this on, to allow it sharper and clearer political expression than in any other form of government. Still less can democracy abolish that conflict.

Hence, in our struggle, let no illusion as to the mercy of the bourgeoisie, no trust in the sincerity of their democratic convictions, confuse the class insight of the proletariat. The prize of battle is much greater than a bit of law or only reform, far greater than a bourgeois revolution ever sought. And the proletariat have a far stronger and more formidable weapon than the bourgeoisie ever used. It forged it not out of the democratic idea—and the phrase mongering of an impotent declining class. Like the young hero in Wagner's *Siegfried*, it views this with distain:

> Away with this gruel!
> I do not need it;
> With pasteboard, I cannot forge a sword!

And it will forge its world-saving sword out of strong class organization and with heroic class consciousness!

2

The Operation
of Bourgeois Democracy

While certainly evincing a deep skepticism as to the ultimate outcome of bourgeois manipulation of the political
system, nevertheless in "The Era of Democracy" de Man,
undoubtedly under the influence of the momentous 1905
revolution in Russia, had been content to advocate zealous
if wary proletarian exploitation of the opportunities offered by bourgeois democracy. In the analysis he undertook in a series of "Socialist Travel Letters" from England
in 1910 there is a significant shift of his position, presumably reflecting his Leipzig indoctrination, in the direction
of assimilating all bourgeois parties. Precisely because of
the fatal attractiveness of progressive politics to the gullible
proletarians, the basic fallaciousness of that attempt to
make capitalism work must be exposed: "Under present
circumstances the worst political enemy of the English
working class is liberalism."[1] As we shall see, his subscription to this corollary to Marxism was to have fateful consequences for his ideological development.

The significance of de Man's experience in the English-
speaking world as a whole was great, though ambiguous.
By his own report he was deeply impressed with both the
civic virtues and the political capacities of England and, a
few years later, the United States, and he was simply
shaken by the American lack of class consciousness. While
the theoretical implications of the latter were, as we shall
see, momentous, ultimately he was to operate on the basis

[1] "Sozialistische Reisebriefe V: Hyndman," *Leipziger Volkszeitung*,
Feuilleton-Beilage, 12 August 1910.

of the historical specificity of Continental institutions, in terms of which the political systems of the Anglo-Saxon powers were regarded as simply irrelevant, if perhaps admirable.

SOZIALISTISCHE REISEBRIEFE: II[2]

The electoral campaign is finishing. Thank God! The extraordinary interest that the outcome of this decisive political struggle commands, the favorable conditions for the study of political life in England that it affords, the consciousness of sharing in a moment of world-historical significance—all this does not prevent one from experiencing a certain feeling of satiation, indeed of surfeit, even before the end of the second week of the voting. The greater the interest in the outcome of the election, the less is it possible to sustain the excessively long span of interest that is demanded by the daily repetition throughout more than two weeks of the act of voting in the various electoral groupings. And then—I must admit that the appearance and behavior of the people on electoral day itself, however interesting it may have been to observe, in the end made no edifying impression on me but rather brought me closer to disgust than to admiration.

It is fully obvious that the nature of the political contest between the two great bourgeois parties, which at least in London nearly monopolize the field of battle, is a competition to ensnare the votes of the worker by means of cheap advertising tricks, such that the party that has the least scruples and the most money will win. For in the end, the essence of political wisdom within the English electoral system is this: to transform the money power of the owning classes into political power in such a way that the workers' right to vote is made into a means to preserve their intellec-

[2] *Leipziger Volkszeitung*, Feuilleton-Beilage, 1 and 2 February 1910; London dateline, 29 and 30 January.

tual and political dependence on the bourgeois parties. The English Liberals just as the Conservatives have brought this art to perfection over many decades, and the entire way in which the campaign is prepared and carried out is directed to facilitating this practice in the most subtle ways.

Praise of the democratic character of the English constitution is heard often enough in Germany—especially from the Liberals and from those Social Democrats who stand under the spiritual influence of bourgeois democracy; and it should not be denied that the form in which the English bourgeoisie embody their class interest comes far closer to the political ideal of bourgeois democracy than the half-absolutistic way in which Prussian-Germany is governed in the name of a politically incapable bourgeoisie by the Junkers, the military, and the bureaucracy. But the Social Democrat in England will in fact be reminded often and urgently enough that the democracy that is here incorporated into political institutions is a world away from what glimmers as the ideal of political organization for socialists. In a certain sense, one can say that England deserves to be called a democracy only in the sense of perhaps the city republics of Greek antiquity, where the political relations of citizens, to be sure, were patterned after democratic principles, but at the same time the mass of the dependent and unfree workers were excluded from this democratic community of the citizens on the basis of their economic position. Certainly it no longer has the appearance that this is the case, at least since the time when the British labor movement succeeded in winning some rights to the franchise. But that is more appearance than reality. It is clear that so long as this right to vote is not used by the working class for its own goals, it serves only to increase the political power of the various strata of the bourgeoisie. And the English franchise is constructed just so that it places almost unsurpassable obstacles in the way of every attempt to use it other than for the advantage of the bourgeoisie.

I received an instructive example of this outlook of the English bourgeoisie one evening when I was present at the announcement of the incoming electoral results at the National Liberal Club. This club, the biggest of its kind, represents in particular left-liberal tendencies. (Upon another occasion I shall come back to the nature of these clubs, so important and characteristic for English life, bourgeois organizations hermetically sealed to the outside, which provide their members with the use of rooms for various kinds of social occasions.) A member of the club who knew me took me into the spacious and splendid "smoking room." Perhaps three hundred members were sitting, most of them political bigwigs of liberalism, among them Mr. John Burns,[3] listening with rapt attention to the announcement of the electoral results, which came by telegraph and were called out by a member. It was naturally most interesting to observe the applause and other reactions of this special audience. When the candidates for the Labour party were mentioned—who, as is well known, in this election fought in almost every case in fact for the same principles as the Liberals[4]—the applause was not less than for the Liberals themselves. The old gentleman who called out the results in the hall in general did not identify them as candidates of the Labour party but used for them "Liberal and Labour." He even did that for our comrade Keir Hardie,[5] whose victory over his Conservative opponent was especially loudly greeted. But it was quite different with the socialist candidates, who had fought against the Liberals and Conservatives with their own program; these were met with jeering. Toward the end of the evening, the Liberal who had won

[3] Renowned for his flamboyant rebuttal to charges of sedition in 1886 and for his leadership in mediating the great London dockworkers' strike of 1889, Burns, 1858-1943, was elected to Parliament in 1892 among the first three Labour representatives, but by the election of 1910 had become associated with Lloyd George's reformists within the Liberal party.

[4] The 1910 election was centered on the constitutional question of the power of the House of Lords to reject legislation, notably money bills, that had been passed by the Commons.

[5] A founder of the Labour party and longtime M.P., Keir Hardie, 1856-1915, resolutely rejected the adequacy of Liberal reformism.

in Northampton, where our comrades Quelch and Gribble[6] had gathered a few thousand votes for the program of
the Social Democratic party, appeared. He was greeted
with lively applause and requested to say something about
the electoral outcome in his district. He reported in a few
words about the elation of the party workers who had
helped him to victory over the Conservative, and added
that the most satisfactory part of the whole thing was that
now one could hope that the socialist candidate was beaten
for all time. Stormy applause roared through the hall.
Never have I experienced so clearly as at this moment how
much stronger English socialism really is than appears to
be the case from the count of votes for its candidates. The
English bourgeoisie know better than the workers themselves the power that lies behind the socialist labor movement.

The evening street scene of London in places where the
electoral results are made known is most interesting. Pro-
jectors are set up at the district headquarters of the larger
political groupings and at the editorial offices of the daily
newspapers, etc., to present incoming electoral results
from about ten o'clock in the evening until one in the
morning. Hundreds of thousands stream together, and despite the specially arranged extra schedule, the trolleys,
underground, and other means of transportation are over-
taxed the whole night. The behavior of the masses, who
express their feelings in the most varied ways at every result that is announced, allows observation of the national
characteristics of the English as a group rather than as individuals. In comparison with a similar crowd in Germany,
it is first of all apparent that the masses here are much
more demonstrative, more passionate, and livelier in the

[6] Harry Quelch, 1858-1913, a prominent and proletarian member of
the Social Democratic Federation which de Man had joined; the fourth
"Sozialistische Reisebriefe," *Leipziger Volkszeitung*, Feuilleton-Beilage, 21
July 1910, was devoted to Quelch. I have been unable to find further
identification of Gribble.

expression of their emotions, to which the greater freedom that they here enjoy understandably contributes the most. Voluntary discipline, which, to be sure, is manifested here only in the shouting together—in general, repeated and long-held hurrays as signs of applause, low booings for the opposite, political songs and such—is effected here much more easily than in Germany. Every time the noise of the crowd dies down, facetious sallies crisscross the air, some with clever allusions to some particularities of the contest in the electoral district in question, some with wordplays—alliteration is used with special skill by the English—in all of which the border between salty humor and insulting rudeness is practically never violated. If a rather long interval ensues between the announcement of successive results, the projector presents political caricatures, pictures of well-known politicians, etc., and also projects jokes and questions, which never fail to have an effect upon the public. For instance, the projector of a Liberal newspaper asked, after announcing a Liberal victory, "Now, friends, show us how you can shout hurray!" The shout of hurray immediately burst forth and was not ended until the "boo" of the opposing Conservatives was quite drowned out. Or, after a row of Liberal defeats, the question appeared on the white screen: "Are we downhearted now?" to be answered immediately with a thundering "No!" by a thousand voices. In short, it must be observed that the greater political freedom that as a rule places no obstacles in the way of mass demonstrations has as consequence that the masses as such are more intellectually nimble, react more easily, more quickly, and in a more appropriate way to stimuli, and are better trained in voluntary discipline than in Germany, where mass demonstrations as a rule are suppressed by the police or, when this is not the case, are directed with the help of an authoritarian drill often appearing as quite policelike and bureaucratized.

And that freedom teaches freedom to the crowd is proved by the fact that not the slightest disturbance marks these excited gatherings of masses of people of the most diverse political colors. Naturally, the freedom permits innumerable instances of the proximity of people who continuously show opposing feelings and who take part in passionate political debates, in which naturally an always increasing portion of the bystanders join. But I have never seen that such discussions, to which the English are much accustomed—I will later find occasion to report on the distinctive way in which the English behave in this respect in public meetings—degenerate into brawls or simply reckless name calling, and I have never seen reference to such a case in the newspapers. If a few people were to dispute over something in the street in Germany, of course a policeman would immediately be there "to restore order" by brutally provoking and hustling the people until he can drag a couple of them to the station house. The London bobby—as the police are here pleasantly called—is content, smiling with good humor, to observe the people without mixing in otherwise than perhaps to whisper very privately into the ear of those bystanders close to him his own opinion as to the matter in the form of a laconic and witty remark.

Of course, it is not thereby said that the London bobbies are any less than the Berlin "Blues" or the Leipzig "Greens" an instrument in the hands of the ruling class to restore "order," especially when it appears to be threatened by any revolutionary action of the working class. It is only that the way in which the English police fulfill their function is infinitely more subtle—and especially from the standpoint of the ruling classes—than the provocative and violent way of the German heavenly brotherhood, which is inspired by the spirit embodied in noncoms of the German barracks. I will come back on another occasion to the distinctive character of the English police, but the presentation of this principal difference between Germany and England is already instructive enough. In the end the parallel between the bobbies and the Blues basically reflects that between the two forms of government, the liberal bourgeois and the reactionary Junker, in general. These are the two democratic forms of political oppression of the proletariat in the capitalistic era; the first is the most reasonable, the second the most brutal.

This does not mean that the London police cannot and have not behaved in a brutal way. But this takes place not as a rule but only under extraordinary circumstances, that is, when it is really thought to be indispensable. And then they do it just as in Germany. I saw this on electoral evening in Haggerston. A crowd nearing ten thousand had assembled around nine o'clock in the evening in front of the town hall in Shoreditch[7] where the results were to be proclaimed and in whose neighborhood a Liberal newspaper has installed a projector for the announcement of the electoral results from the whole country. I went there with a group of about two hundred comrades, men and women from the socialist committee room. We made up a little demonstration: an improvised red flag was carried in front, and the socialist campaign songs sounded joyful and hopeful in the workers' streets through which we traipsed. I had noted beforehand that the police whom I had seen in the neighborhood of the voting booths of the district seemed arrogant and militaristic; in a word, they appeared and behaved Prussian, quite different from those in the City or other central parts of the metropolis. I found the explanation right away, that they feel themselves to be the servants of the public in those quarters where only rich people are likely to live, while they are conscious of their position as masters here in this workers' district, furthermore known as "red." When our parade approached the town hall square, I was shown not to be wrong. The red flag was removed, rolled up and hidden as soon as a strong police patrol was noted. But now a column of police attacked our handful and began to knock around its fleeing

[7] Haggerston was an electoral district within the borough of Shoreditch in London's East End.

members in so brutal a way that I could well imagine myself in Germany. I can at least say I have felt "on my own body" the international relationship of the instruments of oppression of the class state.

The socialist labor movement is handled by the ruling classes in England in complete contrast to socialism and to the labor movement. I will express myself more clearly: socialism as a social and philosophical theory does not yet appear here as threatening to the body of the bourgeoisie so long as it does not find supporters in bourgeois intellectual circles. Millionaires, clergymen, and countesses even find that just a little socialism—naturally trimmed especially to this end—is not unbecoming. In short, socialism here still is socially acceptable, which it has not been for a long time in Germany. The English bourgeoisie long ago made its peace with the workers' movement so long as it is not socialist, that is, with the old-style trade-union movement. It has tried time and again—the whole strategy of the present Liberal government with respect to the Labour party has no other goal—to switch the leaders over and to capture them politically and intellectually in general. But socialism that is supported by the working class—the union movement that will be socialistic—that, you see, is a dangerous thing! Here there is no choice: the socialistic workers' movement must be scotched.

The "democratic" English suffrage is first of all something less than universal; not to speak of women, perhaps the greater part of the male proletariat is excluded. Only men who are either houseowners or who rent an (unfurnished) house for at least two hundred marks a year—that is, only the better situated part of the proletariat, may vote. Moreover, for the nonowners, residence in the electoral district for more than a year is required. It works out so that perhaps 40 percent of the adult men in Great Britain have no vote. In exchange, a minority among the ruling classes enjoys a plural vote. In law, the English voter represents not his own person but his property—which illuminates as by a flash the true nature of this "democratic" plutocracy—and he can give a vote in each of the districts in which he has land or house, whether or not he lives there. If he is at the same time the holder of a university degree, he has in addition a vote as a member of his university district, for the universities have their own representatives in the lower house. Most of the bourgeois plural voters in Germany have given up the practice of their voting rights in far-off districts, but the English bourgeoisie exhibit a much stronger political interest and do not draw back from the loss of time and the costs of travel. This is also the main reason why the elections do not take place here on one day, and in fact there have been very few plural voters in this election who have not exercised their plural rights in full.

Perhaps the procedures of voting are even more important than the franchise itself in favoring the bourgeois parties. This is already apparent in the preparation of the lists of voters. This takes place in a very spotty way, for there is no obligation to report one's residence to the police in England, and there is ample room for the caprice of the authorities. Every voter who is a renter and not a houseowner must justify anew his claim to be registered on the voting lists each year, lest he lose his vote. Naturally it depends very much on whether there are financially solvent political organizations to undertake the transportation of voters favorable to their side; or course, the workers' organizations are at a disadvantage in this respect. But a still greater obstacle is provided by the nearly insurmountable electoral costs. I am not speaking here of the fact that the M.P. receives no pay and that there is an attempt to forbid the payment of stipends by the unions to the Labour M.P.'s, but that the electoral costs themselves are levied on the candidates, that is, on their party organizations in most cases. The whole official electoral procedure is directed in each district by a government official, the "returning officer," especially appointed for this purpose. The steep honorarium and the total expenses of this official and of his helpers must be paid for in equal measure by the candidates. These costs differ in accordance with the size of the district, but amount in the average to perhaps twenty thousand marks per electoral district. It is understandable that with this system, the workers' organizations must think twice before they put forth a candidate in a district. Should he be only an also-ran, the fun is a bit expensive, and the prospect that the only real effect of the candidacy must be to reduce the electoral costs of the opposing Liberal and Conservative candidates from a half to a third hardly improves things. It also happens that the way in which the electioneering is carried out, as I have described it briefly in my previous letter, also makes the costs of campaigning much higher than in Germany.

Further, there are neither runoff elections nor proportional representation in England; the relative plurality decides the selection of the candidate. This circumstance is perhaps the most important of all in worsening the position of the workers' organizations. Where there is no prospect of conquering the majority—and every new party is naturally first of all only a minority—their participation easily has the effect that one bourgeois candidate who has received less than half of the votes recorded will be elected. So it also develops that at this election, and perhaps even more than before, large numbers of voters who otherwise might vote socialist, but who are not social-democratically trained enough to reject the shortsighted application of the principle of the lesser evil, vote for the Liberals in order to prevent the Conservatives from slipping through.

These are only a few particulars that should throw light on the cunningly plutocratic character of the English electoral system. A host of others could be supplied—such as perhaps the unjust division of the electoral districts, which is nearly as scandalous as in the German Empire. But certainly the above suffices.

It is never more apparent than on the day of election itself that in the last analysis the money powers have the greatest political might in England. I have wandered around in various London districts as an observer on election day, and also undertook a walking trip in Essex County in order to gain a view of the conditions in the countryside. What I have seen of the direct and indirect corrupting influence of money on the body of electors just disgusted me. I do not mean that votes were simply bought. Certainly that must happen not seldom, but it is not seen. Canvassing from house to house, which I described in my last letter, is certainly likewise used by the bourgeois candidates very often as an opportunity to impress the voters with something other than purely political arguments. And cases of the intimidation of voters by land- and houseowners have been made known by the hundreds by the Liberal press, which ascribes the greatest part of Conservative victories to such maneuvers. But this is hardly the worst way in which money makes itself felt as a factor of political power. Often alcohol appears as a means, either as whiskey or as beer—for in England where beer is extremely strong, the difference is not very significant. It is not only voters who are treated to free beer but also young boys, who are then sent forth with the candidate's pictures, colorful bunting, flags, electoral slogans in favor of the generous candidate, to "agitate" in the streets until late in the evening. Their principal activity takes place in front of the entrance to the polling place. These are mostly schools or similar official premises, just as with voting for the Reichstag in Germany; the voting goes on from eight in the morning until eight in the evening. Strong detachments of police keep back the crowds, which hang around these places during the whole day—especially in the workers' quarters—and which are largely made up of the youths already mentioned, more or less stirred up by drink. To each voter who enters the polling place, they yell out the name of "their" candidate for whom he should vote, while each party naturally tries to outshout the other. At the same time, whole packages of leftover campaign "literature" are thrown at the head of the man who in the next moment will be exercising his "sovereignty," and flags, placards, and similar objects are thrust at him. It is a good thing that ballots do not need to be distributed, since within the polling place each voter receives a ballot upon which the names of the candidates appear and on which he indicates his preference by a cross. There is a deafening and blinding tumult, which stands in sharp contrast to the calm that generally reigns in front of the polling places in Germany.

The way in which the voters are "whisked" to the polls also made no ennobling impression upon me. Transportation was provided by the bourgeois parties here even more than was the case in Germany at the time of the "Hottentot" election.[8] This was especially facilitated by the fact that the elections took place on different days, so that the same carts and automobiles could sometimes be used for the work of transportation for two weeks long, each day in a different district. In general, the voters were not only brought from their homes to the polling place but also taken back again. Few workers of Liberal or Conservative persuasion let the opportunity slip by to take a trip in the automobile or in the carriage of the noble lord who had placed his vehicle in the service of the candidate of his party. It is sometimes funny to see the proud nonchalance with which from time to time hardly aristocratic-looking proletarians make themselves comfortable on the upholstered cushions of the limousines, while the liveried servant who drives makes a superhuman effort not to lose his obligatory dignified mien when the canaille, "sovereign" on this day, stretch out their feet with their filthy workmen's boots on the velvet-covered seats, or spit a squirt of tobacco juice into a corner of the car. It is less funny to see brewery

[8] The reference is to the Reichstag election of 1907 in which the emotional issue of German imperialism in Southwest Africa mobilized the Navy League, the Pan-German League, and colonial and veterans' societies to energetic measures that unexpectedly led to a resounding defeat for the Social Democrats.

wagons go by—naturally decked with the blue colors of the Conservatives—in which half-drunk workers from the great breweries are being driven to the polls. The same wagons then take the voters, after they have been asked if they have voted for the "right" candidate, back to their homes. This towing around is carried out on a much larger scale in the countryside. In the country districts I visited on election day and where, as is nearly always the case in southern England, all farming is concentrated in the estates of great landowners, the owners and rich fellow party members, who have come from the city to their aid with automobiles by the hundreds, bring "their" workers and tenants into the villages where they may vote.

3

The Singularity of
the Belgian Labor Movement

In the fall of 1910, the young de Man received an invitation from the rising socialist leader Emile Vandervelde to head up a Belgian Labor party program of workers' education. As secretary-general of the newly established Centrale d'Education Ouvrière, he found himself in a strategic position to participate in the training, both vocational and ideological, of the party cadres, an opportunity that he particarly welcomed as contributing to the creation of socialist class consciousness. On the basis of his ideological convictions, particularly as reinforced by his experience in Germany, he viewed the pragmatic, reformist stance of the Belgian party with considerable impatience and scorn, and as a party militant attempting to promote adoption of a radical-Marxist policy, he wrote part of a long critique of the practice and politics of his comrades that appeared in 1911 as a supplementary number of Kautsky's *Neue Zeit*.

While the polemical objective of his article was to discredit reformism, the argument involved accounting for this orientation in terms of a Marxist analysis of the distinctive historical configuration of Belgium, in the course of which he attempted to allow for the efficacy of "national-psychological, religious, and historical factors"[1] while preserving his subscription to historical materialism. The logical stratagem he used was of course to interpret these factors as only "the historical precipitate of the economic development of many centuries,"[2] and at this point in his ideological development he tucked out of sight any difficulties that might arise from this formulation. Nevertheless,

[1] See below, p. 51.   [2] Ibid.

his experience in binational Belgium and in Germany and England had already convinced him of the irrefragability of nationality, and in a sentence whose implications were later to be developed, he had already remarked that "if socialism were nothing other than a so-to-speak mechanical mirroring of the capitalist mode of production, it would also have to take the same form everywhere to the degree that that mode of production is the same in all countries where it has been established."[3] At this point in his ideological development, he was content to insist that a vulgar-Marxist, simplistic interpretation is certainly inadequate, and it was only exigencies of the future that were to bring him finally to recognize that the variables now introduced must be defined not as intervening, but on the contrary as exogenous.

The fact of nationality was of significance not only in de Man's theoretical reasoning but was also evident in other ways in the passages below. His own deep identification with the Flemish masses is visible both in his concentration on their plight in the Belgium he knew and in his distrust of the dominant French culture, in which in fact he was very much at home. The material on the late-medieval blooming of Flanders was based on his own doctoral dissertation, "The Cloth Industry of Ghent in the Middle Ages," for which he had received a *summa cum laude* from the University of Leipzig.

DIE EIGENART DER BELGISCHEN ARBEITERBEWEGUNG[4]

The Belgian Enigma

Knowledge of the singularity of Belgian reformism, that is, really of the Belgian labor movement in general, and of its

---

[3] "Sozialistische Reisebriefe V: Hyndman," *Leipziger Volkszeitung*, Feuilleton-Beilage, 12 August 1910.

[4] In H. de Man and Louis de Brouckère, *Die Arbeiterbewegung in Belgien*, supplementary volume to *Neue Zeit*, no. 9; Stuttgart: Paul Singer, 1911, pp. 3-4, 8-10, 24-25.

historical-economic conditions, tests—if not the applicability of the Marxist method of historical interpretation itself—certainly the capacity of the investigator to use this method correctly. Whoever subscribes to a mechanical interpretation of this method, which of course is fashionable only among its opponents; whoever thus believes that Marxism consists in explaining the political and cultural characteristics of a country, the strengths and the nature of its labor movement, only on the basis of its present degree of economic development, will in any case find Belgium an insoluble puzzle. For there are enough contradictions that simply cannot be ignored.

Belgium is economically highly developed, but culturally very backward.

It is the most industrialized country of the world, but it is governed by a clerical-agrarian party.

The economic class conflict between the possessing and the nonpossessing classes is nowhere greater than here; but the conflict on which political life turns is the ideological opposition of the *Kulturkampf* for and against clericalism, and the line of economic class division does not run between the bourgeois parties but, so to speak, diagonally through them.

The economic conditions for the development of the workers' movement are nowhere so favorable as in Belgium; it has not only the greatest industrial development but also the greatest density of population of the world; the smallness of the country and an extraordinarily thick network of trains allow for movement from any given place to the capital in at most two hours; the mineral resources of the country make mining and the ironworking industry derived there from the leading industries, so that economic concentration is in general exceedingly far advanced; the mass of capital accumulated through centuries of commercial and industrial prosperity and, of late, also through the exploitation of a rich colonial area, brings, moreover, an especially rapid tempo to the continued economic development of the land; but the organization of the work force in trade unions remains in its infancy.

The socialist party is nowhere more completely made up of proletarian elements alone, but the spirit that reigns here is in many respects even more petty bourgeois than in France.

The instance will be less puzzling if one regards it, not from the superficial schematized standpoint that alone passes as orthodox Marxist with the revisionists, but if, at the danger of being called a heretic by the revisionist guardians of so-called Marxist "orthodoxy," one tries to understand the present situation of Belgium and of its workers' movement not only on the basis of the current economic state of the country but also from its entire history. In other words, to look at the present economic situation of the country indeed as the momentary substructure of its current ideological and political superstructure, but at the same time to take into account, in the determination of the formation of this superstructure, of those national-psychological, religious, and historical factors, which in the end are nothing but the historical precipitate of the economic development of many centuries.

To solve the whole problem of Belgian circumstances in accordance with this economic-historical method founded by Marx means of course to write the history of Belgium at least in its broad outline. We will content ourselves here with the more modest task of sketching, according to this method, the most important events that determine the singular reformism of the Belgian labor movement. . . .

The Accumulation of Spiritual Poverty

As has been stated, the fact of the extraordinarily early primitive accumulation of capital—of seven hundred years of capitalism—suffices by itself to explain the seven-century accumulation of physical poverty that oppresses this proletariat. And this terrible physical poverty suffices by itself to explain the spiritual poverty from which our people have suffered.

However, it is not only the fact of this seven-century capitalist development, but also the tempo and the distinctive way in which this development has taken place, that have marked the formation of this physical and spiritual poverty. The fact that should be first noted is that the tempo of economic development of the most important provinces of the country slowed down from the fifteenth century on, and from then until the beginning of the modern capitalist epoch, or the early nineteenth century, experienced a period of depression or of relative stagnation in which the capital from "primitive accumulation" was, so to speak, stowed away and applied largely for goals other than those of industrial production. And this stagnation has been far more disastrous for our proletariat than the free development of an uninterrupted and progressive industrial capitalism would have been.

This can all be illustrated from the history of the Flemish provinces, which, moreover, can be regarded as typical in that they are at one and the same time the cradle of Belgian capitalism and the classical land of Belgian proletarian pauperism.

The manufacture of cloth by the domestic system, on which the blooming of the Flemish cities of the Middle Ages rested, reached its high point in the thirteenth and fourteenth centuries. Then it collapsed very rapidly. The causes of this decline are manifold and of too complicated a nature to be analyzed here. The most important are the shift in trade routes at the end of the Middle Ages, and the guild organization into which the industry was forced at the beginning of the fourteenth century but which did not meet the needs of the newer methods of production that became dominant in the fifteenth century.

Hence there appeared rather large numbers (as measured in those days) of unemployed, principally in the cities but also in the country, where the urban clothiers established many works, such as filling mills and spinneries. Many workers were thrown into vagabondage and henceforth lived from charity. The luckier found other work—naturally not as skilled workers but generally only as laborers. But even if they found work in the linen manufacture newly established as a cottage industry in the country, this meant a distinct worsening of their situation. For as workers in the urban cloth industry they had had (in the guild organization which they had won in decades-long, bloody struggles) a defense against the oppressive tendencies of the primitive capitalism to which they sold their labor power. Henceforth they no longer had this protection. Henceforth they stood completely defenseless against capitalist exploitation—until the beginning of the modern labor movement, it can be said.

Nevertheless, these sectors of the proletariat, employed as unskilled workers in the cottage industry of the countryside, were still much better off than the hundreds of thousands who could keep a hold on life only by means of charity that almost exclusively came from the cloisters and other churchly institutions. This systematic utilization of ecclesiastical charity for the support of a social stratum everywhere thickly peopled—including not only the marginal population but in large part workers, mostly from the cottage industry, who did not earn enough to be able to live—is still today one of the worst plagues of the life of Belgian workers. In any case, it has been from the beginning a taproot for the power of Belgian clericalism.

Flemish capitalism created a destitute proletariat during the very heyday of its development in the thirteenth and fourteenth centuries. In the period of economic stagnation that followed (from the fifteenth to the nineteenth centuries) it was replaced by clericalism, which supported this propertyless class. Capitalism was shown to be more dangerous "dead" than "alive." Live capitalism had thrown the great mass of the people into physical poverty despite their resistance. But dead capitalism grafts spiritual onto physical impoverishment—the stupefaction of the masses through clericalism; it makes and keeps them defenseless and pliable, it works them into the most manageable human dough that modern factory capitalism can discover in any country in its path of conquest through the world.

. . . I will note here only that there is no compulsory education of any kind in Belgium, that according to the latest census (1900) 19 percent of the whole population over eight years of age can neither read nor write, and that nowadays about 11 percent of the recruits are completely illiterate. Moreover, the existing elementary schooling is so miserable, and the knowledge of at least half of the population that is not technically regarded as illiterate is so elementary, that they are not in a position to further their understanding through independent serious reading.

This situation is worst among the Flemish working population. In the Flemish part of the country, I have more than once given talks before audiences 80 to 90 percent completely illiterate. These percentages are of course rare and are found only in areas in which the population is made up almost exclusively of unskilled workers (as in the brick-making villages in the Scheldt and Rupel basins) or of those working at home (such as the rope makers in the "land of the Maas"). But illiteracy is common enough among the town workers—indeed the proletarians of the big cities are worse off in this respect than the farmers. Thus the census of 1900 reports the total of illiterates in the capital city of Brussels as 22.27 percent of the total population.

French Influences

. . . Walloon Belgium, the capital of Brussels, and the French-speaking Flemish bourgeoisie are allied with French culture through language. France, especially Paris, exercises a powerful attraction as a model. Brussels is the metropolis lying closest to Paris, closer than Lyons or Bordeaux. French newspapers, printed in Paris during the night, are sold mornings in the streets of Brussels. Many people here read no other newspaper. And the newspapers of French speech edited in Belgium are in many respects nothing more than provincial French papers. They pick up political articles and news from the French press as if the events had taken place in Belgium. If a murder takes place in Marseilles, the readers of the Belgian daily press, including the socialist papers, will be informed in a more detailed manner than if Bebel[5] has given an address in the German Reichstag or a few hundred thousand English or German workers have gone on strike against their employers.

It is thus no surprise that the workers' movement, specifically in the Walloon part of the country, shows strong traces of French influence. The political awakening of the Walloon labor force has taken place almost exclusively under the influence of ideas of French origin. These ideas by no means arise only from the spiritual arsenal of proletarian socialism but from nearly all of the revolutionary movements and social models that were brought forth in France in the second half of the nineteenth century, and that for the most part are of petty-bourgeois origin. For instance, it is noteworthy that during the great hunger rebellion of the Walloon workers of the year 1886, in which, by the way, agitators who came from France played a role, the leading demands of the unemployed were of a political, not an economic, nature. The foremost was the republic. When one considers that the constitution and the political institutions of the Belgian monarchy are really much more republican than those of France, and that in any case the introduction of republican institutions would bring only a formal change in a Belgium under the domination of the bourgeoisie, it is obvious that a transfer of French republican trends to Belgian conditions has taken place. The first socialist party organization that was

---

[5] August Bebel, 1840-1913, the renowned Social Democratic leader and editor of its official organ *Vorwärts*, an early hero to de Man.

founded in Wallonia—and indeed it was founded by the republican agitator Defuisseaux, who had come over from France—was called the Republican Socialist party.[6] It had a great influence among the miners of the Walloon province of Hainaut and for a long time remained separate from the other workers' movements, especially from the Flemish, which had developed under the influence of German social democracy (usually transmitted via Holland). During the later negotiations for unification that led to the founding of the workers' party in its present form, the Flemings were repeatedly accused of not putting their principal emphasis on the suppression of the monarchy. Thus the Walloon organizations have been of a purely political nature for a long time. While mutual societies in Walloon Belgium are, to be sure, of relatively early origin, although taking after those already existing in Flanders, the trade unions, notably that of the miners, were founded in the middle of the nineties through the differentiation of previously established political groups. The outlook of the Republican Socialist party lives today as strong as ever among the Walloon workers.

It is obvious that the spiritual ascendancy of an economically and socially somewhat underdeveloped country such as France over an industrially and socially hyper-developed country such as Belgium—in other words, the ascendancy of the outlook of the French petty bourgeoisie over the Belgian proletariat—has not been to the advantage of our movement. This circumstance, by the way, makes the puzzle of the proletarian movement and its petty-bourgeois outlook puzzling no more.

[6] Alfred Defuisseaux, 1823-1901.

4

The Lesson of the War

World War I presented de Man—by personal experience
and passionate conviction saturated in internationalism
and antimilitarism—with the agonizing necessity of rationalizing the decision he had taken, after participating in
the abortive efforts of the International to stave off the war,
to volunteer in the army of hapless Belgium invaded by the
Germany he had idolized. The greater the horrors he encountered and committed in the trenches in Flanders, the
greater was his necessity to persuade himself that these sacrifices, of conscience and of bodies, were not made in vain.
This viewpoint made him vulnerable to the thesis of the
neutralist socialists of Zimmerwald and Kienthal who proclaimed the capitalist-imperialist roots of the conflict while
calling for an immediate halt to hostilities. De Man's way
out from this dreadful embarrassment was to revise his appreciation of the significance of political institutions,
changing from his earlier view that liberal capitalist regimes were only superficially distinguished from reactionary capitalist ones. Now he set himself against this idea that
"since all capitalist states are ruled by an imperialist class
and all governments are the expression of the will of this
class, there is no difference between Wilhelm II and Woodrow Wilson."[1] He was fully conscious of the fact that this
shift in viewpoint involved profound ramifications for
Marxist ideology, although at this point he was speaking of
a limited "revision" of Marxism rather than the thoroughgoing and principled critique of that ideology by which he
was to make his international reputation through the publication in 1926 of his *Psychology of Socialism*.

[1] See below, p. 72

If under the impress of this compulsion he delivered
fervent praise to "democracy" as such, it is important to
note the particular perspective of his appreciation. In the
first place, his shift in viewpoint involved essentially the development of an *instrumental* appreciation of democratic institutions, on the basis that they made possible the eventual
triumph of the socialist movement. The autocratic governments of the Central Powers had nullified the power
and broken the spirit of their indigenous socialist parties,
and it would be only by means of a democratic political
revolution that their workers would be enabled effectively
to implement their socialist drive. Without democracy, it
was possible for the ruling classes to stave off the power of
the workers; with democracy, the victory of socialism was a
matter of time. Hence a socialist was necessarily a partisan
of the political institutions of a democratic regime.

But even in the flush of his enthusiasm for such a regime, de Man was quick to emphasize that democracy was
not to be identified with the institutions of a bourgeois parliamentary state. Faithful to his earlier criticism, he insisted
that formal political institutions must be assessed from a
substantive viewpoint, and in another departure from classical liberalism he extended the ambit of democratization by
insisting that the relations of work life must also be subject
to its application.

A second major consequence of de Man's experience
during the war involved the development of a more profound appreciation of the *integral* significance of democracy to the fulfillment of socialism. Presumably up to this
point he had implicitly accepted the Marxist conviction that
in the postrevolutionary world the "government of men"
would wither away to the "administration of things," in the
sense that in the absence of the clash of antagonistic class
interests, politics would henceforth involve only the voluntary, rationally based disposition of resources for the common good. Thus trammels to the exercise of the popular
will would have been removed—and the unquestioned assumption of the overwhelming preponderance of the revo-

lutionary proletariat deepened the democratic component of socialism. As we have seen, in the *Era of Democracy* he had argued that the institutions of political democracy were part and parcel of social democracy.

The political dimension became, however, something more than a corollary to the triumph of socialism with the cataclysmic dilemma represented by the emergence of the Soviet regime. De Man's reaction was strengthened by his extraordinary wartime experience in Kerensky's Russia (to which he along with two other Belgian socialist leaders had been sent by the all-party Belgian government in an effort to keep the revolutionary Russian regime in the war), as well as by his personal experience of the factionalism and intransigence of various Russian revolutionaries (which he saw from the vantage point of the dominant German socialist movement of prewar years). The Belgian socialist repudiation of Communist "revolutionary defeatism" now added impetus to his unreserved and unhesitant rejection of the Soviet regime as brutal and autocratic; in whatever name it spoke, the reality was a travesty of socialism.

It should be emphasized that it was not issues of constitutionalism nor of the forms of revolutionary government per se but rather the degree of the substantive exercise of coercion upon the masses in terms of which he formulated his political criterion of democracy. Hence in anticipation of the fateful ideological quandary posed by "socialism in one country," de Man's argument was unequivocally that the specificities of Russian historical development removed it as a candidate for autonomous revolutionary transformation into a socialist society. Indeed, even in the countries of the West more favored for such development, he was doubtful about the possibilities of immediately implementing a significant degree of real, i.e., democratic, socialization, and in the first sentence of the text below he makes reference to the hubbub he had caused at the Easter 1919 congress of the Belgian Labor party in declaring: "I do not believe that a socialist society is viable with a proletariat so wretched, so enervated, so devoid of

cultural appetites, and so ignorant as the working class of
Belgium today. Let us beware of resorting to demagoguery
or trying to fish in troubled waters. Until we bring about a
complete reorganization of the capitalist mode of production, let us make sure that there is production, and let us
not put useless hindrances to its progressive evolution."[2]
While he indicates below his long-term optimism for meaningful, democratic socialization of the means of production—as against legalistic, inadequate nationalization—the
issue of workers' control was to remain a permanent preoccupation.

Curiously, it was in capitalistic America that de Man
found the institutional framework closest to the realization
of the democratic values that he defined as the very kernel
of socialism. Indeed, at the moment of writing the text that
follows he had decided, on the basis of an exceedingly positive image of America that he had formed by service there
during the last six months of the war, and equally because
of the heart-rending disappointment he was undergoing at
the fiasco of Versailles, to abandon the Old World and to
seek salvation in the New. The experiment was not to succeed, although his American experience did leave a permanent precipitate in his ideological outlook, particularly
by providing an alternative model that cast doubt on the
adequacy of the conventional economic interpretation of
the European socialist movement. In the present context
its significance was to demonstrate, as a counterweight to
Russia, the political and social components indispensable to
the construction of a democratic socialism.

LA LEÇON DE LA GUERRE[3]

My intervention at the Easter congress of the Labor party
as to changing our methods of workers' education has

[2] *Au Pays du Taylorisme*, Brussels: Peuple, 1919, p. 105.
[3] *Le Peuple*, 7 May to 3 June 1919.

earned me congratulations and bitter reproaches. They are
both just about equally agreeable to me, since they prove
that I have attained my end. That was to make our militants reflect as to the lessons that postwar socialism can
draw from the events of these last five years.

I do not put on any false self-esteem to hide the fact that
my ideas of today are very different from those that I had
in 1914. I even believe it is my duty to reply to the wish of
several of my friends who have asked me, as did Arthur
Geerts[4] at the congress itself, to express the reasons for my
change in outlook, in a more complete and detailed way
than I could have done at the rostrum of the congress.

I would not dream of asking for the hospitality of the
columns of the *Peuple* for confessions of such a personal
nature if they did not involve questions of interest beyond
any personal concern. In a general way, it seems to me that
our comrades who stayed at home during the war have
only a vague idea of what the influence of the war has been
on those who experienced it as soldiers. Even if my case is
characteristic of only a few of these, it doesn't seem to me
less opportune to discuss it, if only as a contribution to the
discussion on postwar socialism that Auguste Dewinne[5] has
opened in the columns of our newspaper.

In order right away to avoid any misunderstanding, I
must declare that, even though I was an officer and associated with governmental action during the war by two official missions abroad—to Russia in 1917 and to the United
States in 1918—I have never been among those who lost
their moral autonomy by the intoxication of official patriotism and militaristic chauvinism. I was a socialist, antimilitarist, and internationalist before the war. I believe I am
even more so now. I am perhaps so in a different way, but
certainly not less deeply nor less wholeheartedly. It is precisely because I regard socialism as an urgent reality and as

[4] I have been unable to identify this man.
[5] 1861-1935, longtime editor of *Le Peuple* (information supplied by the
Institut Emile Vandervelde).

even more ineluctable than hitherto that it appears to me
from an angle different from my opinions of 1914.

The revision of my ideas is due above all to the fact that
for three years they were literally put to the test of fire. My
outlook was remade in the trenches. The trip that I took
with Vandervelde and de Brouckère[6] to Russia during the
revolution, and the one that allowed me to pass six months
in the United States the following year, only confirmed the
outcome.

The three years that I passed at the front, starting as an
infantryman to finish as a lieutenant of trench artillery,
were for me a period of pitiless analysis and of unhappy
reflection. For a dozen years I had devoted my life to the
ideal of universal fraternity. The best part of my activity
had been devoted to the struggle against militarism, from
the time I entered the "Young Guard" to when with my
unfortunate friend Karl Liebknecht[7] I founded the International Federation of Socialist Youth. Pursuing the ideal
of becoming a "citizen of the world," I had lived six years in
Germany, Austria, and England, and had traveled in
nearly all the countries of Europe. It was to Germany especially that I owed the essence of my socialist and academic
outlook. When the war burst out there is no doubt that I
had more friends in the German army than in the Belgian
army for which I volunteered the first day of the invasion.

It is certainly easy to say that, not having been able to
prevent the war despite all their efforts, the socialists of the
countries attacked—and Belgium was beyond question,
and treacherously, so—had as their duty to defend their
national independence. But the time had passed in which it
was possible to believe that the most complex questions

[6] Emile Vandervelde, 1866-1938, perennial *patron* of the Belgian Labor
party; Louis de Brouckère, 1870-1951, in prewar years coleader with de
Man of the Marxist wing of the party. The mission in question was reported in Vandervelde's *Trois Aspects de la révolution russe*, Paris-Nancy:
Berger-Levrault, 1918.

[7] 1871-1919; murdered together with Rosa Luxemburg while they were
in prison as leaders of the abortive Spartacist uprising in Berlin, January
1919.

could be resolved by reciting the text of a resolution from an international socialist congress. For a truly internationalist socialist the case of Belgium, as symbolic as it was, could be only one of the aspects of the problem of war. This latter soon passed beyond the framework of purely national questions. The more it became worldwide, the more the conscience of the socialist militant was tormented by new questions that arose on all sides. Wasn't it in the end a conflict of purely imperialistic appetites engaging the British and the German empires? Didn't the Germans have the same motives in fighting against czarism as we did against kaiserism? In believing to give my life in order that permanent peace and democracy might be brought to Europe, was I not simply going to die so that Nicholas would enter Constantinople and George V Baghdad?

I hasten to add that the doubts that these questions—and many others that can be imagined—stirred up within me were always laid to rest by analysis. The conclusion of each moral crisis that I had was that I had done well in taking up the rifle on the fourth of August, 1914, and I came to this conclusion rapidly enough so that these doubts did not prevent me from doing my duty as a soldier with dispatch.

But I do not want to anticipate my conclusions. I restrict myself to recognizing that for three years the thesis of the "internationalists," deriving the duty of socialists from the proposition that the war was only a conflict of imperialistic ambitions, tormented my conscience. How could it have been otherwise? The arguments with which they supported their case were exactly the same as those all of us had used ourselves before 1914 in our propaganda against war. Those who spoke had always been our fellow fighters, and those to whom we had taught socialism returned against us, whom they called traitors to the proletariat, the formulas that we had taught them. The indelible horror of the butchery of which we were the witnesses and the authors, the privations and the injustices of which the proletarians of the trenches were victim, all this tended to make us even more attentive to the voice that, from above the battle, spoke to us of the international fraternity of the workers and of international action against the imperialisms. How could I have not listened to it?

The greatest disappointment that I have received since my return home—and I have experienced a few—is to see that my friends who remained at home seem to have no doubts as to what was the meaning of these tragic moral crises. Thus an excellent prewar comrade, an out-and-out internationalist, apparently thought he was pleasing me in saying that he had always "excused" my volunteering through understanding that I had wanted to see things "from close up" and had given in to the desire for adventure. What a pretty spectacle and fine adventure I would have been able to avoid! I restrained myself from saying to my questioner what I thought of his generous hypothesis. I accepted the outrage as a deserved punishment. For he was one of my favorite students from the national [i.e., Belgian] socialist school, and his outlook, incapable of understanding a feeling other than those to which a supposedly Marxist "class morality" had given the formula, had been formed in my own school.[8]

Undoubtedly I would have astonished him very much if I had said that, of all the sufferings that I knew at the front—and I speak of them without false modesty, since millions of men underwent them—the worst was not the constant threat of death, nor the privations, nor the moral solitude, not even the filth, the cold, and the mud. It was having to fight for a cause so different from that a socialist would have freely chosen, a task that became a permanent problem of conscience. One had to be ready to die at any second, to kill and mutilate men, to make widows and orphans, and still to be in a state at each instant to reply to the great WHY? which came back to me as an echo of what I myself had said against the war before it had broken out.

---

[8] The Centrale d'Education Ouvrière, of which de Man had been secretary-general from 1910 to 1914; under his direction it had attempted to give a Marxist indoctrination to the party cadres.

And to reply by the single consideration that chance had
made me a Belgian citizen rather than a subject of Wilhelm
II.

It is this that I call the proof of fire through which my
socialist conscience has passed. A tragic testing, in which
death was the interrogator! It now was something quite
other than making theoretical formulas in the peace of a
study, or proclaiming them from the height of a professional podium. One had to know whether they were the
truths justifying the sacrifice of one's life—and that of
others.

In this burning crucible there remains much that is
purified and tempered like steel, the ideas that seem to me
today to be fundamental to postwar socialism.

I no longer think that we can understand the new facts
of social life with the help of a doctrine established on the
basis of earlier and different facts. I no longer think that
the theory that sees contemporary wars only as the result of
economic conflicts between imperialistic governments is
right. I no longer think that economic phenomena alone
can furnish us with the weft of all historical evolution. I no
longer think that socialism can be realized independently
of the development of political democracy. I no longer
think that to come to socialism it suffices to appeal to the
class interests of the industrial proletariat, disdaining the
support that certain interests and ideals common to the
whole nation or to all mankind can give to us. I no longer
think that the proletarian class struggle, which remains as
the principal means for the realization of socialism, can
lead to it without admitting certain forms of class and party
collaboration. I no longer believe that socialism can consist
simply of the seizure of the basic means of production by
the state, without profound transformation of the procedures of administration to bring about the unlimited development of social productivity. I no longer think that a
socialist society can be sustained tomorrow if it gives up the
stimulant that today is furnished by the competition of pri-

vate enterprises and the unequal reward of labor, proportioned to its social productivity. I do believe in a socialism closer at hand and more certain, but also one that is more realistic, more pragmatic, more organic—in a word, more human. As all sound philosophy starts with criticism of knowledge, I will speak, in my next article, of the new way in which I envisage the value of theory for action, and so that there shall be no doubt as to my apostasy, I shall entitle it: the revision of Marxism.

THE REVISION OF MARXISM

I experienced an intense pleasure in hearing comrade Geerts, who was polemicizing at the rostrum of the Easter congress against what he called my renunciation of Marxism, when he cited these words from Vandervelde:

> How many times since the beginning of this war haven't we heard that silly declaration that Marx and Marxism should be held responsible for the failings and deviations of German social democracy! But if there is a group in Germany or in the rest of Europe which has known how to keep in the midst of the turmoil the independence of its thought, the international unity of its action, the firmness of its doctrine, staunchly hostile to any kind of war of adventure, domination, or conquest, it is precisely the group of disciples most directly connected with Marx, the most skilled representatives of Marxism.

Thus Vandervelde expressed himself the first of May, 1917, at the tomb of Karl Marx at Highgate. I was there. And I do not hide a certain pleasure in self-esteem in having heard Vandervelde cite my name soon afterward, in a sentence that Geerts neglected to read to the congress:

> Do I have any need to recall that indeed since the day in which German imperialism declared war on

Europe, it was Marxists of strict observance, such as Jules Guesde in France, Hyndman in Great Britain, Plekhanov in Russia, de Brouckère and de Man in Belgium, who were among socialists the first to bring a remorseless condemnation against the pacifism of nonresistance? And, on the other hand, in Germany, where a whole people rushed to the frontiers with the blind furor of the elements, who then had the courage to take the lead or to assert self-possession? It was Liebknecht, Rosa Luxemburg, Klara Zetkin, Kautsky and Eduard Bernstein, the socialist minority, who are the disciples and fulfillers of Marx.

Moreover, Vandervelde would have been able to cite other Belgian names.

Before the war, we were a small group of Belgian militants speaking in the name of Marxism, who had the custom of meeting a couple of times a year. There were Louis de Brouckère, Fernand Dardenne, Léon Delsinne, Isi Delvigne, Guillaume Eekelers, E. Preumont, H. Vandemeulebroucke, and I. But Louis de Brouckère took up his gun the fourth of August, 1914, just like me and like Fernand Dardenne, who died as a hero at the front. Sergeant Vandemeulebroucke collected his stripes and his decorations there as well, and this former director of your Socialist Young Guard upon his return to civilian life hurried to separate himself from the pacifist adventures by which certain groups of our youth let themselves get involved. Preumont died after having, as a war correspondent, done all that he could to support the morale of our soldiers. Eekelers, while completely a "Stockholmian,"[9] helped the Belgian government find workers to make munitions. And when I came back home after the armistice, what an agreeable surprise it was for me to find that my friends Delvigne and Delsinne had both, although in

---

[9] I.e., a supporter of the neutralist socialist viewpoint expressed at the Stockholm Conference of 1917.

quite different circumstances, and although isolated from one another, experienced a change of outlook entirely parallel to that of de Brouckère, Vandemeulebroucke, and myself!

Now if you ask any one of these comrades I would be very much surprised if you didn't hear these two things said: first of all, their doctrinal viewpoint, especially with regard to the theories of Marx, has been modified during the war in a more liberal and a more realistic direction. And second, their Marxist outlook of prewar days, far from preventing this evolution has, on the contrary, helped them better to understand the general problems that took shape before their eyes, and made clearer and less confused the gradual change of their ideas.

If there seems to be something of a contradiction there, it is only apparent. I even believe that we have witnessed a universal phenomenon of change in Marxism, as, moreover, Vandervelde has indicated. The majority of the names that he cited in his speech at Highgate were those of Marxists who had made a personal effort of interpretation of the theories of Marx, and, thanks to the intellectual autonomy that this effort gave them, succeeded in enriching the literature of scientific socialism by works that, with the help of the method founded by Marx, carried further certain Marxist theses and corrected certain other ones. In this regard one could, moreover, put the name of Emile Vandervelde on the same level as that of Kautsky or of Plekhanov.

There are, however, some men who speak in the name of Marxism and who are now in the camp of bolshevism, that caricature of socialism, as Branting[10] has so well said. But one searches in vain among them for a name that has become famous by original works. They are epigones who, prostrated at the feet of the master, believe they are com-

[10] Karl Hjalmar Branting, 1860-1925, Swedish socialist leader, chairman of the Stockholm Conference, later prime minister several times.

municating with the spirit by adoring the letter. They are
Trotsky and other Bernsteins [Bronsteins?][11] who believe
they can claim Marx because they apply formulas, learned
by heart from his works, to entirely different situations
from those Marx had in mind when he conceived them.
They are those who speak of the expropriation of capitalism and of the dictatorship of the proletariat where capitalism and the proletariat scarcely start to be established,
and of internationalism, where nationality itself has still to
be realized. They are those who do not know or who forget
that Marx himself never ceased to consider the realization
of political democracy and of national autonomy as conditions antecedent to socialism. In any case, one can't help
thinking, with respect to these ultra-Marxists, of the witti-
cism attributed to Marx who said that, if he had to choose
to be identified with a school of thought, it would certainly
not be Marxist!

What has given and still gives its value to Marxism is the
fact that it constitutes a method of scientific research rather
than a system of definitive results. Many things that the
prophetic genius of Marx was not able to foresee have
taken place in the half-century elapsed since the appearance of his masterworks. If the system of Marxist formulas
is to be adjusted to new conditions it is apparent that it is
necessary to make as profound changes as the natural sciences had to bring to the theories of Darwin. But there remains of Marx that which remains of Darwin: first of all,
the permanent merit of having introduced, in the area of
knowledge that he studied, the idea of an evolution obey-
ing scientific laws; then and above all, the method, which
consists in making use of economic facts to explain the

[11] It seems unlikely that de Man meant to include the revisionist Eduard
Bernstein, 1850-1932, "in the camp of bolshevism," but it is conceivable
that he detected a commonality in the efforts of both man and party to
maintain the authority of the Marxist tradition. Or it may be that the pen
or the typesetter substituted Bernstein's name for that of Lev Davydovich
Bronstein, 1877-1940, otherwise known as Trotsky.

great forces that make for historical progress, and to recognize the formidable motive force that is found in class interests arising from the mode of production in use.

The results to which this method leads are not more im-
mutable than those of any procedure of scientific investigation. Its value, as that of any instrument, depends on the
way in which it is used. The way in which it helped the
Marxists cited by Vandervelde to understand the general
phenomena of the war period shows that it is far from having its use exhausted.

Nevertheless, for it to continue to be useful it must be
continually emended in the light of the new facts of history. For my part, the war period brought to me very important changes of which I will speak upon another occasion. But what matters even more is that it is understood,
once and for all, that all scientific method, all theory, whatever it may be, can be applied to the study of facts. Before
the war we had not seen that clearly enough. In approaching particular circumstances, we all too often used abstract
categories as if they were the facts themselves, like a
chemist who confused an element to be studied with the
formula describing its general properties.

It is this that the "internationalists" have done in connection with the war.

Before the war of 1914, by virtue of a theory that proceeded inductively from a series of antecedent facts, we
had shown that in a capitalist regime war was the outcome
of an economic competition among states afflicted with imperialistic expansion. Events have shown that this conception was fundamentally correct.

But when the war of 1914 came, it was no longer a question of war in general, but of war in particular. It was no
longer a category, but a fact. A most disagreeable fact,
which we vainly tried to prevent, but which appeared nevertheless in a most tangible form, as I can assure you from
my experience as a foot soldier and trench-mortar spe-

cialist. It brought a whole series of questions of action that had to be resolved.

What did our "internationalists" do at this point? They retired to their Olympia and said: "I do not know of *this* war. I do not care to know who was the aggressor, what are the objectives of the people and the governments in conflict, what would be the consequences if a given belligerent group were to win. The only thing I care about is war, the responsibility for which falls upon capitalism, and to which one must oppose socialism. They're firing at you? They're launching torpedoes or lobbing shells at you? Your women and children are being killed? It's a shame. It's the fault of capitalist surplus value. Marx has put it in a formula. It's very well put: look at page 240 of the second volume of *Kapital*. You say that in the meantime it's vexing that your face is being bashed in? It's possible. Bring about socialism, expropriation, the dictatorship of the proletariat; look at page 63 of the *Communist Manifesto!*"

Thus abstract formulas were used to represent the war to us as an aggression of capitalism against the international proletariat. But the reality was that the proletariat of all countries made war in alliance with the capitalists of their countries. The reality was that capitalist imperialism had created the general conditions making the war possible, but this war had nevertheless been provoked by the deliberate aggression of two semiabsolutistic and completely militarized governments against two small and defenseless nations. The reality was that the victory of the Central Powers would have deprived Europe, and perhaps the world, of that minimum of democracy and of liberty of which socialism has need, just as man has need of air in order to live.

The reality was that the war finally became a conflict engaging all the self-governing peoples with the remaining governments of divine right. The reality is that from the defeat of the latter has emerged, not socialism at all (far from it! who would have expected it?), but a Europe without emperors and without czars, freed from the nightmare of the pointed helmet and from the dynastic yoke that oppressed the nationalities of the central and eastern countries; a Europe in which, indeed, the path is open for socialist realizations as soon as the people want them, since henceforth there are only leaders elected by them.

That is what it has meant to those of us who had judged the situation according to the facts. As for those who have let themselves be hypnotized by the dogmas of a badly understood theory, they must still show that, since all capitalist states are ruled by an imperialist class and all governments are the expression of the will of this class, there is no difference between Wilhelm II and Woodrow Wilson.

Socialism and Democracy

One of the hardest lessons that war gave me is that I, like the majority of the prewar Marxist socialists, had always underestimated the importance of political democracy for the liberation of the working class.

The method of historical materialism founded by Marx had too much accustomed us to see only the economic side of the facts of social life. On the other hand, Marxism had been stamped too strongly by the socialism of Germany and Russia, two countries where the lack of democratic institutions and, what is worse, democratic traditions, had necessarily had repercussions on the workers' outlook. And finally, concern to emphasize the difference between the vigorous class movement of the proletariat and the deplorable decadence of bourgeois democracy, gradually giving up the traditions of its revolutionary origins as its fear of the workers' revolution increased, had led us too often to confuse the prostration of the bourgeois democratic movement with that of the principles in the name of which it spoke. These are the essential motives that explain the mocking scorn that I confess having shown before the war, like many other socialists, for the old fogies who still dared to speak of the "immortal principles of 1789."

And nevertheless, these principles had not yet passed out of fashion, as many among us believed. It was for them that millions of men in the ranks of the armies of the Entente fought. It was in their name that Kerensky led his troops to the Galician offensive, and President Wilson raised the formidable army that came to give the *coup de grâce* to the last monarchies of divine right. I do not know if there are socialists who would assert that these millions of men have been mistaken in letting themselves be taken to slaughter for the sake of democratic slogans which, to listen to them, serve only as a camouflage for imperialistic aims. But even if it is so, the hold of these slogans on the masses which, let us not forget, make up the flower of the working class of England, America, and France, would appear all the more salient and formidable.

For my part, I recognize that I have been strongly impressed by the fact that these working masses have consented to much greater sacrifices for ideas such as the autonomy and inviolability of nations, justice in the relations among states, and the self-government of peoples, than those that up to now they have made when their material class interests were at stake. Even if they have been wrong—and I am convinced of the contrary—the fact would not be less patent. Thus perhaps the Belgian working class would have found itself better off if, instead of concentrating the best of its energies for thirty years on the conquest of universal suffrage, it had devoted an equally energetic effort to the establishment of the eight-hour day or to improvement in wages, for instance. But even if this was a mistake, it was an admirable mistake, a mistake that, in my eyes, makes the working class that committed it more worthy of love. For in acting so, it showed itself more devoted to justice than to well-being, or better yet, that Belgian socialism does not conceive of material well-being without the freedom and equality that political democracy alone can guarantee.

During my sentry duties I often compared this attitude of the Belgian proletariat, which made three general strikes to attain universal suffrage,[12] with that of the German proletariat, which roused only platonic and inefficacious protestations against the bourgeois *coups d'état* which, as in Saxony in 1897 and at Hamburg, Dresden, and Lübeck in 1905, took away from the working class the equal vote at the very moment when it was in process of giving that vote to the social democrats. I remember old Bebel at the Jena Congress of 1905 stigmatizing this servile passivity of the German workers and wrenching applause from the six hundred representatives of German social democracy by his heartfelt cry, disgusted with the brutal materialism of the post-1871 generation, "Hunde seid Ihr ja doch!" ("You are simply dogs"). And I said to myself that if I had been right in advocating before 1914 in Belgium the organizational methods that had made of social democracy and unions in Germany formidable instruments of strength, I had been wrong in not saying out loud enough that these instruments receive their value only by reason of the revolutionary pugnacity and political virility of the masses that they incarnate.

It was the lamentable failure of German social democracy, giving way as a party of opposition to military imperialism on the fourth of August, 1914, that opened my eyes. And the bitter reflections it engendered have, as I said at the Easter congress of the Labor party, "brought back my outlook to the Belgian worker's spirit."

My disappointment was as profitable as it was unhappy. For it led me to this conclusion, that a minimum of freedom, of political democracy, is necessary to socialism for its existence and for its flowering. "This minimum of freedom," I said in 1917 in a speech, of which the *Internationale*

[12] The three general strikes were of 1893, 1902, and 1913; universal manhood suffrage was in fact attained by virtue of the first crisis, but was substantially nullified by the simultaneous grant of a plural vote on the bases of property, education, and marital status. Equality of suffrage was finally obtained in 1919; women obtained the vote in 1921.

Korrespondenz of Legien and Baumeister did me the honor of making a German translation, "existed in the Western democracies. It did not exist in Germany. The proof of that is that, despite the power of organization and depth of theoretical knowledge for which German social democracy has always served for us as a model, it lamentably crumbled as a revolutionary force from the first day of the war, because it was the product of a country of military despotism, deprived of any revolutionary tradition and of that atmosphere of liberty without which there cannot be real civic heroism, without which there will be in the place of well-tempered character only the spirit of slaves."[13]

But why have we fought, if not for this "minimum of democracy"? It was not for socialism; Wilson, no more than Clemenceau or Lloyd George, did not have that inscribed upon his banners. We have not even been expecting that the victory of the Entente will lead to the universal and complete installation of political democracy. That has not yet been realized anywhere in Europe, and it has not even been fully carried out in the United States. But in Belgium, as in England, France, and America, we have at least that minimum, as indispensable to socialism as the air of the atmosphere is to man and which—as events have shown—we did not have in Germany, nor in Russia.

Of course we too have at home annexationists, militarists, and imperialists, just as the Germans do. But the big difference between Germany and us is that with us, in the West, thanks always to this "minimum of democracy," there was an opposition having, over and above strength, the freedom and the "will" necessary to counterbalance these noxious tendencies, while with the Central Powers, those who should have acted against imperialism made themselves its servants and its accomplices. Despotism and militarism had stifled among the people the qualities of character necessary to fight back. It is for this reason that,

[13] "Address to the Soviet of the Officers and Soldiers of the Volhynian Regiment," delivered in Petrograd, June 1917 [de Man].

not having succeeded in preventing the war, and not being able to dream of realizing socialism during the war, we viewed the defeat of the Central Powers as the only means to assure Europe of certain conditions indispensable for the realization of democracy, and without which socialism itself would be only a decoy.

It seems to me that I hear comrades who cry out: "You don't mean that it was for this that we fought?" Indeed yes, comrades, and I think it was well worth the effort. It is easy to take a heroic posture in declaring that only the socialist ideal justifies such sacrifices. But to whom is it given to be able to realize, with the one act of sacrifice of his life, his ideal on earth? If socialism merits dying for its own sake, then it should be the same way with everything that is indispensable for its coming. But who would dare deny that in bringing down the Prussian eagle which for four years held us in its talons we were doing the only thing that was in our power to maintain and to establish in Europe that democracy that is a condition for socialism?

Socialists such as Jean Jaurès[14] who never separated the cause of political liberty from that of economic emancipation, and who proudly claimed the heritage of the "bourgeois" revolutions of England, America, and France for the proletariat, have seen rightly. It is because their conception has prevailed in the proletariat of the great Western democracies that Europe is henceforth made up only of nations that govern themselves.

Socialists, such as the majoritarians of German social democracy and Russian bolshevism, who have considered that socialism has no need for democracy for its realization, are wrong. It is their responsibility that Central and Eastern Europe today offer us a picture of distress and disorder in which the proletariat clutches in vain to a dictatorship that can be maintained only by oppressing in turn its

[14] 1859-1914, French socialist leader, assassinated as a pacifist on the eve of the outbreak of World War I. His humanistic approach to socialism had now come to be revered by de Man.

former oppressors. Those who have won by liberty and by the law can expect to live by liberty and by the law. Those who have conquered by the machine gun will perish by the machine gun.

THE CONQUEST OF THE STATE

I have already said, in a preceding article, how my reflections on the causes of the moral bankruptcy of German social democracy had led me better to appreciate the essential importance of political democracy for the realization of socialism. I wish to continue today this sketch of my mental evolution during the war in saying what was my psychological reaction to my trips, to Russia in 1917, and to the United States in 1918.

In Russia I saw socialism without democracy. In America, I saw democracy without socialism. My conclusion is that, for my part, I would prefer, if I had to choose, to live in a democracy without socialism than under a socialist regime without democracy. That does not mean that I am more democratic than socialist. That very simply means that democracy without socialism is always democracy, whereas socialism without democracy is not even socialism. Democracy, being the government of the majority, can lead to socialism, if the majority comes to be in favor of it; socialism, if it is not based on the government of the majority, is a despotic regime, which means either civil war or stagnation.

But one of the things that impressed me most vividly during my stay in Russia was the incapacity of the socialist movement, which, however, claimed to be inspired by pure Marxist doctrine, to bring any innovation whatsoever to political and administrative matters. There were, to be sure, the soviets. The word was new, but the thing was very old. To the extent that they were not "factory councils," recalling the stage in industrial evolution that preceded the union movement with us, they were copies—and bad copies—of the committees of public safety of the French Revolution, kinds of local and miniature parliaments, where there was much oration, little action, and no administration. Experience has, moreover, shown how this organization was incapable of resolving the complex problems requiring the rapid decisions in specialized areas and the precise responsibilities that preoccupy the conduct of the state today, just as in any other industry. In the social area, the soviets have brought us the reign of the disbanded soldiery, lyingly baptized as the dictatorship of the proletariat; in the political area they have led to the government of ranters and of doctrinaires; in the military area, to the most shameful disorders, such as that of Stokhod in 1917, when two Russian divisions were made prisoner because their soviets could not agree on the tactics to follow; in the technical and administrative area, to the most abominable disorder and to the stoppage of production. Everyone knows the story, characteristic of the "sovietization" of the railroad system, of the two trains that met in front of a shunting track and submitted to the soviets of the two neighboring stations, called together by telephone, the question as to which should be shunted aside to allow the other to pass. Russian industry has seen even worse instances, and it is understandable why Lenin now sees himself obliged to appeal by means of extravagant promises to the technicians of the "bourgeoisie" who happen by forgetfulness or chance to have escaped the massacres in the midst of which up to this point they have learned to live.

To be sure, there were some initiatives that were not just cheap imitations of 1793 or 1848. For instance university professors and managing directors were forced to clean the streets of Petrograd, and banks "socialized" by grabbing the contents of their safety vaults. But I pity socialists who imagine that it is by such acts of disorderly and emotional demagoguery that we are going to build the New Jerusalem.

The counterpart to this Petrograd Soviet as I knew it in
1917, a malodorous mixture of ragtag guard and debating
club in course of gestation (Albert Thomas[15] rightly said
that even the odor drifting there recalled the Paris Com-
mune of 1871), was the administrative departments in
which the socialist ministers, dubiously assisted by inexpe-
rienced secretaries, hurled themselves in vain against the
inertia of personnel held over from the former regime,
who were irreplaceable for lack of alternative trained personnel. During the first months of the revolution nothing
was more absurd than to see, for example, the former officials of foreign affairs, chosen, titled, and decorated by the
czar, carry out (if that is the expression) Kerensky's policy.[16] It is true that some months later Lenin put an end to
this sabotage by showing its authors the door, or by putting
them to the wall. But no more than Kerensky could he replace them, so that all that changed was that, instead of
doing a bad job, none was done at all.

I do not dream of denying, however, that the problem of
the administrative and political capacity of the working
class is manifested, in the countries of Western Europe in
much less unfavorable terms than in Russia, or than in the
country of Bela Kun,[17] this fine fellow who by means of
proclamations made of Hungary a Communist paradise in
which the proletarians were so happy that when they had
to defend it against a handful of Rumanians and Czecho-
slovakians, they all skipped camp together. The working
class of the Western democracies of course contrasts with
the Russian proletariat in numbers, organization, and education. However, who would dare deny that, if in any country of Western Europe the workers' party was presently
swept into power, in attempting to change the organization

[15] 1878-1932, French socialist leader.
[16] Aleksandr Feodorovich Kerensky, 1881-1970, the leading figure in
the Russian Provisional government of 1917.
[17] 1885-1937, Hungarian Communist and premier of the revolutionary
regime of March-July 1919.

of the country it would find itself placed before problems demanding a political, administrative, and technical capacity far beyond that which the working class has been able to show up to the present time?

I would not be a socialist if I did not believe that this capacity is to be found in embryo in the proletariat—on condition that the expression includes beyond the manual workers those, such as the technicians, the white-collar workers, the engineers, the scholars, and the artists, who today sell their intellectual labor power on the market of the capitalist world. But so that this embryo can develop and give other than just momentary yield, a long period of adaptation of the working class to the new tasks of social management will have to take place.

The conquest of political power by the workers' parties seems now to be close in the majority of the large European countries. Let us rejoice in this, but let us not forget that it is only an optical illusion than can lead us to confuse this conquest with the realization of a socialist society. This will be only the first step. The real task will only start when we have the tools in hand. It will then be evident that the question that is henceforth to be put to the proletariat setting out for the assault for political and industrial power is a double one. It is not only to know who will possess the instruments of this power and for which ideal they can be used. It is also a question of making sure that these instruments are capable of serving whatever ideal there may be. In order better to organize production and better to divide its fruits, it is necessary to begin by assuring its functioning, and by making possible the unlimited increase of social productivity. And since for this we must inevitably make use of the political power that will put the majority in a position to realize its views, we must henceforth consider in what sense we must transform the state if we want it to serve in this transformation.

This last problem will become all the more pressing as the universal crisis of parliamentarism shows us from day to day more clearly that the capacities required in order to govern—in the more extended meaning belonging to this term—are very different from those that make up the armament of the lawyers who fill our parliaments with the echoes of their eloquence. Democracy and parliamentarism have been confused for too long a time. The latter is only one aspect, and scarcely an essential aspect, of the government of the nation. The complexity of the administration of things increases to the degree to which the ambit of the activity of states, provinces, communes, and agencies is extended, and as the output of all enterprise requires a greater division of functions and responsibilities. The functions of ministers are reduced to those of political agents of liaison between the administrative, legislative, and executive powers. Their original function as heads of administration has become a myth. It is rather their bureaucracy that administers them. Where public agencies have taken over the management of industrial or commercial affairs, as a general rule they have shown themselves to be inefficient, routine, and wasteful, until it has been understood—and the socialism of the European continent has just begun to understand this—that the authority of representative organs should, in these cases, be reduced to a simple power of supervision and of censure, leaving to the technical management of the agencies an autonomy comparable to that which prevails in private industry. Lastly, in parliamentary life itself the system of parties has brought about a kind of fossilization. What was, originally, a guarantee of the balance of political forces in the nation, has become an instrument of professional intrigue, to the point of nearly constituting an obstacle to all progressive legislation. Recourse to the referendum, combined with the consultation with representative bodies of specialized jurisdictions, and the introduction of a greater administrative and budgetary autonomy in the public services, seem more and more the only means of reconciling parliamentarism with the true expression of the popular will, whereby all legislative measures would be judged according to their intrinsic merits and all administrative service according to its results.

Now that socialism is passing from the era of agitation to that of realization, it must regard its problems openly. It cannot pretend not to know that if the state, as it is organized and equipped today, were to be invested at one and the same time with the right of ownership and with the function of administering most of the public wealth, it would put an end to certain of the evils of private capitalism only to increase some of the others. If the latter consist in a lessening of social productivity, combined with the establishment of a dictatorship without that guarantee of progress that is assured by the right of minorities to organize, the cure will be worse than the disease. In any case, it seems to me that we must declare that henceforth we will be seeking to avoid this reef, notably by making a very clear distinction between the owning state and the administrative state. This will still be only a necessary, but not a sufficient, condition. I will speak of others in a following article.

CLASS STRUGGLE AND SOCIAL COLLABORATION

The lessons of the war have led me especially to change the idea of the class struggle as a means for social action. "I no longer think," I said in a preceding article, "that to arrive at socialism it suffices to appeal to the class interests of the industrial proletariat, disdaining the support that certain interests and ideals common to the whole nation or to all mankind can give to us. I no longer think that the proletarian class struggle, which remains as the principal means for the realization of socialism, can lead to it without admitting certain forms of class and party collaboration."

I hasten to say that this opinion is not based at all on the belief that the common life of sufferings and sacrifices led by the bourgeois and the proletarians fraternally united in uniform, or even in civil life by common resistance to the enemy, would have created a new outlook with tomorrow's generation. At the beginning of the war I knew people, notably socialists, who naively believed that a kind of golden age was thus going to be realized, in which human fraternity and mutual esteem were going to transform our former political and social struggles into a kind of idyll. I never forbore from laughing in their faces. The fraternization of classes under the flag? Ah what a delusion! It sounds very well in a speech, but go ask someone who has lived at the front to tell you in all candor what he has seen in reality. Perhaps there was something of this kind in France or in the other countries where everyone served under the flag. But in Belgium? There have doubtless been a certain number of bourgeois and of aristocrats in the army who have done their duty nobly. But their sacrifice does not change at all the fact that from the beginning the bourgeoisie made up a very small minority, thanks to the privilege by which it had, until just a few years ago, escaped from the burden of military service. The heroism of a few does not wash away the class shame, which has made an army of the poor defend the capitalist paradise. When after the Yser[18] there was greater and greater resort to educated men for service at the rear, in headquarters, and in noncombatant units, the drift took place naturally enough. The best of what the bourgeoisie had contributed to the Belgian army had left the front. As there were plenty of positions to be filled and since there was only a small minority of educated people in the army, the Belgian army of the trenches was again, from 1915 on, the army of the poor. It was scarcely possible to find enough candidates with the indispensable minimum of education for commissioned or noncommissioned officers. Others became headquarter secretaries, motorcyclists, chauffeurs, supply officers, clerks in the innumerable offices of the rear, interpreters, radio operators, railroad superintendents or even

[18] Battle of the Yser, in which the Belgian army with French support withstood a major German attack, 18-27 October 1914.

gunners in the heavy artillery—the heaviest possible, as King Albert said. In the trench-mortar battery to which I was finally attached, there were only three out of the 182 men who were neither peasants nor workers. And all three had stripes, you can believe it. In these conditions, if the fraternization of classes took place in the Belgian army, it must have been at Calais or at Sainte-Adresse,[19] for at the front one never saw it at all.

As for the effect of the life of the trenches on character, it requires an intransigent idealism to believe that such music softens manners! I'm afraid that on the contrary it created, aside from a very small elite of those athirst with idealism, a mass of several million men brutalized by sufferings, fatigue, and tedium, with whom the practice of killing had reawakened the bestial instincts which only await an opportunity to manifest themselves in the social struggles of the future and in the recrudescence of criminality. Some distance from an idyll, I would say.

As for the moral effect of the war on the civilian population remaining at home, I am not in a position to draw conclusions. However, the comrades who have lived under the occupation appear to me to be very skeptical about it. And I can understand this, when I see around me constant proofs of the wholesale demoralization which has given an even more revolting appearance than hitherto to the onslaught of appetite; when I assert that the possessing classes of Belgium decidedly do not intend to give up the honor of being the most backward in the whole world and the last to allow the working class to wrench concessions from them; and when I learn that the Belgian bourgeoisie has not even shown enough social conscience under the occupation to give up depriving, through their bank notes, starving people of food that was a necessity for the children of the poor and a luxury for the property holders.

[19] Calais was a principal supply center for both the Belgian army and the British Expeditionary Force; Sainte-Adresse (near Le Havre) was the wartime seat of the Belgian government (information from the Institut Emile Vandervelde).

For that matter, I do not imagine for an instant denying that the war, as much through its moral influence as its economic effect, has, far from reducing the class struggle, on the contrary intensified it everywhere, even in a country like Belgium in which the problems of reconstruction nevertheless impose a rather strong bond of national solidarity. One must be blind not to see it.

Therefore, if it is only a question of asserting this fact, or of generalizing it by stating that class struggles have always played a primordial role in the great mass movements, which are the weft of the fabric of history, we are immediately in agreement, not only among socialists, but indeed with men of all classes who uphold truth.

But there is a *struggle of classes*, a historical fact, and a *class struggle*, a doctrine of socialist action. This latter seems to me subject to revision.

To be sure, the socialist revolution of tomorrow will be essentially the work of the proletariat, moved by its class interests, as that of 1789 was that of the bourgeois and peasant Third Estate. But does that mean that the realization of socialism will be the automatic outcome of the action of a single social class, which will only have to obey the dictates of its own interest in order to establish a reign of justice? I do not think so.

A "bourgeois" scholar—and not one of the least—who follows the progress of socialist democracy with a well-informed sympathy, made a remark to me the other day that coincided singularly with my own thoughts: "Your prewar Marxism," he said, "is a singular and illogical mixture of materialism and idealism. It proclaims that social progress is realized primordially by the action of the masses who act in accordance with their class interests, that is, from the common interests that arise from the particular role that they play in economic life. Granted, and I've never denied it. Therefore, when you Marxists say that the present-day proletariat in pursuing the conquest of power for the realization of socialism has only to obey its class interests, you are smack in the middle of deterministic logic.

Up to this point you are materialistic. But then, when this proletariat will have seized power, expropriated large-scale capital, and abolished classes, what will become of it? What motives will it obey when it will no longer have its class interest to guide it, since it will no longer exist as a class? In order to reply to this question you are obliged to rig the working class out in ideal virtues, sufficient to transform the devils of today into the angels of tomorrow. And there you are smack in the middle of the most cloudy idealism. I myself could wish for little more than to believe in this metamorphosis. But do you really believe that things will be that simple?"

I had to acknowledge how right my questioner was. I have even gone further than he in declaring that I do not believe at all in that magical jump from the material into the ideal. I have been forced to recognize that the class interest of the proletariat, while being a sure guide for organizational and propaganda action today, will not, however, resolve any problem at all when the hour of decisive social realizations will have sounded. The proletariat does not have a monopoly of wisdom or of disinterestedness. It has not even come so far as to tear away from the bourgeoisie its monopoly of high scientific and artistic culture. In the strict meaning of the word it is limited to the class of producers, and does not even include the social categories that exercise the functions of management and coordination, which are essential to all large-scale production. In countries like Belgium, the agricultural classes and the professions remain outside its movement. And can one declare with impunity, on the other hand, that even at the present time the working class draws its inspiration for action only from the consciousness of its material class interests? I do not think so. If that were true, there would be no more difference in the outlook of Belgian, German, Russian, and American industrial workers than there is in the type of factories in which they work. But it's not like that at all. The intellectual resources from which the proletariat draws its ideas, even its moral and political ideas, are not limited to its class. They are the heritage of a long past common to all social strata, enriched by the treasures of an artistic and scientific culture, which developed independently, if not of social life, at least of the material interests of a particular class at a given moment. They carry the imprint of national institutions, of religious or moral beliefs of given surroundings, of the whole spirit of an epoch. To take away from the workers' outlook the human element it has beyond the limits of social class is to reduce man to a puppet, to the absurd abstraction of the *homo economicus*, which has hands only to produce and a stomach only for digestion.

But there is something more. By the extent of the sacrifices imposed on the nation, the war made evident to everyone that the domain in which the interests of the various social classes meet is much wider than prewar Marxism held. I am not thinking here only of the common interest of all the members of a nation in there being a minimum of universal education, or of security and of public health, or that the cities are provided with food, fuel, water, air, and guarantees against fire and flood, that the means of transportation and communication are assured, and a thousand other things as well; although a social cataclysm such as we have experienced and still experience does suffice to show that, all things considered, the lowliest worker finds himself bound in every phase of his daily life by at least as many bonds of solidarity to the social community as to the class of which he is a member. But is there not an interest common to all humanity, that the earth produce the greatest possible wealth and that the productivity of labor be increased? Does the industrial proletariat alone have an interest in preventing the mass destruction of lives and goods by war? Doesn't all humanity, aside from a few profiteers, find itself united by this desire? And when the working class itself finds itself driven by strike or lockout in battling for its right to life, doesn't it constantly make appeal to the interest of the community that production and transportation not be stopped, in order to break down egoistical resistances? And finally, is it not clear—let us look at Russia and Germany!—that the working class intending to found a new order by law has the same interest as everyone else that the existing laws, from the moment they are based on the consent of the constitutional majority, be observed, and that order be maintained, save in the well-defined cases in which the fundamental documents of democracy (the Declaration of the Rights of Man and the American Declaration of Independence) declare that rebellion is a duty?

It is for all these reasons that I believe that the class struggle must not exclude certain forms of collaboration, such as, for example, the present participation of the Belgian Labor party in the government of the country. It is for this reason especially that I believe it would be to diminish, impoverish, and compromise socialism if its appeal were to be limited to the material interests of the working class. In each nation, and in humanity as a whole, there are wells of idealism, which can and should be tapped. And in the next, last article I shall sketch how I conceive of the new socialism, humane and integral, the threshold of which we approach.

The New Socialism

It would not do good at all to disguise the fact that European socialism has lost the unity it seemed to have before the war. In Eastern Europe there is bolshevism, which wants to establish socialism on the dictatorship of force. In Western Europe there is democratic socialism, which conceives of the new social order as the result of the freely expressed will of a majority. If between the two tendencies there was only a passing national hostility created by the war, or the organizational dualism that arises from the competition between the Internationals of Moscow or of

Bern, one could be mistaken as to the importance of the conflict. But there is something more. As for what concerns me, I see an abyss between the two conceptions that no compromise will be able to bridge.

My objections to bolshevism are completely different from those that prevail in the bourgeois world. Of all the evils that afflict us I know of none less tolerable than the fashion of redbaiting upon all occasions. It is all the easier a sport since the immense majority of those who engage in it have no more idea of bolshevism than the solid citizen of Brussels who, when he was jostled the other day in the tram, scolded the guilty party: "Hey, you Commie, do you have to walk on my corns?"

As for those who know a little more what it's all about, they reproach the Bolsheviks for being socialists. What I blame them for is that they are antisocialist and above all antidemocratic.

At the present time if there are any credulous bourgeois remaining who see in bolshevism only the fruit of German gold paid to traitors, and in the Spartacism[20] of the other side of the Rhine only a skillful maneuver of the German government in order to frighten the Versailles Conference, they have tenacious illusions. Only a short while back there were those who tried to kill socialism by presenting its adherents and leaders as traitors, careerists, and scoundrels. But socialism is not dead, far from it. As for bolshevism, it seems to me that its progress is in direct relation to the brutal stupidity of those who have undertaken the mission of opposing it by using precisely the means—the suppression of liberties and the stubborn conservation of privileges—that gave birth to it.

We will escape its destructive action by studying objectively the causes that have elsewhere made it grow, and by trying to suppress them among us to the degree that they

[20] This was written shortly after the great left-socialist Spartacist rising in the Ruhr mining districts, put down with severity by a German Social-Democratic minister of war.

exist. It is a social illness created by the war just like the Spanish influenza, and the germ is just as widespread. To try to kill this germ by means of the judge, the policeman, censorship, the machine gunners, and the flame thrower would be like killing the influenza microbe by striking it with an umbrella.

But where have bolshevism and its sundry Communist and Spartacist variants taken root? Exactly in the countries in which, up until most recently, political and social tyranny has prevailed. Despotic socialism is the rejoinder to the despotism of the czars and emperors. In contrast, in the countries with democratic constitutions and traditions, socialism is also democratic. Wherever one finds, banked or burning, fires of Bolshevik propaganda, one can always discover their cause in the existence of specific grievances so urgent and with such a lack of normal means for redress that the spontaneous resort to violence appears to those who suffer them as the only means with which to succeed.

To recognize the social causes of bolshevism is to show why it is avoidable for the proletariat of countries in which, as in ours, the working class has at hand henceforth a means other than violence to better its condition and to realize its social ideal. Indeed, here it has the right to organize in the economic area and to conduct political propaganda which, as soon as it will have attained the majority, will give it the power to make and to execute laws and to found a new justice.

This future social order will not be any more unchangeable than the old order. If it were, that would be the stoppage of civilization, the progress of which can be conceived only as a continual transformation of the forms of common life. But the essential superiority of political democracy over all other forms of government—despotism, aristocracy, oligarchy, dictatorship, etc.—consists precisely in that it alone makes possible this unlimited evolution.

I know very well that in the present state of affairs the ideal of a government of all the people by all the people is far from being attained in any country, however democratic it may be. The minorities still are always those who govern; majorities are always outside government, just as they are outside high culture. But the governing minority —the politicians, the bureaucracy, the press, the banks, finance, the management of the great social and industrial organizations, etc.—is larger than under any previous regime. Access to it is not limited by any caste or hereditary condition. The means whereby it governs forces it to obtain the consent of the governed. It obtains this by using all the means that form what is usually called public opinion: the press, the school, the church, propaganda of every kind. The diversity of interests represented requires that the liberty of this propaganda be extended to all classes and all parties. Thus democracy, as differentiated from the old governments, can live only by ceaselessly increasing both the number of those who take an active and deliberate part in government, and the capacity to judge of those whose consent is necessary to the minority, which can be maintained only by the support of public opinion. Democracy has its faults and vices like all political systems; it is subject to malfunctions and weaknesses; but it has a virtue that makes up for all this in carrying within itself the principle of its own cure, since it can be maintained only by growing and perfecting itself.

If a triumphant socialism were to be tempted by the apparent ease of establishing a dictatorship by brute force and were to renounce democracy, it would commit suicide. It needs democracy, not only in order to conquer power but to deserve it after it has conquered it. It will have to be careful to avoid hidden reefs. The worst is statism—which, if we are not careful, threatens us with a more abominable tyranny than any despot, since it englobes acts not only of political but also of economic life. There are two guarantees against this danger. The first is the development of cooperative and union organization, outside of the state; this above all will make it possible to furnish a serious coun-

terweight to the ascendancy of bureaucratization upon the
organization of industrial democracy. But of what use
would it be to replace the tyranny of the state by corporative monopoly? In any case salvation must be sought for its
own sake in the second guarantee, which consists in the
maintenance and development of the rights that any constitution will assure to minorities: freedom of opinion, organization, the press and speech, freedom to oppose within
representative organizations. If socialism were incompatible with these freedoms, that would prove that it does not
deserve to exist.

I would insist even further on my concern to see
socialism, in its course of realization—which can be soon
—adapt its administrative procedures to the new demands
of social productivity with a minimum of scrapes, gropings,
and mistakes. I have already indicated the very great re-
pugnance I experience as to the seizure of the basic means
of production by the state, such as it is today. But I do not
see any means of making the state be transformed other
than by competition with private capital. It is only if it finds
itself summoned to build on these forms of administration
permitting it, by the means sketched in my article on the
"Conquest of the State," an output at least equal to that of
private enterprises, that we can succeed in cauterizing bureaucratization. It is Herculean labor that is not finished in
a day, for it involves changing an entire way of thinking. It
is for this reason that I give preference to a system of competition rather than forced expropriation as a means of
transition. There are scarcely any areas, such as that of the
elimination of parasitic landed property, where the latter
can be accomplished without grave disadvantages. In industry and transportation, I would like to see the state (or
bodies publicly financed and controlled) be transformed in
competition with private capitalism. The experimental
character of this policy permits the gradual adaptation of
its administrative procedures to economic needs. Thus one
would be able to eliminate the vices of capitalist monopoly

without giving up the immense advantages of competition as a stimulant to productivity. Of course it would be necessary to break with the old Communist dogma of the equality of wages and to establish a kind of payment for work which, in relating an individual's income to the social productivity of his service, would constitute a further inducement for increased output. The socialism at which one would thus arrive would be better than an antithesis to capitalism.

It would be a synthesis, borrowing from capitalism its tendency toward increased productivity, and from democracy its ideal of liberty, equality of rights, and universal solidarity, to bring about the supreme reconciliation of the two equally fertile, but hitherto antagonistic, principles: individual freedom and social unity.

Unless I am very wrong, the democratic socialism of tomorrow will be much like this. And that will be worth more than what has been done up to the present time in Moscow, Budapest, and Berlin.

In this article, as in the five others that have preceded it, I have been able only to sketch the outlines of the change in outlook of a socialist deeply influenced by the experience of the last five years. I have wanted to make this confession of faith before departing for a distant and perhaps long trip. When these lines appear, I will have already left Europe. If they provoke some discussion, I will no longer be able to participate in it. I console myself for this in thinking that what led me to write them is not the self-esteem of the builder of definitive formulas but the simple desire to furnish to my fellow fighters some material for thought, by propounding a few problems to whose resolution I anticipate devoting some time. They can do with this what they wish. Until I come back to retake my place among you, I wish you good work and all the success that the travails and efforts of the Belgian working class deserve.

5

Letter from America

During the course of his pilgrimage to democratic America, de Man was to be sadly disappointed, for the United States of postwar reaction, with the Palmer raids, the exclusion of the five elected Socialists from the New York State House of Representatives, the labor defeats in the coal and steel strikes, and the flag waving of the American Legion, was not the America of Wilsonian idealism, seen in the image of the pioneer tradition, of social experimentation, and of generosity of spirit that he had come to admire during his wartime experience. He spent a full year in the New World at this juncture, first passing a remarkable winter as the leader of a surveying expedition in Newfoundland, then traveling through Canada to Seattle in the expectation of directing a newly formed Labor College sponsored by the local union council. He passed the intervening summer largely in the company of a colony of Wobblies—members of the Industrial Workers of the World—on an island in Puget Sound, and took an active part as well in the political campaign pitting the Farmer and Labor party against the "Lumber Trust." In the event, labor was soundly thrashed both in strike action and in politics, and de Man was most lucky to be invited to teach social psychology at the University of Washington. But with the outcome of the election, pressure was put on the university to restrict the activities of this dangerous foreign radical, and under the circumstances it was with a sense of relief that de Man accepted a coincidental offer from Vandervelde to direct the Ecole Ouvrière Supérieure, a further, intensive development of workers' education in Belgium.

Nevertheless, his somewhat disabused views of America

still gave him a vantage point that served to extend his theoretical horizons. Ultimately he was to use the anomalous lack of class consciousness in America as a decisive consideration demonstrating the inadequacy of the Marxist framework to account for the development of the European socialist movement. At this time, however, although he reveled in the experience of social democracy, he still retained the view that, with the cessation of mass immigration and the closing of the frontier, "For the immense majority of American workers there is today scarcely more opportunity to rise from the proletariat than there is for the European workers. The class struggle, therefore, has in fact begun."[1] The possibility that there might be a permanent differentiation in the configuration of historical forces despite the similarity of economic system was only gradually to be assimilated in de Man's theoretical outlook.

Nevertheless the phenomenological exceptionalism of America was undeniable, and in the letters from the United States and Canada that he sent back to the Belgian socialist press during the course of his sojourn, he laid emphasis on the palpable reality of many a striking contrast to the world that his readers knew. The conclusion of the letter reproduced below indicates the development of a perspective that removed its author some distance from the conventional Marxist interpretation. A further step in the assimilation of this experience is represented by the passage contrasting the outlook of the German and American workers included in chapter 9 below, pp. 214-16.

LETTRE D'AMÉRIQUE:
CE QU'ON NE VOIT PAS AU CINÉMA[2]

I have now doubled the distance that separates me from the rue des Sables [Brussels address of *Le Peuple*] by

[1] "Lettre d'Amérique: l'Handicap Europe-Amérique," *Le Peuple*, 2 October 1920, p. 1.
[2] *Le Peuple*, 20 July 1920, p. 3. I have been guided by a previous transla-

moving my household from the east of Canada to the west of the United States. I intend to spend several months on the Pacific coast, particularly in the Northwest, with Seattle in the state of Washington as my headquarters.

This is probably the part of America that at the present time has the most interest as a locus of social experiment. The West, and particularly the Northwest, is and has been the birthplace of most of the progressive movements in the United States. Here is the cradle for the New World of woman's suffrage, of direct popular legislation by the referendum, and of the legal minimum wage. It is here that the labor movement represented by the Industrial Workers of the World, the "one big union" movement, originated. The first sympathetic general strike in America was called in Seattle in February 1919. In this part of the country also has occurred the first effective alliance between the trade unionists and the farmers. Last of all, the Pacific Ocean has become, since the war, the center of that great world conflict among imperialist interests in which the proletariat of all nations is most deeply concerned. Seattle, which is a sort of junction point for the United States, Japan, and Australia, thus makes an excellent observation post for the study of these questions.

Of course what is seen of the life of the Far West in the movies the whole world over gives no idea of this whatsoever. But there really is something here other than wild landscapes, giant trees, and rattlesnakes, and the most interesting fights that take place here are not the ones in which actors disguised as cowboys shoot at one another with revolvers.

The big cities of the Pacific coast represent the last word in progress within our present industrial system. Certainly in no other place on earth is the standard of living so high for everyone, thanks in large part to the power of the trade unions which include just about 100 percent of the work-

tion of this article appearing under the title "Real America" in *Living Age*, vol. 306, 11 September 1920, pp. 649-651.

ers. Although the city of Seattle has more than three hundred thousand inhabitants, there is neither poverty nor poor relief. Even the humblest citizens occupy their own cottages, each surrounded by a garden, with the result that though the city has about the same population as Antwerp, it covers more ground than Antwerp and Brussels together, and is, except in the business district with its skyscrapers, filled with greenery. There is one car for every eight inhabitants, and there is probably not a private home in the city without a bathroom and a telephone.

The conditions I have just described are not confined to the large cities. Thus I write this letter on the way back from Yakima, a little town in the Columbia Valley. This is the center of an agricultural district which irrigation has created in less than fifteen years from a wilderness where only a few redskins hunted buffalo. The redskins are still there, and one of their "reservations"—half the size of Belgium—comes up to the boundaries of the town. But most of them are now farmers, and when they come to the movies they are more frequently seen driving a car than on horse.

Our Belgian peasants would certainly stare to see how the white farmers live hereabouts. Let me give a single figure. The town of Yakima has 34,000 inhabitants and more than 9,000 cars, or one for less than every six of the population. The houses of the farmers (mostly fruit growers) are like our suburban villas. All of them have electricity, running water, baths, telephones, flower gardens, and a garage together with a car. I have just spent several days in this district in charge of a propaganda campaign for the Washington Federation of Labor, and I visited several farms every day.

I did not enter a single farmhouse that did not have a library, and let me say parenthetically that socialist authors are well represented. This valley is in fact an active center of the Non-Partisan League, which among the farmers stands for about what the Labor party stands for in Bel-

gium. In nearly every farmhouse I found a piano or a
phonograph. I spent a week at the home of one of these
farmers, a man no better off than any of his neighbors. He
had no hired help and worked his farm with the assistance
of three young sons. He had a regular office, with a telephone and a typewriter. In his library, besides the best
English authors, an encyclopedia, and several works on ag-
riculture, I saw Hugo's *Les Misérables*, Tolstoy, Henry
George, John Stuart Mill, and quantities of Socialist Party
literature including Karl Marx. His two daughters played
Beethoven in the evening while the men sat on the veranda
in their shirtsleeves, smoking their pipes and discussing
bolshevism, the socialization of credit, or Upton Sinclair's
latest novel. More than once during these evenings my
thoughts drifted back to certain farms in Limbourg, where
I was quartered during the war, and I asked myself what
effect it would have upon our Peasant Union if our villages
could each send a delegate to spend a short time among the
farmers of Yakima, and learn what organization and education can accomplish.

This is a country that demonstrates that it is not poverty
that creates the most vigorous class consciousness, and that
a regime of capitalist exploitation is most menaced where
the common people have attained the highest degree of
material well-being and education, as they have in the
American Far West. All this country is just now the scene of
a great revival of class consciousness, both among the country population and among the workingmen of the cities. It
is a surprising phenomenon, especially for a period immediately following a war. Its most characteristic expression is
the alliance of the trade unions and farmers' organizations
to support an outspokenly collectivist program. This
movement has already revolutionized the political situation
in a group of states west of the Mississippi, including North
Dakota, South Dakota, Wisconsin, Minnesota, Idaho, Ne-
braska, Colorado, Montana, Oregon, and Washington. It
has not yet gained a wide foothold in the East and South,

but is extending rapidly in those directions. Even at the present moment it profoundly influences the general policy of the country, and it is the great new fact that disturbs the slumbers of old party politicians upset to see this third predator threaten their monopoly of power.

During the last two months I have been studying the growth of this movement and the conditions to which it owes its birth. I am convinced that it is destined to have a marked effect on the history of both the United States and Canada. I dare predict that it is going to revolutionize the social constitution of all the new countries of the Anglo-Saxon world, and bring them, perhaps by paths different from those of European socialism, but not less surely nor less rapidly, to a cooperative republic of producers.

I will be writing again of the joint movement of workers and farmers, for now that the world has become so small and all the continents make up, so to speak, a single economic unit, this is an event of world politics that may not be ignored by the workers of Europe.

6

Workers' Control

Unlike many ideologists, de Man spoke from an intimate knowledge of the workers' life conditions and social psychology. Although his own family background had been distinctively nonproletarian and although he never worked in a factory himself, nevertheless his decades-long involvement with workers' education in Belgium and in Germany, his commissioned investigation into the social consequences of mass-production techniques in America, and his lifelong preoccupation with the pragmatics of "socialization" made him a pioneer industrial sociologist. While his empirical investigations into the social context of industrialization were expressed in *Au Pays du Taylorisme*[1] and *Joy in Work*,[2] the ideological implications of the process of socialization were perhaps most explicitly developed in the presidential address he gave at the Belgian trade-union conference concerned with the implications of "workers' control" held in 1921, the text of which follows below.

The importance of this topic in de Man's eyes and his heterodox approach to its analysis are revealed by his extraordinary statement that "all of the social problems of history are no more than variants of the eternal, the supreme, the unique social problem—how can man find happiness, not only through work, but in work."[3] Another

---

[1] Brussels: Peuple, 1919. This report was based on de Man's participation in a team investigation into "scientific management" in the United States, sponsored by the Belgian government in the spring of 1918; in his official capacity as a specialist in labor relations, de Man spent three months visiting factories and talking with union officials, managers, and labor-relations specialists.

[2] London: Allen & Unwin, 1929; first published as *Der Kampf um die Arbeitsfreude*, Jena: Diederichs, 1927.

[3] *Psychology of Socialism*, London: Allen & Unwin, 1928, p. 65.

passage sets this statement in a more general context: "the old struggle for the rights of man, taking on a new form as a struggle for joy in work, has shifted the problem to some extent. In one sense the aim of this struggle falls short of the abolition of capitalism; in another sense, it is much more than this. It is less, insofar as many of the worst causes of the workers' distaste for their work can be done away with even without an abolition of the capitalist profit-making economy; it is more, insofar as there are other causes, deeper causes, rooted rather in industrialism than in capitalism, and the task of overcoming these would still face an industrial socialist society."[4]

The cogency of these considerations has become more visible with the passage of time and especially with experience in the nationalized enterprise. Within command economies the most explicit, if still cautious, recognition of many of the problems diagnosed by de Man is to be found in attempts at decentralization and self-management in Yugoslavia. In the West, social innovation has taken two notable forms. The first is *Mitbestimmungsrecht* or *autogestion*, by which substantial labor representation on the board of directors is designed to funnel input from employees into the formulation of policy. While such representation has undoubtedly influenced some basic decision making, the largely formalistic and episodic role of such boards has served to reduce the psychological impact of the innovation. Closer to de Man's formulation have been the scattered efforts on the part of firms engaged in large-scale manufacture to introduce self-directing teams of workers charged with the responsibility for certain stages of production. The results, while interesting, have not been awe inspiring. It would seem that, for good reason or not, the industrial world has a long way to go to approximate the goal of "changing the government of things, social life itself" rather than changing merely the names, the people, or the formulas involved in conventional authoritative administration.

[4] *Joy in Work*, pp. 221-222; see below, pp. 218-219.

LE CONTRÔLE OUVRIER[5]

Comrades, before starting the discussions that are on our agenda today, I would like to take advantage of this plenary session to identify a few points that are not without importance if we wish our discussion to bear fruit. I believe that even before entering into discussion it is indispensable that we obtain some further clarity with respect to the object of our consideration: the definition of workers' control or, at least, the definition of the manner in which we are going to study the realization of workers' control. I am ready to admit to you in advance that it is impossible, in the present state of affairs, to give a definitive and precise definition of what is understood by workers' control. The idea itself is changing, because it arises from circumstances that are still changing, that are completely subject to the process of evolution.

Even with respect to Belgium itself I believe that we will be able to give only a very tentative definition at the end of this Semaine Syndicale, and it would be futile to want to attempt it beforehand. However, it would be useful to establish certain limits to the discussion and to clear up terminological misunderstandings before we begin.

That these misunderstandings exist I know from personal experience. I have already had this experience in trying to come to agreement with the speakers, notably with those comrades designated by the Belgian trade unions, so that they could know what they should talk about to their audiences.

In order that our discussion may be fruitful, we must give to the words "workers' control" a larger meaning than that we usually employ. In their proper meaning in French, the words "workers' control" would be synonymous with what we currently call the right to inspect, that is, the simple supervisory right given to workers in the

[5] *Comte rendu sténographique de la Semaine Syndicale tenue à Morlanwelz du 4 au 10 septembre 1921*, Monday session, 5 September 1921; Brussels: Lucifer, pp. 11-17, 44-60.

sense of surveillance or the knowledge of certain matters hitherto known only to the employers. This is the most restricted meaning. We must substitute for it the much broader conception that is becoming more and more used in the international terminology of the labor movement. It is that which takes the word "control" in the Anglo-Saxon sense of the word, a control that means management, governance, intervention. To do justice to the idea that is more and more on the way to becoming established in the world labor movement, it would be better to say workers' management. Workers' control—as ideal, principle, and ultimate goal—thus is, if we take the English meaning of the word, easy enough to define: in short it is the application to production of the principles that are the essence of democracy in political life; that is, if you wish, it is democracy applied to the organization of economic life; it is the management of the workshop, of the firm, with the consent of the governed, a government organized by the common will of those who work there.

This workers' control, in its final and comprehensive meaning, of course includes many things that will not come into the ambit of our discussion today. In the end, this workers' control is only an economic or industrial aspect of the great social reform that we call socialism. Union action itself is only one means to attain this, since the realization of this ideal—in application not only to the transformation of the processes of administration within industrial enterprises but also to the very form of ownership of the means of production—is a political and legal transformation at the same time that it is an economic one.

These forms of ownership can be modified only by political intervention. The socialization of the capital of an industry, on the one hand, and the democratization of its procedures for internal management, on the other, are two parallel but distinct movements. It is difficult to conceive of realizing the one without the other. But socialization as transformation of the right of ownership of the means of production is an object of the special interest of the political labor movement; it is above all by legislative action that we will be able to realize it; while democratization of industrial management, the introduction of democracy in the workshop and the factory, arises essentially from union action. It is especially this aspect of the democratization of industry that we will have to study during the Semaine Syndicale.

We will study the question not so much as a theory as from the point of view of processes of realization. Theory is variable, inconstant, and often very vague; theory itself arises from circumstances, from events. It is above all with regard to the theory of the union movement that one can say that in the beginning were events. Leading ideas indeed affect events, but only because they arise from events. The theory of workers' control will be established clearly only to the extent that this control is effected in an unambiguous manner.

Our attention should thus be directed especially to the conditions leading to workers' control, and it is in this sense that our program of this week should be understood.

We must then study not an ideal situation, but the practical means that up to the present time have been leading to its realization. For the nature of our investigation it is less important to establish where workers' control ends than where it begins.

I believe that one can say in a general manner that workers' control begins—that there is workers' control in embryo—as soon as organized workers, supported by the union's strength, intervene in the internal management of work in the workshop, the factory, the colliery, the shipyard, or the office.

To take a concrete example, which was suggested to me by my fellow speakers: one can ask if the "collective compact" and the national Joint Commission, as we know them in Belgium, are forms of workers' control. Note that I am here comparing the national Joint Commission and the col-

lective compact because the two institutions resemble each other in that both record an agreement, forming a contract for a period, fixed or unspecified, between the representatives of the organized workers and the employers with respect to general conditions of work within an industry.
Is this workers' control?

I believe that one must say no. No in all cases in which the agreement or the commission only defines conditions of work, leaving the matter of their application to the free play of the power of the employers and the workers. But we shall see during this week in the studies that refer to Belgian industries that the majority of the agreements and even of the commissions accomplish more than this. They naturally must concern themselves with the application of the general agreement to individual work contracts and with the very execution of these contracts. In general it is by the creation of bodies supervising this application that workers' control arises, from the fact that these bodies include, in most cases, direct representation of the workers in the selfsame places in which they do their work.

Let us take an example. Let us suppose that the metallurgical workers of a region come to an agreement with the employers, or with an employers' association, as to minimum wages. This happens in real life. This agreement still is not a form of workers' control, because it has been agreed to outside of the firms. It fixes general conditions for what can be called the sale of manpower, but its action stops the moment the agreement has been concluded, the moment the worker enters the workshop.

But suppose that in order to assure its execution this same agreement holds that the employers must recognize as the spokesmen of the workers a workers' association or representatives specially elected in either workshop, firm, or union. These representatives will have to check that the piece rates established within the factories conform to the conditions agreed to by the employers. By this fact they must discuss, even within the firms, questions of wages and the methods for the calculation of wages, sometimes even with respect to costs; they will have to discuss, from the standpoint of the application of the agreement, new methods of manufacture, the introduction of new machines, to the degree that these questions influence wages. In order to assure the execution they will have to discuss and negotiate about the hiring and firing of workers. In brief, this is a case—and we will see later on that the instance is real—where the workers acquire the right to discuss specific conditions of work within a firm in order to carry out the terms of the agreement. From this moment on, even without there being any right of surveillance, even if the employer does not have to submit his accounts, there is a beginning of workers' control.

Thus institutions exist that we must study at our Semaine Syndicale if we want to understand the paths by which workers' control is realized. In the case cited, there is the beginning of the democratization of industry, since the employer, up to now the absolute master, must concede a bit—sometimes a very little bit, but one that will grow— from that absolute right that he has always reserved for himself to decide on the organization of work itself.

Let us take another example to show where workers' control begins. Please excuse these somewhat technical details, but I think that it is good to establish them precisely, for popular ideas are far from being exact in this respect, I can assure you. Suppose that a regional agreement, like the one of which I have just spoken, was limited to stipulating the conditions of work without making any provisions as to methods of application, or even suppose an industry where there is no collective agreement at all. But in this industry there is a factory where the union organization, while not having a general contract, has brought about recognition by the owner, or the manager, of representatives of the workers who work in that factory. These representatives can be the shop stewards of the period preceding recognition. The recognition of these stewards may or may not be incorporated in a written contract; it can be tacit, and the result of the very fact of their coming together as permanent negotiators. Or perhaps it can be incorporated in the shop rules, which is one byway leading to an agreement to recognize the union. Whatever the case may be, from the very fact that the worker representatives are recognized, from the fact that they have the right to intervene, if only by the single means of recommendation, there is a beginning of workers' control, and consequently an institution that our study must include.

A last example. Suppose that in the coal-mining industry there is no national collective compact. I take on purpose an industry the real situation of which is close enough to this hypothesis. Suppose, I say, that in the coal-mining industry there might be simply a mixed commission in which the representatives of the unions and of the employers determine work conditions in the mines. Well, in my opinion there isn't any workers' control thus far.

But suppose that in order to minimize the chances of conflict this national joint commission sets up procedures that include the election, with the participation of unions, of workers' representatives recognized by the employers as commissioned to examine all the questions or grievances resulting from the application of the decisions of the commission. Workers' control starts here, since there is a designation of representatives entrusted with supervising within firms the execution of the decisions of the commission.

The above is certainly not a complete or definitive definition even of the lower limit of workers' control. But I think that we would do well to note provisionally the idea that I have just presented, if we wish to avoid wandering in long and vague considerations.

I think that we should here consider the joint commissions and the collective agreements only from the viewpoint of their conditions of execution, and especially from the viewpoint of the institutions of workers' representation within the firm for which they provide.

Let us try to complete this definition by saying a few words about questions that are outside the conceptualization of workers' control, and that must in consequence remain outside our discussions. First of all, if one takes workers' control in the broadest sense, one can conceive of its realization from the standpoint of a total political reform: socialization, public ownership, nationalization, technocratic management, communal management, etc. I have already said that I think that these reforms must remain outside our discussions as political and legal measures. But I will add another reason to this one: certain forms of collective appropriation, notably certain forms of communal and national administration, are simply transformations in the kind of industrial ownership that often involve no change in the processes of the internal administration of production. This has already been seen in those cases where there has been a simple transfer of ownership to a collectivity of certain means of production, of certain industrial capital, without any change whatsoever in the organization of work. In this case the workers have simply changed the boss, but the boss' procedure remains the same.

Another question that I suggest leaving out of the present debate is that of producers' cooperatives. We will see by the reports of workers' control in certain foreign countries, that for some industries—for example, construction—there is a very strong movement for industrial democracy through the spreading of a means of action that we know as producers' cooperatives. We anticipate hearing of workers' partnerships[6] in Italy, of guilds of construction workers in England, where one is on the way toward workers' control by using the old processes of cooperative produc-

[6] *Commandité*: a legal form stipulating limited liability of partners.

tion, lightly modified by the intervention of employers, technicians, the state, etc. Theoretically the extension of producers' cooperatives can be conceived of as a means to arrive at industrial democracy. However, experience has shown us that industries in which workers' cooperation can attain serious competition with capitalist producers on the free market are very rare.

Moreover, what I have said about socialization can be said about producers' cooperatives: very often, it comes down simply to a change in the form of ownership, which does not necessarily imply any change in the processes of administration. Only too often we have examples of producers' cooperatives in which the internal organization of work does not differ at all from that we know in private enterprises, where really there has been only the substitution of one form of managerial control for another.

In the last place, I think that it is necessary to exclude from the domain of our study of workers' control all of those institutions that, although including representation of workers within firms, have not been won by workers, by unions. For example, we shall see that in certain countries, notably in the United States, employers have established factory councils for the most diverse motives, sometimes praiseworthy and sometimes abominable. These organizations bring a direct representation of the workers, but they are not based on union strength. They have been granted by the good will of the employers, and their power is consequently limited by his good pleasure. This is a form of democratic or so-called democratic administration that is not contractual. But, workers' control must be contractual: that is, it must be based on the balance of power between workers and employers, bound by a contract, unless it is to be only a snare, simply a variant of control by the employer.

Please excuse me for having been a little long in these remarks, undoubtedly arid since they are about defining a term. But I think it is well worthwhile getting ideas a little

in order first of all, before starting the discussion of a subject so vast and so little studied.

But I do not intend that you accept at first sight the
definition that I have proposed. You will do with this what
you please. However, I do believe that it is only in the
senses in which I have just developed these ideas that it will
be possible to have a truly fruitful discussion at the present
time. . . .

The subject that I am going to take up, the "psychological aspect of workers' control," may perhaps seem to you a
bit forbidding. There is no reason to be alarmed by this
word "psychological," which has the fault only of being a
bit academic. My intention, in a nutshell, is to show you certain consequences of workers' control from the viewpoint
of the human element involved in production. In the end,
that's all that the word psychological means.

When we propose to study the psychological aspect of
workers' control or of any other institution, we wish to treat
the question from the viewpoint of the soul of the men who
are involved in that institution. I think, moreover, that in
entering into the path of workers' control the union
movement is going to encounter more and more often
questions of a moral content, psychological questions, indeed what can be called the psychology of technology; in a
word, everything relating to human attitudes, behavior,
and their "manipulation," to use an unattractive if expres-
sive word. It must give to these questions a much greater
importance than they have been granted up until now.

Let us recognize that the deliberate undertaking of
union action with respect to the human element, the attitude of the individual worker in the factory, has been
completely lacking until now. One can even say that up
until now such action with regard to the organization of
work within the firm has in general hardly been perceptible.

Right up to the beginning of the phase of workers' control, the attitude of the union as to the execution of the

work contract within the firm has been entirely negative. The union has not said: we are going to produce and work in such-and-such conditions. It has rather said: we are not going to work, unless we are given certain compensations, unless we are given certain wages, and unless the length of the workday does not exceed a certain number of hours. If we look at the relations existing between the action of unions and the organization of work in industry, I think that one can divide the evolution of the union movement into three great phases. The first, which I will call the primitive phase, is that of intermittent resistance, in which the intervention of the union is limited to the organization of a strike. The second, contractual phase is characterized by the making of collective contracts establishing minimal conditions to which specific work contracts must conform. This is the phase in which most of our unions are at the present time. The third is the phase the theshold of which we are now approaching, that of workers' control, in which the union, not content with concluding all sorts of agreements—kinds of armistice treaties with the employers—is preoccupied with setting up institutions the purpose of which is to check the application on the shop floor of the principles recorded in the agreements.

In the first two phases, that of pure and simple opposition, and the phase I have called contractual, the action of the union remains, in short, negative from the viewpoint of the organization of industrial production itself. In origin unions are defensive rather than offensive bodies. They owe their solidarity to the desire to maintain a given situation. They are founded largely by craftsmen whose place is threatened by proletarianization and by the development of machine production.

The majority of the militants here present will remember the first phase through which their own occupational organization has passed. In almost all cases, oppositional groups were formed to prevent a reduction in wages, an inevitable consequence of the industrial revolution of the

nineteenth century, which changed the skilled craftsman
into a worker who has lost his occupational title and who
finds himself condemned to more and more mechanical
work.

The very name of many of our old union organizations is
suggestive. Many of them are called society or fund "for
defense" [de résistance]. The same thing can be found in
other countries. The oldest English and American unions
have almost all retained in their name expressions such as
"protective association." These unions attempt to maintain
a vested position, that of the independent craftsmen,
threatened by the machine.

The most characteristic examples of this first phase of
union development are found in England. Neither are
they absent in Belgium, for if we look into our memories
we will see that the union movement in Belgium has been
created by craftsmen threatened by machine production,
by that decline of which I have spoken above.

Think for example of the hand weavers, who were terri-
bly affected by the crisis that broke out toward the middle
of the nineteenth century following the introduction of
mechanical weaving. Think also of the book industry,
which was one of the first to be organized in unions for
similar reasons. Other industries were in an analogous position, for instance bronzeworking or cabinetmaking.
Think also of the cigar workers, the glass blowers, and of
craftsmen in certain luxury trades, such as diamonds and
hat making. When we consider the list of old manual occupations that have been mechanized in the course of the
nineteenth century, we note that they are precisely those
whose workers were the first to be organized in the form of
unions in Belgium.

These unions had an intermittent effect, limited almost
entirely to the conduct of strike movements. It is for this
reason that they did not generally have a widespread base:
just about the only form of regularly available compensation that they knew was the viaticum—the travel allowance,

a very symptomatic bounty, for in case of conflict it relieved the local labor market by taking workers away.

In the first phase, all things are provisional: there are no collective contracts; strikes are ended by verbal understandings, very rarely by written agreements. These do not take the form of permanent concessions; they are overthrown as soon as the balance of forces changes.

The present phase, from which we are beginning to emerge, is that of the collective contract, in which the union keeps to this negative function of restricting itself to establishing certain limits to exploitation, but this time by a lasting act. This phase is characterized not only by the making of collective contracts but also by organizing on a widespread basis, with the naming of officials, permanent staffs, and consolidation into large industrywide unions.

The coming phase, that of workers' control, as I tried to suggest this morning, does not result from a theoretical concept, the wish to try out a new idea, but from events themselves. It is on the way to being realized as a natural, almost ineluctable consequence of the preceding phase, that of the collective contract. Indeed, all of the realizations of workers' control that are found up to the present time in various countries have taken place little by little out of the need to organize supervision within the firm of the execution of the contract stipulations, without knowledge, and almost certainly without there being conscious pursuit, of a doctrinal goal. Let us take some examples.

The collective contract obviously cannot determine individual wages in any country or in any industry; it can establish only the general criteria to which wages must conform. In industries where the products are very diverse, where the mechanical processes and types of variability in the market or in technical processes make it impossible to establish specific rates on a nationwide basis, only certain minimum standards can be defined. In this circumstance supervision of the execution of agreements becomes at least as important as the drawing up of the agreements themselves. Suppose that a union, having concluded a contract establishing a minimum wage, has obtained to supervise its execution recognition of representatives who can question with the employer, the engineers, and the foremen its application to piecework. Is it possible to think of this situation without recognizing that the representatives will necessarily come to take up not only questions of wages but also the relations between the wages and the processes of manufacture, the relations between the wages and the new methods of work that may be introduced? As soon as this is the case, workers' control has begun to be exercised over a part of the internal administration of industry which, up until then, had been the exclusive domain of the autocratic employer.

And this is brought about by the action itself of the agencies that are indispensable to assure the execution of collective contracts.

It is the same with work discipline. It is a commonplace to say that whoever—individual or organization—signs a contract giving certain rights assumes by this very fact certain duties. It is needless to look far for examples of negotiations or of clashes in which the attitude of the employers consists in insisting upon the duties of the workers with respect to the organization of work, upon services to be done, upon various obligations that result from signing a contract. As soon as the representatives of the unionized workers are permitted to debate these things, they have an influence on shop discipline, and to some degree the unity of the authority structure of the shop, based until now on the absolute authority of the employer, has been broken. A form of authority, or responsibility, has been introduced that no longer owes its origin only to the delegation of the power of the employer to the foremen or to the division heads, but also to the industrial democracy formed by shop stewards elected by their fellow workers. I do not want to anticipate the conclusion of our studies, but we doubtless

will see some examples among the representatives of the
ironworkers of the Center.[7]
These representatives of the ironworkers, obliged to
check up on the effective output of work in connection with
the regulation of wages, by this very fact take away a part of
the supervisory functions of the presumptive foreman.
This process, which has just started, will, if carried out
generally, come to mean the introduction of the system of a
foreman elected by the workers, that is, the administration
of discipline within the workshop exercised by representatives of the workers and, indeed, by union representatives.
And this results, whether one wishes it or not, from the
linkage of events arising themselves from the increase in
union strength.
Likewise, you have collective contracts that have, as all
good contracts do, clauses concerning hiring, preference to
be given to union members, the right of organized workers
to refuse to work with nonunion workers, etc. Here also
the situation resulting from the contract gives to the union
the power of supervising its execution and henceforth, the
union or worker representative takes over in this case too a
part of the functions and the rights of the employer concerning hiring and firing of workers. Look at what happened in Germany, where the law concerning factory
councils provides in certain cases for consultation with
workers' representatives by the employer each time there is
a question of changing the organization of work, where the
factory councils require that the employer justify with the
workers' representatives, by the presentation of documentation referring to costs, sales, the state of the market, etc.,
his intentions with respect to the lessening of work, the discharge of workers, or the closing of his factory.
I have not wanted to present here a sketch of the manner
in which this new union right has been carried out; I have

[7] A region of heavy industry, especially of coal mining and iron and
steel mills, in the vicinity of Charleroi, Hainaut.

simply wanted to show that it emerges from events, that it has done so, will always do so, independently of the wishes or preferences of those who write up theory.

In acquiring the right to participate in the internal administration of factories, to take a place next to the employers in saying how the work will be organized, what kind of discipline there will be, how hiring will take place, what new processes are to be used, what measures are to be taken for the determination of wages, etc., the union movement ventures into an entirely new domain. Now it is leaving the negative phase that I have tried to describe, and it assumes responsibilities as a body participating in the administration of production. Now the union is no longer concerned simply with general questions that envisage the work contract only as a general agreement establishing base lines; it intervenes in a domain in which it's a matter of the individual as the human element, in which it takes over a part of the functions and responsibilities of the head of the firm as a manager of men.

Every one of us has heard many a time the employers formulate in their way the idea that the unions have not until now undertaken this positive work: "You are always claiming rights," they say, "but you never accept duties." This is the refrain of a song that most of you must know well enough, and it is needless for us to waste our time in long polemics about this subject. For the unions we should, however, be able to respond that we attend to first things first, and that before speaking of duties we must begin by winning a minimum right to existence, that before demanding that unions guarantee performance it is necessary to begin by giving the worker the means for self-development by reducing the workday, relieving him from overwork, giving him a minimum wage that allows him to live, etc.

We would also be able to say that as long as the employers refuse to allow their prerogatives as managers of production to be affected, they should accordingly keep for themselves the whole responsibility that flows from this authority; that to ask unions to take on responsibility in the organization of work, notably concerning the amount and character of service of their members, is an illogical and unreasonable thing, unless they are given an appropriate measure of authority with respect to the establishment of what the specific conditions of production should be.

In reality it must be said that, if the union movement has not interested itself directly in the question of the worker's capacity and service rendered, it has had an indirect influence of the highest social importance in this area. It suffices to recall the part that many of our organizations have taken and continue to take in the development of technical training. It is not irrelevant to recall here notably, by way of example, all of the institutions formed to this end by the province of Hainaut under the influence of the working population. And it might be noted that it is precisely in the industrial provinces, where the working population is largely under socialist influence, that the most remarkable institutions have been formed in Belgium to increase the quality of the worker's performance.

One can likewise reply to the employers that, merely by the fact that it has created the worker's dignity, that by its solidarity and organization it has given the worker an individual pride arising from his class pride, the union movement has furnished to the worker a stimulant not without consequences from the viewpoint of his attitude to the workshop and to the quality of his service.

But all that is polemics. If we wish to see the total situation apart from mutual complaints, I don't think that it can be denied that in the course of the nineteenth century and at the beginning of the twentieth century there was in general, although to a variable extent according to the industry, not at all a lowering of the individual output of the worker—this is impossible to determine, output depending notably on the technical processes of work—but a weakening of the personal psychological motive that makes up the human factor of production, a lessening of work satisfaction, and consequently of the desire to produce. As a matter of fact, there is even a relaxation of discipline, and even perhaps a consequent lessening of production. This is perhaps debatable for certain industries; I do not lay claim to a universal competence, but for the several industries that I have been able to study in various countries I have no fear in claiming that there was an almost continual tendency toward the relaxation of work discipline.

Let us not debate here the necessity of discipline; we could hardly go beyond commonplaces unless we were to probe the problem further than we can in fact do here; let us simply note that in production, as in everything that requires the collaboration of a great number of men, good order, punctuality, voluntary subordination to the welfare of all, to the necessities of production, are a condition sine qua non of the means of subsistence, of the survival, of any social regime whatsoever. This applies as much to socialist or union governance as to a capitalist system.

I will add, moreover, that the universal crisis of demoralization unleashed by the war and all that has followed it has, I think, singularly contributed to the aggravation of this state of affairs. But it has not created it; the war has simply accentuated a trend that existed before and that would continue to be manifested without it.

At the bottom of all this is that there has been for a long time in most occupations a decline in work satisfaction, a lessening in the individual self-respect of the worker as a producer.

If the union movement has some of the responsibility for this, it will accept it. But let us seek out the objective causes, and we will find that the union movement and the decline in work satisfaction are not in a relation of cause and effect, but are both effects resulting from the same causes. The union movement and the decline in work satisfaction arise in a parallel way from the same situation, which might be called the deskilling of work, that is, the more and more mechanical, more and more monotonous character of industrial operations in the majority of industries where the extension of mechanization and concentration of production have been experienced.

This subject deserves consideration, for it is extremely important from a larger viewpoint than that of the action of unions. No social system, no civilization can survive when those who produce find less and less pleasure in production.

This word "civilization" means something: we all felt this at the height of the crisis through which we have just passed, and we still feel it now, when it seems that civilization will founder unless it is radically transformed. There have been some beautiful, high civilizations in the world. There was Greek civilization and the handicraft civilization of the Middle Ages, which gave us the most beautiful works of art and during which humanity was most oriented to a common ideal. It is especially during these civilizations of handiwork that man had satisfaction in producing, the worker working with self-respect because he found happiness in his work, while today he seeks his happiness more and more outside of his work.

Let us try to find the causes of this situation, freeing ourselves from the very superficial view of the vulgar. Thus the employer has his ready-made explanation: the worker is lazy and becomes more and more so, because socialism and the union movement preach laziness to him. Employers who are far from being stupid or evil people say this, and I believe that for most of them it is a sincere opinion. They are vexed with the lack of self-respect, with the carelessness and negligence of their workers in the factory; they are truly indignant at an attitude that, because they misinterpret it, they cannot understand. They see that the worker is acting otherwise than they would act, and they erroneously conclude that the worker is acting in a given way for the same reason that the employers would if they were placed in his situation. But tell these employers, who often rightly complain that a worker does not give in the shop what he should give, to see this same worker work in his garden after hours. Very often they will find out that this man who has been taking it easy in the shop will be working in heavy sweat in his garden plot, although he works in less pleasant circumstances from the standpoint of equipment, sometimes on a soil from which he receives hardly any economic return. Why? Because there the worker is working for himself. That means a great deal.

The Greek or medieval craftsmen, of whom we spoke a moment ago, worked for themselves also. This means that these men had gratification from their work, because they possessed their own means of production, their own tools, and they bought their own raw materials; they worked, not for wages, but to sell the product of their labor to the consumers themselves. And, what is perhaps even more important is that these craftsmen saw the entire product, from raw material up to the finished work, be shaped and finished by their own hands. A man working in these conditions—for example a cabinetmaker buying his wood and completing a piece of furniture—experiences work satisfaction, if he is normal and healthy, because in working he satisfies one of the most fundamental drives of man, the drive that distinguishes him most clearly from animals, the drive to create. The greatest happiness is the satisfaction of our highest impulses, and there is not a higher one than the drive to create, the constructive instinct.

This man works with satisfaction and works well because he puts his soul into the product of his hands. He manages his own work. His work is himself—not only his strength, but also his judgment, his taste, his intelligence. Of all these consequences of machine production, of factory work, and of the deskilling of work, none has contributed more to kill work satisfaction than that which has taken from the worker almost all the influence of his intelligence and his will on the way in which his task is accomplished.

The craftsman himself concentrates all of the productive functions within one person, in one will: performance as much as planning. He exercises not only his hands but also his judgment, his initiative, his conscious will, that is, what is highest and most accomplished within his mental make-up. But all of you know that in the specialized jobs of today's factory these functions of judgment and of initiative tend more and more to be concentrated in the hands of a specialized group of technicians, to be distributed from on high throughout the entire chain of command from sources in offices where the worker never enters and of whose activities he knows nothing.

There isn't a better illustration of this situation than that furnished by Taylorism. Didn't Taylor state that one of the most essential points of his doctrine was that it was necessary to take away from the discretion of the worker any sort of influence whatsoever on the work that he was doing, to concentrate all functions that require reflection in the technical offices? This comes down to reducing the worker literally to the role of the performer of certain elementary mechanical operations, of the sort that are carried out by automatic machines. Taylor has even extended this idea to the point of saying that with this system a trained gorilla should be able to carry out all industrial work.

We know very well that, in practical terms, things haven't been carried to this extreme. But this example illustrates in a striking manner the general tendencies toward which we move everywhere to the degree that mechanization develops. You all know the consequences from the standpoint of the manual worker. One of the worst is boredom with work, the loss of all opportunity for the worker to exercise his skill, his initiative, to utilize in his work the highest powers of his mental faculties.

This is indeed a huge problem, comrades, for which workers' control does not supply the whole answer. To set up a social organization that, in place of destroying the psychological motive that drives man to create, enables him to find happiness in work is the cardinal problem of the social crisis that we are undergoing, and it is not by any isolated measure that we will be able to solve it.

Certainly there is a whole array of solutions that could be

called external: the development of education, technical training, recreation, and especially the improvement of workers' housing. Within certain industries, for instance among the English miners, who exhibit chronic discontent at the present time, there is an enmity that no increase in wages, no material reform, can dispel. This enmity will exist as long as these people must live in an environment that prevents the satisfaction of their cultural, recreational, and civic needs—and that these needs can be satisfied will seem ridiculous to anyone knowing the classic coal-mining settlements of that country.

But this is not the complete solution of the problem and, from certain viewpoints, it is not even a solution at all. For if the internal state of the factory or the shop is such that less and less satisfaction is found there, then the more the man finds satisfaction when he is outside the factory, the more he will resent his unhappiness in being there. The same thing can be said of the reduction in the hours of work to a limit, like the eight-hour day we have achieved in Belgium, which could be called a physiological limit. A workday that does not go beyond this limit is obviously an essential condition for any work satisfaction at all, but it is not it that makes for work satisfaction. From the moment we have realized this reform, from the moment we have reduced the workday to that which is compatible with human health, the great problem for the labor movement is no longer to know how many more hours we are going to wrest from work, but how we are going to change the hours devoted to work in such a way that they become satisfying hours.

In order to make factory work more tolerable, solutions have been tried that must be considered as palliatives, which treat the symptoms rather than the illness. There have been efforts to embellish certain factories and to provide for more air and light. Obviously there are an enormous number of things to do in the factories that would improve well-being, and the employers would gain by increased production. For example, there are those who use rather infantile means, like the American factories in which the phonograph is played while work takes place. It's a little like officers who give grog to their men before they make an attack. It is certain that the loveliest phonographs in the world will never be a permanent stimulant, the stimulant that will replace work satisfaction.

There are other, more elegant solutions, notably the combination of various forms of work for each individual—but this is obviously subject to realization only in a much improved state of affairs. Thus certain sociologists dream of a requirement for every intellectual or sedentary worker to change every day, for a minimum number of hours, to industrial or agricultural work, and a requirement for all industrial workers to be occupied, for a certain number of hours per day, with outdoor work, such as the intensive working of a garden plot. Belgium, the country of intensive cultivation of the soil and of dispersed working centers, is above all others the best situated country in the world for the realization of this program. There is hardly another country where its realization appears more logically as the outcome of the situation that already exists for a great part of our working class.

But all these partial solutions do not touch on the fundamental cause. It's not all this that can give our factory workers the satisfaction with work that quickened the craftsman of the Middle Ages of whom I spoke a little while ago.

There is a much more direct way of giving to the worker this satisfaction in work—to allow him to employ his capacity to discriminate, to make him feel that his work engages his intelligence, his highest faculties. Workers' control will enable us to obtain this immense advantage by making the worker an active element participating in the internal organization of the factory.

The realization of workers' control implies a set of little reforms that, taken separately, appear trivial, but that constitute in reality the keystone to a new social structure, the foundation of a new workers' outlook, capable of bringing this indispensable work satisfaction! Nothing more discourages the worker than to feel, in most factories, that he has no means whatsoever to influence the specific processes of work, not even to transmit directly to the management suggestions for technical improvements. On the part of the employers there is an indifference that is harmful to their own immediate interests. They do not realize the profits they could make, with respect to production, from a system of internal organization that would enable them to use the intellectual abilities, indeed the inventive genius, of their workers.

I am sure that in the whole world there is not an industry or workshop where it would not be possible to obtain a considerable improvement in the worker's output from one day to another by simply putting into practice the suggestions of workers. The latter are in a position—we know this from experience—to suggest to the employers a whole array of improvements helpful for the whole group of workers, and they will do this the day when the organization of work will be such that the worker will feel more at home in the factory and more closely associated with the work that is done there.

Before closing this speech, I would like to add a few words on the subject of certain psychological consequences of workers' control, which might be called extrinsic, at least with reference to the embryonic form of workers' control that we know up to the present time.

If workers' control should be put into effect some day, under the pressure of union forces, it will not be able to exist or be maintained except under the condition that we will be able to count on the collaboration of the technicians. Before an audience such as this one, it would be like breaking down an open door—after the experience of Russia, Italy, and elsewhere—to state that the taking over of political and union power by the class of manual workers will permit us to establish a new regime of production and to maintain it in a viable state only if we can count on at least the sympathetic neutrality, if not the active cooperation, of the technicians.

One of the big errors of many of our militants is to imagine the "bosses" as a bloc symbolized by one and the same feature. In actual fact there are scarcely any bosses left in the true sense of the word, at least in big business. The boss who is at the same time the owner and the technical manager of his plant is becoming more and more an object of curiosity. It is indispensable to make a distinction between the pure capitalist component, the financial component represented by the corporation or the bank, and the component we generally consider as the boss but who is in reality a technician of management, simply the executor of the wishes of the real capitalists.

There are, it is true, many things in common between the outlook of the capitalist and that of the managerial technician, even when the latter is not financially interested in the firm. This community of views extends even to the lower grades of the technical chain of command, down to the simple engineer or the foreman. For example, often the technician will agree with the capitalist in complaining of the workers' lack of zeal. He imagines that if he himself had to carry out the tasks of the worker, he would work more conscientiously, with greater application. Moreover, I think that in fact one is misjudging no one in recognizing that the greatest number of technicians work at least as hard as do the majority of workers. Doubtless it is sometimes rather hard to express in hours of toil the quantity of work accomplished by the majority of those who have the management or responsibility for production jobs, a fact that makes such a comparison rather difficult. But the individual service, in energy used, not only of the technicians but of the boss or manager, is often greater than that of the manual worker.

I add that the motive of their work is not always material

profit. It is an error to believe that captains of industry
never think of anything but money, of their dividends.
Men who have attained high positions in business—I am
not speaking of investors nor of the boss's son, but of those
who exercise authority and who are assigned real
responsibilities—remain in these positions, as a general
rule, because they are capable and because they work hard,
often more than eight hours per day. They imagine all too
easily that the worker, who does not have a direct interest
in the success of the business, is lazy because the men who
themselves manage this business possess thereby that joy in
work that the worker has lost as a consequence of his position in large-scale machine production. The technician
himself knows full well that he has the thinking, coordinat-
ing, deciding role. The psychological motive that predominates with him is the self-respect of the producer.

But this same motive, which differentiates the attitude of
the technicians from that of the worker, forms at least as
deep a difference between the technicians and the parasitic
capitalist.

Let me speak here a bit from my personal experience. I
once found myself in the situation of having to do a technical type of work, entailing a considerable degree of initiative, for a capitalist company. On the one hand, I was very
aware of the difference between my outlook, dominated by
the interest that I brought to the personal work, and that of
the workers whom I had to employ and who did not have
this stimulus because they did not exercise their own initiative. That is the great difference between the outlook of the
technician and that of the average worker today. The technician's outlook, at least for the one who has a job involving
authority and real work of coordination, is normally as-
suaged by the satisfaction of organizing production. This
difference separates the technician from the worker. But it
likewise separates the technicians from the capitalists, and
it is here that things become interesting. At the time of
which I speak, I was painfully aware of this antagonism
with respect to my employers, and I knew by the conversa-

tions I had with my engineering colleagues who were in the
same situation I was, that this feeling was far from being
peculiar to me. We felt ourselves as far from the capitalists,
from the financiers who employed us, as the workers themselves. Management and the shareholders did not have the
production viewpoint at all. The workers knew only their
wages, the capitalists knew only their dividends. It was extremely humiliating for us who were doing the really creative job to feel that we should give the best of ourselves,
that we should take an interest in and devote ourselves to a
work that would not even be understood by those who paid
us; and, in short, those who would gain would not be ourselves at all but those drawing dividends. From all this
arose a feeling of injustice, of an affront less tolerable than
simply a material frustration. This feeling created a veri-
table chasm between the technician and the capitalist, even
deeper than the one that exists between the technician and
the worker. The latter arose above all from the fact that
with the technician the predominant motive is satisfaction
in-work, but with the worker this motive no longer exists.
This rift will be smoothed out when we possess a democratic organization of industry that will give back to the
worker an ever increasing part of the managerial functions
of production.

I think that perhaps one of the most important and most
immediate consequences that the spread of workers' control will entail is to create for the technician and the worker
in the shop, by the common task of organizing production,
a zone in which it will be possible for the psychologial motives of both worker and technician to join in the effort to
bring about an appropriate organization of production. It
is only when we will have this contact with the technicians
on the basis of equality in a common or a federated union
movement that that harmful barrier erected between the
technicians who plan but who do not carry out the actual
work, and the worker who toils without participating in the
planning, will fall.

Another psychological consequence of the development

of workers' control, about which I would like to say a few
words before concluding, concerns the transformation of
the outlook of the union and of its leading personnel that
will be entailed. The psychology of the union movement
has already been changed from the phase of intermittent
resistance to the second, contractual one of which I have
just spoken.

To the first phase belongs the agitator, a man who generally did not have an administrative responsibility because
he hardly had anything to administer, and whose
function—indeed very often a heroic one which gave us
admirable men—was to stimulate the masses, to bring them
into organized groups, and sometimes simply to engage
them in strike action. This function belongs to past history.

Today the great concern of the union representatives is,
if not to prevent strikes, at least to direct those that are
unavoidable. Most of those present have no need for a detailed description of the mountain of material and administrative concerns of all kinds that weigh upon the administrators of our unions of today. Parenthetically it can be
noted that from the psychological viewpoint it is rather interesting to study this passage from the role of agitator to
that of administrator. Sometimes catastrophes have arisen
from the fact that in order to satisfy this new need for administrators it has been necessary to make use of men who
were born to be agitators and who had had their experience in positions where all those completely new characteristics and understandings of the new phase were lacking.

An analogous development is in the process of taking
place right now, wherever workers' control is introduced
into the factory itself. In many industries we have had shop
stewards for a long time. But before the recognition of
unions and the designation of representatives the steward
was, to speak frankly, often only a dues collector. If he was
more than that, he was a union propagandist in the factory; he represented the union to the shop more than he

represented the shop to the union. Moreover in many cases when it was mostly a matter of collecting dues the shop steward was not the best or the most intelligent worker because the latter did not want the duty.

With union recognition the whole situation changes. A man must be found who is able to do something quite other than distributing bulletins, announcing meetings, and collecting dues; a man must be found who, having acquainted himself with the case at hand, is capable of negotiating with the employers or his representatives in circumstances new to him where he encounters others professionally trained to maneuver. I have the impression—I may be wrong—that if we had always succeeded in finding in our organizations men just right for this position, even with the little workers' control that we have in Belgium we would have obtained ten and even one hundred percent more than what has been obtained up to the present time. The mistake we make is perhaps to allow the operation of a kind of natural and uncontrolled selection. The result is that in general the workers of a factory or of a workshop, not having had enough experience—and this is often the case when we have elections in the general union meeting— elect as representatives those who speak the loudest and the most often. But I think that one can suggest here as a principle that if the representative of a shop chosen by his fellows to defend their interests isn't the best worker of that shop, the one who has the best knowledge of his trade and the greatest experience of the ins and outs of his shop— then the one chosen will always have beside him, or even against him, a more influential man, and this man will be the best worker of the shop, even if he isn't a good speaker. I think that the system will give what it is capable of giving when it succeeds in harnessing the man who combines the greatest psychological maturity, the staunchest moral courage, and the best technical knowledge.

Comrades, this is perhaps the cardinal problem of all workers' control. At bottom it is a question of men.

Everywhere I have been to find out about the functioning
of the system of union representation, notably in the school
for shop stewards, I have been told that it is difficult to get
the best men to take on the function of steward. At bottom
this is explained by exactly the same reason that explains
why it is very difficult to find corporals in the army. Many
soldiers prefer to remain privates, and perhaps they are
right. Some wish indeed to become a sergeant, a second
lieutenant, or especially a general, but unfortunately one
must start by being a corporal. Being at the bottom rung of
the chain of command, the corporal, poor fellow, has to assume in the end all the responsibility for carrying things
out, in view of the famous system of the devolution of responsibility. But while having the most responsibilities, at
bottom he is, despite his chevrons, only a simple soldier
who lives all the time with the other soldiers. If he can
make his authority prevail with them it will not be because
of some external symbols but by reason of his superior
worth as a man.

The analogy is striking and, as it is difficult to find good
candidates for corporal in the army, so it is difficult to find
good shop stewards in the factory. The function unites in
fact increase of responsibility with very little authority, and
extends no possibility of success other than by personal
worthiness, based on experience, technical knowledge, and
judgment.

It is often easier being a general than a corporal. It is relatively simple to dazzle audiences by making fine speeches
or tub thumping. It is not always necessary to be an eagle in
order to incite the masses. After the peroration has finished others have to take over. But when questions of cost,
of technology, of the services and characteristics of individuals, and of discipline must be negotiated; when there
are interventions on behalf of people who have quarreled
with the foremen on extremely complex questions and it is
necessary to meet foremen, engineers, and employers on
their own grounds while the poor steward is on a ground

that is unfamiliar to him, then the chevrons no longer count, but the man does. That is why it is difficult to find as many good shop stewards as are needed.

The solution to this difficulty is consciously and systematically to create the means that will help us to form such men. Those who are elected as shop stewards must have a union outlook and be aware of the heavy responsibility they have to fulfill. They must have recognition corresponding to this responsibility. They must not be reduced to the rank that a corporal has in the army. What is more important is to give to the stewards what might be called responsibilities for promotion. It would be disastrous for the union movement to establish a watertight bulkhead between the two parts of its leading personnel: the permanent officials and the shop stewards, who are temporary and not paid. I draw your attention very specially to this point, for it constitutes an essential aspect of the relations to be established between the acts of the union and the acts of its stewards in the factory.

In England an antagonism of this sort has threatened, and continues to threaten, the unity of the union movement, the grouping of the shop stewards often being regarded as a democratic form of organization in the factory contrasting with the "union bureaucracy."

Without flattery I can say that in Belgium the danger of the formation of a union bureaucracy, which is a real danger for any institution that develops a permanent staff, is much less likely than in any other country with a strong union movement. This can be said in honor of the comrades who have in some degree been forced to accept permanent positions. You know as well as I do that there are no sinecures here and that the specialized administrative functions of our large unions take up the whole time of those who serve them. Nevertheless they have managed to preserve the democratic outlook of the masses to a remarkable extent. We do not have a problem of bureaucratization in our union movement.

That is one more reason to plan and to follow a policy that will not permit this bad seed to grow, and that will nip in the bud any danger of the building of a bulkhead between the stewards and the permanent staff. I do not wish to develop this question further; I am only drawing your attention to one point that otherwise might become an agonizing problem some time or another.

Please excuse me for having been so long. I wish to draw only one conclusion from this account. That is that the winning of workers' control, which seems to be a series of modest, partial, scattered, and hidden advances, of which many people know very little, marks in reality the beginning of a great evolution. It is the beginning of a profound overthrow in the human order, in its consequences more fundamental than any other overturning that has been produced in the social and political order up to today.

In saying that I am not underestimating the importance of political reforms. The political preoccupations of our proletariat concern reforms that certainly have their value, but they appear to me nevertheless insignificant when I compare the importance of democratizing the state to that of democratizing work life.

Legislation interests us, affects us directly; moreover we in Belgium know how much we have been hampered in our affairs, even in our union affairs, when our political enemies have been the masters. However, the essential part of our political action is not to create new areas of free action but to record the results and to remove the obstacles that hamper the liberating work of our union organizations. This work is much more important than that which can be adopted by any vote of the Chamber or the Senate.

You go to elections only once every four years; you go to the shop, the factory, the workyard every day. You spend there the best part of your life; you expend there the power of your muscles and of your nerves. Democracy will be realized nowhere unless it is realized there.

I have tried to show you, in the first part of my account,

that the survival of any social order depends on organizing the life of its producers in such a way that they want to produce. Capitalist society is incapable of resolving this problem. Its processes must be changed, and democracy must be established everywhere by introducing the system of workers' control.

There are comrades who like very much to speak of the revolution and who always have in their mouths certain banal formulas by which they conceive of it, such as "the dictatorship of the proletariat." These people will perhaps find that the question of workers' control is not very interesting, that its realization is still far off, even that it has an odor of class collaboration. Let us say it openly: they are exposing themselves to very bitter disappointments in imagining that it suffices to destroy the bourgeois state in order to build a better society.

To change laws is not very difficult! To bring about a political overthrow, to establish dictatorships, sometimes only machine guns are necessary. Unfortunately, in general one ends up only with changing the personnel of the bosses, in changing the name of the regime, in changing the formulas in the name of which one governs afterward—but changing the government of things, social life itself, is accomplished only with difficulty, since the outlook of those who are living that life has not yet been changed.

Before such an enterprise can succeed it is indispensable to change the general outlook, to transform institutions, customs, ideas, not only in political life, but in work life, everyday life. That is not the work of six weeks, of six months, nor even of ten years.

That revolution will be fundamental only to the extent that it is drawn out and toilsome. This is the real revolution, the only one that counts. To be a revolutionary is not to speak of revolution but rather to take it seriously and to work at it.

I think that I have done well in showing you the impor-

tance of workers' control for the entire endeavor. It is good
sometimes to open a window in order to see the horizon, to
throw a glance on the road ahead, and to envisage the consequences of a movement in which one is engaged. In this
way it can be seen that the least reform in the administration of a firm is still a stone in the building of the better
society we wish to build.

This remaking of society depends on a change in the outlook of its members. The workers will acquire this new outlook to the degree that they become producers who will
have satisfaction in working and who will work well because they will have their word to say in the regulations
that determine the forms of their production.

7

The Psychology of Socialism

Deceived in the fervent hopes he had placed in the post-Wilsonian America of "back to normalcy" and in the post-Versailles Belgium of the occupation of the Ruhr, de Man returned in 1921 to Germany, where he first was active in workers' education and later became professor of social psychology at the University of Frankfurt. With the publication in 1926 of his critique of Marxism entitled *The Psychology of Socialism* he became a figure of international import in Continental intellectual circles. At the same time he was regarded as a renegade by the socialist Old Guard and as such was effectively removed from influence within the parties claiming Marxist orthodoxy by a policy of ostracism. For the wider public, however, the singular attraction of the book lay in the fact that, while the object of the attack was familiar, the intent of the author—to radicalize the socialist movement—corresponded to the need of many a socialist sympathizer who in rejecting the ideological temptations represented by the Communist path to salvation found himself frustrated and disconcerted by the increasingly conspicuous gap between radical aspiration and conservative practice in the West. The uniqueness of de Man's approach lay in the fact that he diagnosed the opportunism, reformism, bureaucratization, and "embourgeoisement" of the movement as primarily consequent on the nature of that Marxist theory by which it received theoretical guidance. Alternative and more adequate theoretical equipment would, he argued, enable the movement to escape the contamination of its capitalist environment. Hence a thoroughgoing critique of the philosophical adequacy of Marxist analysis was undertaken in

this volume, and subsequently de Man was to take up both
the theory and practice of an alternative approach.

DIE BEFREIUNG VOM MARXISMUS[1]

> The task of historical materialism, as Marx understood it,
> was to explain how human beings can transform the
> circumstances of which they themselves are the products.
>   *G. Plekhanov*

It is not surprising that socialism is in the throes of a
spiritual crisis. The world war has led to so many social and
political transformations that all parties and all ideological
movements have had to undergo modification in one direction or another, in order to adapt themselves to the new
situation. Such changes cannot be effected without internal
frictions; they are always attended by growing pains; they
denote a doctrinal crisis.

As far as Marxist socialism is concerned, its recent history shows signs of a crisis which cannot be interpreted as
anything more than transient difficulties attending the
process of adaptation to new conditions. The last ten years
have merely served to emphasize a trend which had existed
long before, have made plain to all observers the widening
cleavage between Marxist theory and the practice of those
labor parties which claim to embody it.

All over the world, the trade unions, the cooperatives,
and the labor parties have been driven more and more by
force of circumstances into a policy of compromise, of
moderation, of defensive coalition with their adversaries of
a little while back. By making casuistic distinctions between
means and ends, a logical bridge between the traditional
doctrine and the actual tactic can always be built. But a log-

[1] Chapter 1, *Psychology of Socialism*, translated by Eden and Cedar Paul
from *Zur Psychologie des Sozialismus*, first published in Jena by Diederichs in
1926; London: Allen & Unwin, 1928, pp. 19-37. Reproduction of this
translation, the spelling of which has been Americanized, is through the
courtesy of Allen & Unwin.

ical bridge is not a psychological one. Logically, a policy of class collaboration can invariably be justified by a doctrine of class struggle; yet there may be contradiction among emotional motives when there is no contradiction among intellectual motives. Now, the motives of the masses are essentially emotional. It is sometimes difficult to make the masses understand that, after the lapse of a few years, when circumstances have changed though the end remains the same, it may be right and proper to pursue this end by other means than those adopted heretofore. When, in such a case, new means are employed, there is grave risk that the rank and file may lose confidence in the leaders—that confidence which is the moral tie requisite for all manifestations of a collective political will. The leaders, therefore, do their utmost to demonstrate the continuity of motive by reiterated avowals of faith in time-honored doctrines. Such avowals are symbolical rather than practical. Marxism no longer really inspires political activities, for these are now dominated by circumstances very different from those in which the doctrine originated. The function of Marxism today is merely to supply the socialist arsenal with propaganda formulas, above all with such as are likely to fan the enthusiasm of party members nourished upon the ancient traditions, and to confute Communist accusations of treason to principles. Thus, the principles acquire a conservative function differing widely from their function in old days. Marxist doctrine, therefore, has come to play a part analogous to that played by religious rites in a church which has gained temporal power. Whereas it used to be the motive force of action, it has now become nothing more than an auxiliary means of propaganda. For instance, Marxist socialists, wishing to contest the Communist claim to have a monopoly of Marxist orthodoxy, are accustomed to contrapose their "pure" Marxism, their Marxism of the elect, to the "vulgar" Marxism of the Communists, the Marxism of the crowd. Well now, among the social democrats, the "purer" the Marxism voiced by the leaders, the

more scrupulously "orthodox," the better fitted is it to gal-
vanize the energy of those rank and filers who are still inspired by the revolutionary idealism of former days. But if
Marxism is to remain "pure," it must isolate itself more and
more from practical politics and from the actual trends,
from the great currents, of intellectual life. Consequently,
it turns more and more to textual criticism, to disputes
about interpretation, to the discussion of abstract principles. Whenever it is concerned with actual practice, it de-
generates into casuistry, always trying to justify the action
by the system, and never trying to vivify the system by im-
pregnation with the living fact.

Hence arises that general impression of a lack of intellectual vigor, which is not an indication of a crisis in growth,
but, rather, of senile decay. We detect a loss of logical co-
herency and of self-confidence, such as must inevitably
arise when the guardians of a doctrine are more concerned
to prove that it is still alive than to use it for the conquest of
the world. Young people are particularly sensitive to such a
loss of moral stamina. As everyone knows, they are apt to
be a little intolerant in their demand for a view of life which
shall be at one and the same time a philosophy and a guide
to conduct. Young people, like intellectuals, always look
upon politics as the realization of an idea, as founded both
upon the moral sense and upon reason. Especially nowadays, when wartime experiences have shattered confidence
in so many ideals, the thoughtful members of the younger
generation are yearning for a faith whose sincerity can be
proved by its realization in the practical life of the individual. This is the inner reason why our young people and our
socialist intellectuals have an instinctive prejudice against
Marxism, which they consider too rigid as a mode of
thought and too easygoing as a rule of conduct.

Insofar as these young people become acquainted with
Marxism, it seems to them not so much erroneous as
superfluous. They feel, more or less clearly, that Marxism,
though it may be useful as an economic theory, provides no

answers to the questions which chiefly occupy their minds. For these questions are no longer concerned with the mutual relationships between various economic forms, but with the relationship of individual human beings to economic life and to the community at large. Young people do not so much want a new economic theory or a new way of explaining history, as a new outlook on life, and indeed a new religion. Since Marxism does not offer them this, they turn away from it.

A critique of Marxism, therefore, now brings to the front questions very different from those raised by Bernstein when he set about criticizing Marxism in the closing years of the nineteenth century. Bernstein wanted to "revise" certain parts of Marxist sociology, which seemed to him to conflict with the economic and social development of his days; he wanted to revise the theory of increasing misery, that of capitalist concentration, that of value and surplus value, that of economic crises, that of the intensification of the class struggle, and so on. But Bernstein's criticism of these theories was substantially inspired by the same mode of thought as the theories he was attacking. He did not want to touch the philosophical foundations of Marxism, but only to "develop" the doctrine, by applying the old way of thinking to the new phenomena of economic and social life.

If the Marxism of the social democrats is no longer today the living doctrine of a live movement, this is not because a few of its formulas (such as that of the increasing misery of the proletariat, that of the concentration of capital, and that of the intensification of the class struggle) stand in need of revision. Even if Bernstein's criticism of these formulas had been utterly fallacious, a much more important question would still remain to be answered. Supposing that the formulas are correct, can they serve to guide the march of socialism as Marx believed they could?

Thus, as far as the theoretical success of revisionism was concerned, it was of no moment whether Bernstein or

Kautsky was right in the dispute as to the soundness of Marx's theory about the concentration of capital. The crucial question was, not whether this concentration proceeds in the way described by Marx. The question was: first, whether the concentration of capital affects the social will in the manner predicted by Marx in his theory of social catastrophe; and, secondly and chiefly, whether the decay and disappearance of the middle class (supposing it to occur) would show that socialism was either necessary or desirable. Let me put the matter in another way. Of what use is it to prove that economic crises have assumed other forms than those foreseen by Marx? What matters to us is whether there really is, as Marx believed, a necessary connection between economic crises and the social revolution. Again, even supposing that the theory of the increasing misery of the proletariat is true, what can this signify to one who does not consider that the socialist will of the masses is dependent upon the extremity of their poverty and distress? What, finally, can the intensification of the class struggle matter to one who does not believe that the fight on behalf of class interests will necessarily lead to socialism?

The vulnerable points disclosed in Marxism by these questionings do not relate to the question whether Marx's economic and social inferences are sound or unsound; they relate to the way in which Marx and his followers try to change their method of interpreting history into a mode of action. The plane of criticism is thus transferred from inferences to methods. Now, our historical study of Marxism and the Marxist movement will show us that the method is rooted in the philosophical theories that were dominant during the middle decades of the nineteenth century, theories which may provisionally be summarized in the catchwords "determinism," "causal mechanism," "historicism," "rationalism," and "economic hedonism."

Marxism deduces the socialist objective from the laws of social evolution, which are assumed to have the inexorable necessity of the "laws of nature" formulated in physical science; to this extent, therefore, Marxism is *determinist*. The form in which these laws work is regarded as dialectical, this meaning that they conform to a type of causality in accordance with which (as we see in certain mechanical examples) a force can undergo a change of direction without undergoing any change in nature or intensity, so that it comes to produce an effect which is the converse of its original trend; to this extent, therefore, Marxism is *mechanistic*. It bases its knowledge of the laws of social evolution upon the history of the past, regarding the objectives of human volition as the outcome of certain environing situations ("relationships"). Man being thus reduced to the level of a mere object among the objects of his environment, and these external historical "relationships" being held to determine his volitions and to decide his objectives, we are justified in applying to the theory in question Nietzsche's catchword of *historicism*. Nevertheless, Marx tells us that social evolution, though thus proceeding in accordance with law, does not fulfill itself spontaneously; it proceeds in virtue of the voluntary actions of human beings; these actions are the fruit of a knowledge of the circumstances which determine them; in the case of the fighting proletariat, moreover, they are to be the fruit of a knowledge of the Marxist laws of rational necessity; the Marxist belief that knowledge is the mainspring of social activity entitles us to describe Marxism as *rationalistic*. Marx held, and his followers continue to hold, that the knowledge which determines the social activity of the masses is knowledge of a peculiar kind; it is an awareness of the economic interests which arise out of the relationships of production, and especially out of the conflict of interests between the buyers and the sellers of labor power; thus, in the last analysis, the "relationships" which determine human actions are "relationships of production," and the development of these depends in its turn upon advances in the technique of production; the Marxist belief that social happenings are the outcome of economic causation entitles us to describe Marxism as a variety of *economic hedonism*.

The theory of motives which underlies the whole chain of reasoning, the belief that social activities are determined by an awareness of economic interests, is the basis of the most important and most original positive contributions of Marxism, namely the coordination of the proletarian class struggle and of socialism into one and the same doctrinal system. In the days before Marx, socialism was utopian; the motive for establishing socialism was to be found in a recognition of the moral superiority of a socialist commonwealth. Marx wanted to escape the uncertainties involved in this dependence upon visions of the future, by proving that economic laws make the coming of socialism inevitable. The struggle of the working class on behalf of its own interests, as determined by the capitalist organization of production, will (said Marx) necessarily culminate in the establishment of socialism.

It is this identification of the class struggle with socialism, this belief that there is a necessary connection between the conflict of interests and the liberation of mankind, which has been increasingly called in question by the experiences of the last few decades. Since the day when Marx lived and wrote, it is true that the class consciousness of the workers, based on a recognition of their interests as a class, has grown ever more alert; and it is true that the class struggle has been unceasingly intensified in the industrial and political field: but the goal of a classless society seems farther away than ever. Doubts arise as to the inevitability of the transition to a new social order as the direct consequence of the proletarian struggle on behalf of the workers' interests; and these doubts grow more and more urgent. Enough to point to the way in which the working class is tending to accept bourgeois standards and to adopt a bourgeois culture; to the gradual substitution of the reformist motive for the revolutionary motive; to the increasing intimacy of the ties connecting the workers with the political and economic institutions of the existing order; to the accentuation of national differentiations in the socialist labor movement; to the formation of a bureaucratic upper stratum within the labor organizations; and so on. The problems which are thus brought into the foreground of every discussion concerning the present value of Marxism, lead directly to the central question whether the Marxist doctrine of motives, the theory that the social activities of the masses are determined by their knowledge of their class interests, is still tenable.

Before going farther in the methodological and historical discussion of Marxist doctrine, it will be simpler to let facts speak for themselves—facts which can throw light on the real connection between the proletarian struggle on behalf of working-class interests, on the one hand, and the socialist objective, on the other.

The first point we note is that the historical sequence of events conflicts with the rationalist theory of the adoption of a socialist objective as the outcome of an awakening to the knowledge of class interests. Socialist teachings are not a product of the awakening of class consciousness among the workers; on the contrary, they are an essential preliminary to such an awakening. Socialism existed (as an objective) before there was a labor movement, and even before there was a working class.

Socialist teachings, those of Marx and Engels not excepted, sprang from other sources than the class interest of the proletariat. They are products, not of the cultural poverty of the proletariat, but of the cultural wealth of instructed members of the bourgeoisie and the aristocracy. They spread from above downward, not from below upward. Among the great thinkers and the ardent enthusiasts who were pioneers in the field of socialist theory, hardly one proletarian can be named. Beyond dispute, socialism, though in course of time it has become the objective of the labor movement and supplies that movement with a program, is, historically considered, not so much a doctrine of the proletariat as a doctrine for the proletariat. Were we to accept this misleading terminology of Marxism, which tells us that every specific kind of social ideology is the expression of the outlook of some particular class, we should be compelled to describe socialism, including Marxism, as a bourgeois growth.

In reality, the undoubted fact that the originators of socialist doctrines have almost invariably been bourgeois intellectuals, shows that psychological motives are at work, motives which have nothing whatever to do with class interests. The peculiarities and diversities of these doctrines only become intelligible in the light of an analysis of the spiritual motives which underlie the views of every socialist thinker, or at any rate of every socialist thinker who has a claim to originality. Of course this psychoanalytical biography cannot dispense with a consideration of the social and economic environment of the thinker. We must take into account, not only his general social background, but also his individual economic and social position—which, for instance, is "bourgeois" alike in the case of Marx, university trained and primarily designed for an academic career; in that of Owen, the factory owner; and in that of Saint-Simon, the aristocrat. If, however, leaving the field of individual biography, we pass on to attempt a psychoanalysis or to formulate a sociology of socialist thought in general, we find that socialist doctrine becomes explicable, not as an adaptive reaction of the proletariat to its class situation, but as an antagonistic reaction of cultured bourgeois and aristocrats to the circumstances of their cultural environment. Socialist creative thought, thus envisaged, is seen to take its rise in an affect, or rather in an almost infinite multiplicity of affects, derived from cultural, ethical, and aesthetic sources. These affects, and the resultant thought processes out of which the doctrines arise, are no more to be explained as the outcome of class interests and the class struggle, than the beauty of a painting by Rembrandt is to be explained in terms of a chemical analysis of the pigments and the canvas—though "in the last analysis" the picture consists of nothing more than canvas and paint. Insofar as science has anything to say in the matter, the only science that is of any use here is one which ignores economic interests, and bring the intellectual and moral personality into high relief. Here we need the aid of biography, ranging from the description of the personal environment to psychoanalysis and portraiture; for thoughts are the outcome of personality, not of a parallelogram of social forces as displayed in mass movements.

Agreed that social forces, as generated and brought into clash during the class struggle, turn thoughts to account. The more accurately social processes have been reflected in the brain of a socialist thinker, the more trustworthy his perception of the longings of the masses, the sooner and the more heartily will the masses accept the teachings which embody their desires. Then, what the individual has thought, becomes the symbol of the volitions and feelings of millions upon millions. But the origin of the two elements whereof this compound of will and idea consists, is as diverse as that of the meal and the yeast out of whose union bread is made. The nature of the process of fermentation which finds expression in the socialist labor movement can only be understood by one who realizes that the working masses are the dough, whereas the ideas of nonproletarian intellectuals are the yeast.

Marxism obstinately ignores this multiplicity of socialist motivation, refuses to see the complicated nature of the issues. Otherwise the Marxists would lose their faith in the necessary connection between class interests and ways of thinking. When we study the origin of Marxism itself, we see that the position of the working class (a very different thing, by the by, from the interests of the working class) has served merely to arouse an affective predisposition for the use of ideas which, for their part, had their source in far nobler cultural motives than the desire of talented intellectuals to gain some personal advantage. We are told that the

bourgeois and aristocratic pioneers in the advocacy of
socialist ideals were but exceptions to the general rule that
socialist doctrine is of proletarian origin—whereas the facts
show clearly enough that these "bourgeois exceptions" are
really the rule. To substantiate their illusion, the Marxists
begin the history of socialism with Marx, repudiating the
great forerunners, whose portraits would give the picture
gallery a too obviously nonproletarian stamp. In doing this,
Marxism does grievous wrong to itself. We gravely underestimate the value of personality, if we reduce the highest
form of mental production to a nonpersonal process, if we
regard it as nothing more than a link in the chain of economic determinism, wherein the creative personality is but
an epiphenomenon devoid of independent causal significance.

The recognition of this truth, however, must not lead us
to the opposite extreme of underestimating those motive
forces of the labor movement which find expression, not as
individual thought processes, but as psychological mass
phenomena. One such mass phenomenon is the affective
reaction of the working class which makes the workers re-
sponsive to the ideas formulated by intellectuals.

Here, likewise, Marxism is incompetent to explain how
this mass affect originates. The rationalist foundations of
the doctrine impose an obstacle. To the Marxists it seems
that the class struggle, the struggle for surplus value which
expands into a struggle for socialization, is the direct and
necessary consequence of a particular mode of production,
of an economic category. They regard the struggle as, in a
way, an end in itself. It is not fought under the impulsion
of variable motives, and to secure variable ends; from the
moment when the working masses realize that their interests are fundamentally opposed to those of the possessing
classes, it is directed toward an aim previously inherent and
henceforward self-evident—that of the social revolution.
For Marx, knowledge, awareness, was the primary determinant, the class will was the outcome of class conscious-

ness. We are confronted with a kind of mystical revelation: a revolutionary necessity hovers in the air, as a scientifically demonstrated principle inherent in the developmental laws of the capitalist method of production; the workers, the "midwives" of the revolution, need only recognize the truth of this principle, and they will take the steps requisite to bring about the birth. They are the instruments of a dialectic which already lives as a law in a supraterrestrial sphere before it descends to earth and enters the minds of the human beings whom knowledge will stimulate to the fulfillment of the law. Others besides the Communists (the "vulgar" Marxists) are a prey to this rationalist error, as we may learn from a characteristic passage in Kautsky's *Ethik*,[2] where he speaks of the "moral indignation" which impels the workers to play an active part in the class struggle as being the outcome of their class consciousness. This implies that the workers first acquire the knowledge which underlies their awareness of their class interests, and then only, having recognized it ratiocinatively, proceed to *feel* it as a matter of justice and ethics!

Can we wonder, then, that Marxism has not as yet made any serious contribution toward solving the problem as to precisely how these processes go on in the workers' minds, these processes thanks to which those who live in particular class relationships acquire particular class views? Persons who are a prey to rationalist superstitions, those who believe that knowledge precedes feeling, have no need of any such explanation; they do not recognize that there is any problem to solve. The right way of stating the problem is, of course, to ask in what way the conditions of the worker's life react on his state of feeling, and how his affects guide his social volition. Not until we have made an exhaustive study of the worker's emotive reaction to his social environment, can we understand the part played by socialist theories in this reaction, and the infinite variety of the con-

[2] Karl Kautsky, *Ethik und materialistische Geschichtsauffassung*, Berlin: Dietz, 1922, p. 135.

sequent reciprocal influences. We must therefore, just as in
the case of individual volitions, begin with the study of the
affects, the emotional mainsprings of action, and then go
on to examine the rational motives which provide theoretical aims for the volitions aroused by the affects. This division into a primary analysis of the affective sphere, and a
secondary analysis of the ideational, corresponds just as
much to historical reality as to a logical necessity. In the
course of human evolution, thought has developed into an
ever more important function of emotional and voluntary
processes; so, likewise, the whole course of the inner history of the labor movement exhibits a progressive transformation of feelings into thoughts, of needs into ideals, of
impulses into reasons. Throughout, there has been a
clearer illumination of that which at first was but dimly
craved for and darkly apprehended—illumination by an
awakening consciousness, a growing rationality. The working class fought before it knew. Class war was not born out
of class consciousness. On the contrary, class consciousness
was born out of the class war, and the class war itself was
the outcome of a feeling of class resentment. The workers
do not fight as a class because they know themselves to be
exploited; but they come to think themselves exploited
when, and because, they are engaged in the fight. The
theory of exploitation is the product of a struggle engendered by feeling and not by thought.

Therefore the sociology of the labor movement must always begin with a study of the affects of the individual
worker, as typically produced by his normal living and
working conditions. This investigation will be most en-
lightening if we concentrate, to begin with, upon the workers in medium-scale and large-scale industry. Of course
there are various other strata in the working class (wage-
earning women, agricultural laborers, office employees,
the lower-grade civil servants, home workers, artisans, the
workers in dwarf industries, and so on), whose conditions
of life and psychological characteristics diverge in various

ways from those of typical industrial operatives. But these latter constitute the most numerous section of the working class, and they display, in a peculiarly salient form, the features common to all the workers. They give out the fundamental tone of the class, and are therefore the most suitable specimens to select when we wish to study the class as a whole. Now, such a typical proletarian, an average member of this stratum, is by no means identical with the picture of him drawn by Marxist doctrinaires. As we have seen, socialist philosophy was conceived by bourgeois intellectuals. Their inclination was to idolize the proletariat; and they did this the more enthusiastically, the less they were acquainted with actual proletarians. When a modern socialist intellectual, and above all a modern Marxist intellectual, speaks of the proletariat, it is with a reverent vibration of voice, such as might have been heard when an early Christian was talking of the Savior, or when an 1848 democrat mentioned the People. For to the Marxist, the proletariat is the Savior, the Power, the Will, predestined to satisfy the longing for a better world, the longing for a "socialist hereafter." The proletariat is not a reality but a concept. This idealization of the proletariat is a counterpart to the idealization of the peasantry characteristic of Jean Jacques Rousseau and his followers in the days of the eighteenth-century Enlightenment. In these cases, we get an ideal picture which is as far from reality as a Watteau shepherd was from a genuine peasant of the time. Gorki puts the matter very well in his account of his impressions when, as a young workman, he attended the secret meetings of Russian socialist students and other enthusiasts. "When they began to talk about the People, I speedily realized that I did not share their sentiments in the matter. This surprised me a good deal, and made me mistrustful of myself. For them the People was the embodiment of wisdom, of spiritual beauty, of goodness of heart, an almost divine and unique being, the exemplar of all that was beautiful, just, and great. The description did not tally with 'the

People' as I knew it."[3] An analogous surprise, though in
another setting, is described by H. G. Wells in *The New
Machiavelli*. At Cambridge, in the nineties, his hero, then
an undergraduate, comes under the influence of the
thought trends initiated by the Social Democratic Federation. He regards the proletariat as a "divine being," per-
sonified in a propaganda poster by a workman, "a huge-
muscled, black-haired toiler swaggering sledgehammer in
hand across a revolutionary barricade." A little later,
Remington comes into actual contact with the industrial
workers. He goes to the Potteries, and is much distressed
by the contrast between reality and fancy. "The picture of a
splendid Working Man cheated out of his innate glorious
possibilities . . . began to give place to a limitless spectacle of
inefficiency, to a conception of millions of people not organized as they should be, not educated as they should be,
not simply prevented from but incapable of nearly every
sort of beauty, mostly kindly and well-meaning, mostly incompetent, mostly obstinate, and easily humbugged and
easily diverted. Even the tragic and inspiring idea of Marx,
that the poor were nearing a limit of painful experience,
and awakening to a sense of intolerable wrongs, began to
develop into the more appalling conception that the poor
were simply in a witless uncomfortable inconclusive way—
'muddling along'; that they wanted nothing very definitely
nor very urgently, that mean fears enslaved them and
mean satisfactions decoyed them, that they took the very
gift of life itself with a spiritless lassitude, hoarding it, being
rather anxious not to lose it than to use it in any way whatever."[4] In like manner a German, Curt Geyer, disillusioned
with communism, wrote not long ago of "the alternation
between vegetative well-being (without vision of the future)
and despair, an alternation characteristic of working-class
mentality."

[3] Maxim Gorki, *My Universities*, Moscow: Progress, 1954, p. 38. Professor Irwin Weil of Northwestern University has been good enough to lo-
cate this citation for me. The material quoted in the text, however, was
translated from de Man's excerpt from a German edition of Gorki.
[4] New York: Duffield, 1919, pp. 112, 114-115.

No doubt the bitterness of disappointment may have led these writers to paint their pictures in unduly dark colors. Still, there would have been no disillusionment had there not first been illusion. In any case, such pessimistic descriptions are no farther from the truth than were the original fancy pictures, which were not based upon experience but upon a tissue of abstractions. Among all the varieties of socialist doctrine, Marxism is most prone to create such mirages. To the Marxist, the proletariat is a pure concept, an instrument for the realization of other concepts, one term in the algebraical formula of the social revolution. In this formula, the worker lives only for the class struggle; all his thoughts and all his actions are directed toward the one end. The Marxist intellectual identifies the proletariat (insofar as it is anything more than a purely abstract notion) with the specimens he encounters at propaganda meetings. The fallacy, of course, is twofold. First of all, at these meetings, our intellectual sees only an infinitesimal selection of the workers, which he then proceeds to identify with the "masses." Further, he assumes that the behavior of this select group at propaganda meetings gives a true index of what they, and the workers at large, think and do at the bench, in the home, in the normal environment of everyday life.

This psychological error underlies the fanatical idolization of the masses which, even before the war, was characteristic of the left wing of the Marxists, and since then has been made a principle of political strategy in the forms of spartacism and communism. Mystical virtues are ascribed to the "masses." Thanks to these virtues, mass action will be a panacea for the ills which the organized and disciplined minority has not yet been able to cure! This Marxist cult of the "masses" is the expression of a tendency of certain intellectuals toward the "projection" of their own aspirations (born of their own impatience, and of a reaction against the impotence of the social stratum to which they belong) upon a great X, which at any rate has the advantage—for them—of being an unknown quantity. Experience shows, however, that the mobilization of the masses is by no means able to infuse into the labor movement that element of heroic defiance which the theoreticians among the extremists anticipate. It is the "masses" who, after they have been temporarily set in motion by a transient ebullition of feeling, then force upon their leaders an opportunist policy, a policy in which revolutionary objectives are sacrificed for the sake of immediate material gains. The German revolution of November 1918 is not the only one which, owing to the participation of the masses, has (as German socialists are now in the habit of saying) "degenerated into a movement on behalf of better wages." What the Marxists dream of getting from the masses is really a new leadership; their cult of the masses is another form of hero worship. The unknown masses are imaginatively endowed with all the heroic lineaments which are not discoverable in the organized workers and their leaders. Nothing could be more typical of the psychological springs of this movement for the idolization of the masses, than that its chief exponents have been women. Hero worship is a specifically feminine tendency. Three noted Marxist women have been its chief protagonists: Rosa Luxemburg, in a critical and polemist form; Clara Zetkin, as a sentimental propagandist; and Henriette Roland-Holst, symbolically and poetically, for in this writer's dramatic and lyrical verses we find the most effective symbolical expression of faith in the masses as a form of hero worship.[5]

The actual leaders of the working-class movement, born in the ranks, daily and hourly coming into contact with the masses, are far more skeptical. No doubt their attitude is partly determined by their professional position, which makes them as bureaucrats take an exaggerated view of the

[5] Luxemburg, 1870-1919, noted Marxist theoretician, parting from Lenin notably in emphasizing the "spontaneity" of the masses, a founder of the Spartacist League in Germany in 1916; Zetkin, 1857-1933, veteran German Marxist, a founder of the Communist party of Germany in 1919; Roland-Holst, 1869-1952, Dutch poet of the socially conscious "generation of the eighties."

importance of organizational apparatus. Still, their particular kind of bureaucratic activity does certainly bring them
into close touch with live proletarians; whereas the
theoreticians, the writers, and the journalists who play, or
would like to play, a part in the labor movement, only leave
their studies or their editorial offices to enter the heady, artificial, and misleading atmosphere of party meetings. It is
solely among these intellectuals that we find the originators
of a Marxist cult of the masses, such as flourished during
the decade before the war. I may mention four notable
persons with academic titles: Dr. Rosa Luxemburg, Dr.
Anton Pannekoek, Dr. Karl Liebknecht, and Dr. Hermann
Gorter; also Henriette Roland-Holst, the poet, and Karl
Radek, the author; three more who could write "doctor"
before the name, Angelica Balabanoff, Alexander Helphand (Parvus), and Van Ravesteyn;[6] I might add Dr.
Henry de Man to the number, were it not that I had, even
before the war, laid myself open to the charge of
"latitudinarianism" by a certain skepticism and moderation. So long as my socialist work remained literary and
propagandist, it was not very difficult for me to retain a
due measure of orthodoxy, and to preserve my enthusiasm
for the poster pictures of the ideal proletarian. When,
however, my activities in the workers' educational movement and in the Belgian trade-union movement brought
me into contact with the problems of proletarian daily life,
I found it ever more difficult to safeguard my primitive

[6] Gorter, 1864-1927, Dutch poet and socialist theoretician of the same
generation "of the eighties"; Radek, 1885-1939 [?], veteran Russian Bolshevik, active with respect to the German movement, at this moment lean-
ing to Trotsky, to be purged in 1937; Balabanoff, 1878-1965, Russian
Marxist long domiciled in Italy; Helphand (the name is variously spelled,
and in fact he was also well known by his pseudonym of "Parvus"), 1869-
1924, veteran Marxist associated with Trotsky in 1905, Russian by birth
but Central European by choice, a supporter of Germany in World War I
and the vital intermediary in the return of Lenin to Russia in 1917; Wil-
lem Van Ravesteyn, 1876-1970, Dutch editor, politician, and historian, at
this point returning to the socialist movement after some years with the
Communists (information on Dutch figures supplied by the Institut Emile
Vandervelde).

doctrinairism against the onslaughts of doubts and reservations. The halo had vanished from the proletarian head.
Not that my attachment to the workers had waned, not that
I had become less willing to devote myself to their cause;
on the contrary, this feeling and this desire grow deeper
and stronger as the days pass, precisely because they now
relate to living individuals instead of to a generalized
abstraction. I no longer look upon the proletariat simply as
a mass, which exists for the sole purpose of fulfilling its his-
toric mission to set mankind free. The workers seem to me
all the more lovable, all the more in need of help, because
they have ceased to be the heroes of historical drama, and
have put on flesh and blood, with its biological and social
heritage of virtues and vices, longings and imperfections. I
find it impossible, now, to look upon my fellows as the
mere instruments for the fulfillment of an idea. They are
creatures driven onward by instinct, and their ideas are but
tools for the satisfaction of the bodily and spiritual needs
that arise in social life.

Marxists relapse into the naivety of the outworn primitive democratic adoration of the crowd, when they believe
that the masses originate ideas. Besides, their own practice
gives the lie to any such theory. In socialist practice, the
spiritual sovereignty of the masses is treated as a fiction.
There are leaders and led, the subjects and the objects of
policy. The extremists of Marxism, the Russian Communists, are past masters in the art of "guiding" the masses
with the aid of all the means provided by modern technique for the formation of "public opinion."

Socialist conviction is, first and foremost, a complex, an
emotional state, no less in the isolated thinker who
launches ideas, than in the masses who accept them as
symbols of their own volitions. Only, the nature of the
complex differs in the respective cases. In the individual
thinker, it is poietic and active; in the masses, it is receptive
and passive. Let there be no misunderstanding. I am not
suggesting that mankind should be dichotomized into

those who are mental leaders and those who are mentally led. Such a dichotomy is equally incompatible with extant peculiarities of character, and with the class affiliations of "thinkers" and "masses." We cannot permanently divide the socialist movement into operatives and intellectuals. All human beings have tendencies to lead and tendencies to accept leadership as part of their spiritual makeup, tendencies which may be respectively qualified as typically masculine-active and typically feminine-passive. As temperament varies, one or other element may markedly preponderate. Yet we are not entitled to base on this individual preponderance a binary classification of social types. The only characteristic justifying such a classification is the *behavior* with which this individual or that responds to a particular situation. Among those who manifest a leader temperament in one field of action, there are few who are not inclined to accept leadership in some other field, where different claims are made upon their capacities. For instance: many a born general can in political matters be led by the nose by wirepullers; many a great political leader is a henpecked husband;. many a noted professor, who is a highly original thinker in his own chosen subject, is no more than a "man in the street" upon all other topics. Every one of us, however independent and creative his mind, is sure to be one of the crowd in the matter of some pet weakness. If, therefore, we wish to speak of "actives" and "passives," of "leaders" and "led," we must classify by the objective canons of behavior in some special situation, rather than by temperament.

There can, then, be no question of trying to subdivide the socialist labor movement permanently into an "instinctive" proletarian mass and a "thoughtful" stratum of intellectuals. Of course the "individual thinker" may spring from the masses, and the intellectual may be one of the "led." Poietic and receptive behavior denote different functions in relation to some definite happening which exercises a specific influence upon people's minds; they do not

denote temperamental distinctions or varying class affiliations, per se. If in the following pages I frequently refer to
the instinctive affects and the instinctive receptivity of the
working class, this is only because, as far as the socialist
movement is concerned, the workers at large constitute the
real mass element, whose fight on behalf of working-class
interests is regarded by the Marxists as the source of
socialist conviction.

8

The Crisis of Socialism

With the critical success of the *Psychology of Socialism*—there were those who compared it in import to *Das Kapital*[1]—de Man was enabled in his own mind and by virtue of his international authority to devote himself to active participation in efforts to resuscitate the ailing socialist parties, weakened by the Marxist disease he had diagnosed. For although he became a professor of social psychology at the University of Frankfurt and continued to produce scholarly works on relatively esoteric matters of ideology, his work always had as its goal the winning over of adherents to a new socialist policy more adequate to the conditions presented by twentieth-century capitalism.

But as an ideological heretic in the eyes of the party regulars, and as a foreigner, however faultless his German, he found only spotty support in Weimar Germany, where in any case questions of doctrinal bases of adherence soon paled in significance before the threat posed by Nazism. As he himself was to say later with reference to his life work, "All in all I have produced new yeast, but little new bread."[2] Yet with hindsight it is all too easy to underestimate the unrealized potentialities of history, and in any case the significance of de Man's work transcends the epoch in which it was generated. During these years he produced a constant stream of polemic works for a wide variety of audiences. One of the most trenchant of these

[1] Hermann Keyserling and Bernard Lavergne; Theodor Heuss, later president of West Germany, saw it as the "weightiest analysis of Marx and of his effects that has been attempted from the explicitly socialist side," *Berliner Börsen-Courier*, 23 May 1926.

[2] *Cavalier seul*, Geneva: Cheval Ailé, 1948, p. 148.

pieces, typical of the clarity of his analysis and the urgency
of his concern, was the following address.

LA CRISE DU SOCIALISME[3]

If I am to believe reports you already have had many lectures on this subject. However, it seems to me that not everything has been said. Up until now you have been told
about problems of tactics and of theory, but there has been
only touching reference to the problem that I believe is essential, which is not that of a crisis of knowledge but rather
of a universal crisis of faith, confidence, emotion, and will.

A formulation often used to sum up the symptoms of the
universal crisis of contemporary socialism is that in gaining
breadth it has lost in depth. Or one could also say: a gain in
weight but a loss in impetus.

Let us look a little closer at what there is behind this impression, more or less vague and debatable according to
the meaning given to these terms. We will soon find a more
exact psychological formulation with which we can agree.
In the beginning the essential motive of the socialist action
of individuals was the desire for a radical overthrow—
which was believed to be near—of the whole social order.
All daily activity—consisting, moreover, above all in the
propaganda of ideas and of preparation for revolution—
appeared as a means leading directly to this end.

Since then, by progress both in organization and in deed,
these everyday activities have so changed in nature that the
means have been transformed more and more into goals
themselves. I know very well that in theory one can present, as de Brouckère[4] recently did from this podium, all
the reformist means as in some sense preparatory to a final
revolutionary goal, especially by giving a sufficiently

[3] Address given to the University Association for Social Studies at the
Maison du Peuple of Brussels, 21 June 1927; Brussels: L'Eglantine, 1927.

[4] Louis de Brouckère, 1870-1951, prewar Marxist comilitant with de
Man in the Belgian Labor party, who remained an orthodox Marxist.

abstract meaning to the word "revolution." But I am not
dealing here with what *can be* in theory, but with what *is*,
with the reality of the psychological motives that actually
impel men having specific responsibilities and functions.
But there has been and there continues to be a shifting of
motives in the socialist movement, analogous to that which
is produced in all institutions, in all movements, in all
groups sharing beliefs and opinions, to the degree that
they gain in strength and in breadth, become organized
and differentiated, and prepare to defend the gains they
have made.

For this reason, the more means we possess, the farther
away the original goal seems to become, the more it moves
to the background as a motive for action. There is not
necessarily any loss of faith, but the content of this faith becomes different in practice and by practice. The messianic
faith of the beginning in the imminence of the Great Day
becomes weak. The Great Day has not come, and one does
not believe in its imminence, nor in its certainty, as much as
hitherto. The motives of practical action bear on much less
ambitious goals, in large part even defensive or indeed
conservative ones; one *defends* democracy, the mark, the
franc, the eight-hour day, the unions, reforms already won
and vested interests.

In brief, there is a weakening, not at all of faith in the
justice of the socialist cause, but of belief in the imminence
of its truimph, in the present-day applicability of many of
its formerly urgent demands; in a word, there is a retreat
from the chiliastic or messianic belief that we have had the
custom of considering as the criterion of socialist conviction. Hence the impression of a growing divergence between old doctrine and new practice, of a frustration of the
altruistic motive of conviction by the less elevated motives
of interest and of the will to power.

In the face of this situation some young people see no
other resolution than to condemn the present in the name
of the past, contrasting the present-say attitudes of leaders

to their former opinions. This is really too simple. For at
bottom a phenomenon as general, as universal as the one
the symptoms of which I have just sketched, must have
general and universal causes. The shift of motives which is
at its origin involves the masses just as much as the leaders,
although in a somewhat different way; I am not at all sure
that in Belgium, for instance, the average organized
worker, the unpretentious provincial militant who is the
real pivot of our movement, is not at least as disabused,
since 1886 or 1902,[5] as our socialist ministers. In any case,
before anything else it is necessary to try to *understand* the
entire import of the general phenomenon of the shift of
motives. It is less a question of doctrinal or parliamentary
criticism than it is a problem of collective psychology. This
does not mean that there is nothing to do but say amen.
But it does mean that a good diagnosis is indicated if one
wants to have a good prescription.

But the diagnosis that sees a return to the romantic formulas of yesterday as the only cure is superficial. And that
makes it very dangerous. For in the end, what is the
present-day socialist other than the product of an evolution
the origins and paths of development of which were given
by these formulas? On what basis can today's youth hope to
avoid arriving at the same point if in the course of becoming older, of in their turn becoming eminent, important,
respectable, potential cabinet officers, they take the same
starting point?

The revolutionary formulas have not immunized the
elders of today against the shift in motives; nevertheless
these elders have had to give—and have given—far more
arduous proofs of character than socialist action requires
today of its young militants. In the twentieth century just as
in the nineteenth, twenty-five years plus twenty-five years

---

[5] 1886, the "terrible year" of economic crisis leading to quasi-
insurrectionary activity on the part of Belgian workers; 1902, the year of
an unsuccessful general strike for universal and equal suffrage (finally accorded at the end of World War I).

makes fifty years, and this ineluctable mathematical fact entails just as ineluctable physiological and psychological consequences: one acquires plumpness, experience, wisdom, a sense of responsibility, prudence; following the formula dear to our friend Louis Bertrand,[6] one attaches more importance to good soup and less to beautiful words. To sum up, when the young oppositionists of today will be ministers, the same things will be said of them. At that point they will quote from the speeches of the leaders of 1927 as they now quote from the speeches of the leaders of 1900. The only difference will be completely to the disadvantage of present-day youth, for they are starting by returning to the past, whereas the young of 1900 thought only of the future. Formulations that were then adequate have become outmoded. We are going to see that in a moment. And in the meanwhile, let us state that it is not by returning to old ideas that we are going to rejuvenate the movement. A better means is to rejuvenate the ideas.

In saying this I do not place myself alongside those elders who find youth too oppositional. On the contrary, I find that they are not enough so—or in any case, not in the right way. I would like to see them attack the very doctrines by which the elders have been inspired, and formulate a new doctrine in place of warming up the old one.

I can contribute this evening to this formulation only by a very fragmentary survey of some aspects of the problem. It is especially important to show why its solution presupposes a critique of Marxist philosophy.

The doctrinal starting point of the older generation—those who became socialist before the war—was more or less Marxist. I say "more or less," because the term "Marxist" covers a very great variety of formulas. With Marx himself, and even more with the movements that speak in the name of his doctrine, there has been a clearly

[6] A revered Belgian socialist, 1856-1943, author of *Histoire de la Démocratie et du Socialisme en Belgique depuis 1830*, 2 vols., Brussels: Deschênes and Paris: Cornely, 1906 (dates from the Institut Emile Vandervelde).

marked movement of thought. And to this movement in time there has been added variation in space, owing to the diversity of national environments. But I will not pause here to study these differences; on the contrary I wish to search out the elements of belief common to all the separate variations. Thereby it will appear that Marxism itself is only a particularly characteristic form (because particularly intellectualized and systematized) of certain much more generally held socialist tenets, belonging to a whole age and in part even predating Marx.

The fundamental idea of this socialism of the second half of the nineteenth century appears to me in its turn as a particular form of the belief in continual moral progress, a belief that characterized all the ideologies of that century, bourgeois as much as proletarian. Thus the present-day crisis of Marxist belief is only a special instance of the general crisis of the idea of progress, affecting all the movements of ideas, all disciplines, all philosophies. Of course, in speaking of the idea of progress, I have in mind the specific concept of progress that inspired almost all the thought of the nineteenth century: continual and ineluctable progress of humanity toward more happiness by the continual and ineluctable perfection of the means of production and transportation, hence ideological and social evolution bound to natural laws and knowable through scientific methods. In order to characterize this conceptualization by "isms," one could label its various partial aspects as: scientism, rationalism, positivism, historicism, economic hedonism.

Look at the history of science for the last century or two, or even since humanism, from this broadened viewpoint, and you will see that Marxism, that all so-called scientific socialism of the nineteenth century, is the proletarian form these general beliefs take. In this case they lead to certain particular formulations: technical and economic evolution is the last and determinant cause of social progress; social progress is identified with the transformation of institutions, that is, of the material environment; it is accomplished through the action of this environment on men, by the mechanism of the class struggle governed by collective economic interest.

This Marxist conceptualization represented an immense advance upon the former utopian socialism. One could not better characterize this progress than by saying that it made a scientific synthesis, and thus brought about the practical union, of two hitherto isolated elements: the proletarian struggle moved by interest, and socialism, a goal inspired by an ethical conviction. This is the great historical service of Marxism, a permanent contribution that obliges all criticism, all theoretical revision, to be expressed as "beyond Marxism" instead of recommending a return to pre-Marxist conceptions.

This does not mean that, in order to realize this "going beyond," there should be no submission to the crucible of criticism of the fundamental postulates of Marxism: the identity of the proletarian class struggle and of socialism, of socialist progress with the struggle for economic interests.

In sum, Marxism is an effort of genius, fruitful for many years, to insert sociology into the natural sciences, to explain social progress by natural evolution. To put it more exactly: Marxism wishes to submit social evolution to natural causality, which for it takes the particular form of economic causality.

But it is the very principle of this method that my criticism attacks. I dispute that the social attitudes of individuals and of masses can be explained by causality. I see them submitted, to a very great extent, to the laws of finality. And the governing images that orient this finality cannot, in my opinion, be derived from the causality of the material environment.

Here let me first of all clear up a misunderstanding. In the critique he recently made in Paris of my views, Vandervelde said, according to the report in the *Eveil Universitaire*, that I wanted to reverse the Marxist thesis of ultimate economic causes by replacing it with that of ultimate ideological causes; according to him I would place the Marxist ideological "superstructure" on the bottom and its economic "substructure" on the top.

I must have expressed myself very badly to have been so understood.[7] I made a considerable effort to explain that, on the contrary, there were no ultimate causes, ideological or economic, known to social science. It is precisely this principle of causality that I am attacking. And the method of this attack is psychoanalytic: I have tried to demonstrate that all causal sociological theory is only a scientific disguise of an emotional evaluation of motives, that each sociological system establishes its ultimate historical causes from the present-day motives with which it is concerned.

This does not mean at all that we must, then, give up causal explanation. But here I am opposed to Marx in two regards.

First of all, I think that in order to remain scientific, any method of causal explanation must rest on the demonstrated effect of immediately knowable, specific causes and not on general and conceivable causes. As soon as one leaves the inductive for the deductive method, one has abandoned science for metaphysics. I do not deny the usefulness of metaphysical hypotheses for research, but then they are working hypotheses, simple provisional instruments of research without value in themselves, and not at all dogmatic bases for belief. Political parties are not founded on methods of scientific research.

Additionally, I think that it is necessary to admit a form of different causality, and hence a different method of research, according to which the material environment on

---

[7] The report of Vandervelde's address published by the *Nouvelle Revue Socialiste* of June 1927, contains still another astonishing mistake. It has me say that "the identity of their gainful interests is among workers only a secondary, problematic bond." I said precisely the contrary. The sentence from the *Psychology of Socialism* (p. 209) censured by Vandervelde does not refer to the workers but to the intellectuals [de Man].

the one hand, and human reactions on the other, will be explained. The causal method of Marxism and its hypothesis of governing economic factors remains, without being a dogmatic truth, still useful—under certain conditions that are not important here—for the explanation of the environment. But in order to understand human reactions to this environment, the causal method no longer is enough, as it is a question of phenomena of the psyche into which conscious goal orientation enters. It is necessary to start from the hypothesis of an ethical finality here, since this finality is manifested in the concrete reality of psychological motivation.

To illustrate this by an example: one of the principal theses of my book, the *Psychology of Socialism*, is that socialist ideology is not the product of a unique cause, the proletariat's consciousness of its own class interests. On the contrary, I see it as the product of two factors—more exactly, of the state of tension of two forces—of entirely different origin and tendency. Historically and psychologically, socialist conviction is independent of all class interests, it is inspired by broadly humane ethical valuations, and it is moreover the creation of bourgeois intellectuals; but as a mass movement, contemporary socialism is largely a workers' movement, because the life conditions of the working class, which give it special interests, have created in it a distinctive collective emotional disposition admitting of socialist objectives.

You have here the example of a confrontation of two elements of mutual reaction: the passive element of the environment, the active element of man. In order to explain the emotional reactions of the masses to the environment, I use to a large degree the causal method which awards a very great importance to ascertainable economic factors, but in order to explain the creative process of the idea, of the motive force of the idea, of the idea as goal, I have had to make use of a final-cause method, and this latter cannot dispense with the hypothesis that there is a scale of ethical values independent of the economic interests, private or shared, of humanity.

In short, to explain a change in salaries one can use principally, perhaps exclusively, the economic causality that governs the adaptation of men to the social environment, but in order to explain the convictions of Emile Vandervelde, one must admit an ethical finality, a contrary reaction of the thinking individual *against* the environment, which means that socialism is not only sought, but sought as just; one must presuppose an absolute scale of ethical values. Hence: in order to explain psychic reactions, emphasize ethical finality. To understand the socialist workers' movement, do not regard it at all as the semiautomatic result of an environmental determinism, but as a state of tension between two, sometimes convergent, sometimes divergent, forces: economic interest, class egoism on the one side, ethical conviction, human altruism, on the other.

Hence it is not a question of putting in place of the Marxist dogma of economic determinism an opposed dogma of ideological determinism. On the contrary, one must challenge the claim of causal determinism to explain everything, and one must give place to human factors not determinable by the positive sciences. The economic factor is not thereby eliminated, but it henceforth appears as a *conditional*, rather than as a *determining*, factor.

In other words, the knowledge of the environment, notably of the social environment explainable in terms of economic factors, does not teach us why we should want socialism, why it is desirable and just; it teaches us only to know what is capable of realization, or realizable in one or another form, by one means or another. In short, this knowledge of the economic environment shows us conditions and obstacles to the realization of our goal, but it does not know how to justify this goal.

Marxism can henceforth serve—and only under certain conditions—to describe the environment, and that is why it is a science of the capitalist environment rather than of the socialist reaction of the psyche; it no longer is adequate either to justify or to interpret the immense and fluctuating diversity of psychic motives that make up the socialist movement. Its historical role was to contruct this movement intellectually a priori, before it existed in reality, and thus to contribute to its creation. This role is finished. Now that the movement itself is also an ascertainable and observable reality, moreover a reality in constant evolution, the theory of socialism must be based no longer in the first place on the abstract study of the capitalist economic environment but on the concrete study of the socialist movement, of its motives, its goals, its institutions, and of the reactions of men to this new reality. As de Brouckère has said, "The experience of the workers' movement, analyzed scientifically, gives birth to the new socialist theory."

In this conceptualization, the relation between the class struggle and socialism appears completely different from what it is for Marxism. But in the first place, it is not at all a question of denying the reality or belittling the importance of the proletarian class struggle. This class struggle is a fact that dominates the whole history of our age. I am even totally ready to believe, with Marx, that the conflicts of interest that cause it are going to get more rather than less intense. But I separate myself from Marxism where it identifies this struggle of interests with the realization of socialism. Yet again, where Marx sees a relationship of direct and ineluctable causality, I see a relation of tension, of finality, and consequently a task to be fulfilled rather than an ineluctable development. In more concrete terms: the struggle of the working class for its interests does not by itself lead to socialism. It can lead to it under certain conditions; it might also lead elsewhere, for example to embourgeoisement, to the absorption of the working class by the capitalist cultural environment.

Let us recognize, as it is necessary to do, the fact of the class struggle between the bourgeoisie and the proletariat, let us see it with Marx as the natural result of the conflicts of interests which the capitalist mode of production engenders. All very well. But then, the struggle of the bourgeoisie for its interests is also completely natural, that is, determined by the same laws of social causality, as the struggle of the proletariat for its own interests. Hence in what sense is the proletarian attitude superior to the bourgeois attitude? As socialists we believe in this superiority, which in the end is a superiority of ethical motivation, but in order to establish it we must have a different basis than the statement of the reality of the class struggle; we must have a scale of ethical values valid for all classes, we must have a theory of motivation that is not contained within a theory of causes.

Consequently the unity of the class struggle and of socialism is moved from the domain of causal determinism to be put in that of moral duty and political will. In the struggle of the working class there are two kinds of motives very different in origin and nature. On the one side, there is the interest motive proper, a product of the adaptation of man to the capitalist environment, which, acting by itself, ultimately would lead the worker to lessen the social distance that separates him from the bourgeois, that is, to cultural embourgeoisement to the degree that his material situation improves. On the other side, there is a motive of socialist conviction, product of a reaction of opposition, of moral rebellion against the environment, which is the only thing that makes the workers' movement something other than what Bernard Shaw has called the "capitalism of the working class." And here, furthermore, there is a state, not at all of mechanical causality but of psychoenergetic tension. The practical conclusion is that the realization of socialism by the class struggle is not a doctrinal starting point to be accepted, but a political goal to be willed; the realization of socialism is not simply a question of the victory of the proletariat over the bourgeoisie, but a question of victory within the proletariat of the socialist soul over the capitalist soul; the class struggle is a necessary condition to socialist progress, but it is not a sufficient condition.

But if the class struggle is not all there is to socialism, the idea of socialism itself implies—at least in our age—the idea of the class struggle. Every socialist whether he is by circumstance bourgeois or worker has the same moral duty to support the working class in its efforts at betterment and liberation. And this precisely because the struggle of the working class is something other and more than a struggle of interests, because it is a struggle against injustice, against exploitation and oppression, for the human dignity of the workers, because it is, aside from a reality determined by material causes, a duty postulated by moral motives. One can be a worker conscious of his class interests without being a true socialist, but one cannot be a true socialist without being body and soul on the side of the working class in its economic and political battle.

In examining the matter more closely one thus finds that the theoretical disassociation of the ideas of "class struggle" and "socialism" belittles neither one nor the other of these ideas; that, on the contrary, it is the means of establishing a truer unity than that presupposed by Marxism, since it must be willed by a conscious effort, by the transformation of the "causal" motive of interest through the "final" motive of moral conviction.

The idea of the class struggle is raised and ennobled by seeing in it something other than a question of interests, namely, a question of dignity, of conviction, and of conscious will—a task, a human obligation, and not simply the consequence of an economic interest which will be extinguished at the same time as the social condition that gave rise to it.

And likewise, the socialist idea will be raised and ennobled by making it something other than the cause of a fraction of humanity. Moreover, this is to increase its capacity for recruitment and for influence, and to help the working class itself in finding support for which it has need in order to realize the social transformations that can liberate it.

This support becomes more and more a practical and political necessity of the first order. For there are com-

pletely practical motives that oblige the working class itself
to realize that the action of a party of class interests encounters, on the very threshold of so long-desired socialist
realizations, scarcely anticipated obstacles.

It is in the first place simply a question of social and electoral statistics. Even in the most industrialized countries it
is evident that it will still be a very long time before the
majority appears, if one trusts economic causes to transform a greater and greater proportion of the population
into dispossessed and more and more impoverished proletarians. Without raising here the very sensitive question
of the impoverishment predicted by Marx, the extension
of the industrial proletariat runs up against frontiers that
Marx had not foreseen. There are agricultural producers,
for whom the concentration of enterprise does not follow
the industrial pattern; there is the "new middle class" born
from the increasing division between the brain work of
management and the manual work of execution; and there
are still many other causes that mean that the workers' parties are very near to what one could call the saturation
limit, so long as they intend to represent only strictly proletarian interests. We are aware of the political consequences of this situation, which makes our workers' parties
look for allies in other social strata in order either to govern or to oppose. Even from the narrow viewpoint of the
conquest of power—which is far from being all there is to
socialism—it is becoming more and more urgent to enlarge
the sphere of influence of our movement of ideas, by showing that socialism is something other than the collective
egoism of a given class. Think of the peasants who have retained an outlook of independent and deeply proprietary
producers; think of the nonmanual workers who do not
have the same gainful interests as the working class; think
of the Christian workers shocked by avowed Marxist materialism, and you will understand that Sollmann,[8] one of the

[8] F. Wilhelm Sollmann, 1882-1951.

foremost leaders of the progressive wing of German socialism, recently was able to say that the recruiting ability of socialism would be increased by disassociating class struggle and socialism.

And if you place yourself in the higher vantage point of socialist tasks that start only beyond material victories, and that are a question of capacity rather than a question of strength, do you not see that the workers' capacity to work for a renovation of the social environment is closely bound to the furthering of motives of conviction as against motives of interest? There is not a more urgent or more anguishing problem than this for the practice of the workers' movement. For instance, there is not a single trade-union militant who would dare deny that the great obstacle to the latest realizations of the movement is a psychological difficulty. It arises from the fact that more and more the masses look for the maximum of gain for a minimum of privation whereas formerly gain was only possible by means of privation.

The exercise of power is itself limited by capacity; not only, as is believed too often, by intellectual capacity—a question of knowing—but especially by moral capacity, which is a question of character, of a sense of responsibility, of consciousness of duties as much as of rights. A theory that makes its appeal only to interest would not be able to develop this latter capacity sufficiently, since today the struggle for interest is no longer necessarily a heroic struggle inspired by the idea of sacrifice for the common good. Immediately after the conquest of power different faculties are required in order to exercise it. This is more obvious in the workshop than anywhere else. I have no fear of contradiction in saying that in no country do we exercise a tenth of the power of control and of industrial democracy that institutional transformations, following the war, have given on paper to the factory councils, either by law or by contract. It should suffice to consider this example, which I hold more essential for socialist transformation than any change whatsoever in high places, in order to understand the immense practical importance of this problem of motives, of the growing inadequacy of the appeal to interests.

And since I am addressing university students, let me at least touch on that other pragmatic consequence of my theoretical premises, namely that if the relation between socialism and the class struggle is as I think it, the non-proletarianized intellectual would thenceforth cease to occupy the false position in the socialist movement from which he suffers today. For if one identifies socialism and the proletariat, the socialist intellectual feels himself to be inevitably made inferior, only tolerated in a house that is not his own. This leads him all too often either to discouragement and to inaction, or—without the slightest bad intention—to indulge in outbidding the workers, in rendering to the working class the bad service of idolizing it even to its faults. In contrast, by accepting my theoretical starting point one arrives at a very different situation, more dignified and more authentic, and understands what I mean by a neo-Fabianism that would permit intellectuals to serve maximally the socialist cause in ways other than by becoming politicians.

At the risk of making still heavier this rather indigestible dish, please let me point out a scientific conclusion that seems primordial to me. From my whole way of looking at things it follows that in order to judge and to understand socialism it is necessary to take as the criterion, not the goal relegated to the future, but rather present realization. I have striven to show how the conception of an ideal future socialist society, by which both Marxism and all earlier socialism have been inspired, is a utopia and a psychological illusion—a simple intellectual landmark which has no reality but to the degree that it constitutes a motive of present-day realization.

A certain effort of imagination is required in order to realize what a reversal of traditional values is implied by the acceptance of this perspective. Thus, let us suppose that one day all of the demands of the socialist movement will find themselves finally realized. According to the current conception, that day we will have socialism. Well, according to my conception, that day will mark precisely the end of socialism. Having realized that hope, humanity will continue its effort in aspiration toward other goals, toward another ideal of happiness, and henceforth there will be no more socialists. Socialism is not a future affair, it is a present-day effort, a perpetual creation. The only valid criterion for socialist deeds is not a distant ideal but the present motive.

This is another form of the old thesis of Bernstein:[9] the movement is everything, the goal is nothing. Only I do not say that the goal is nothing. On the contrary I say: no movement without a goal, but the goal exists and is valid only by reason of the movement and has no reality whatsoever outside of it. The goal is a subjective idea, an imaginary marker which moves to the degree that one approaches it. But it is not and will never be an objective condition.

Henceforth the ideal stops being an excuse and becomes an obligation. Will that not be a gain? For my part, I have learned to distrust those who place the ideal too far above present-day tasks; they call "ideal" what they can put off until tomorrow. It is a little like the gentleman who says to you that he is in agreement "in principle"; this is generally a sign that he really is opposed.

You see that by thus clearing away from socialism its element of futurist illusion we give it a singularly vital meaning, rather than emptying it of meaning. But you also see that in accepting this perspective you are putting an end to the paralyzing opposition of the ideas of reform and of revolution. Revolution is, so to speak, absorbed into reform, and no longer has any reality outside of it, but reform thereby becomes truly revolutionary, that is, it im-

[9] Eduard Bernstein, 1850-1932, the famous German Social Democratic revisionist.

plies a radical transformation of motives as much as of institutions; from simple, auxiliary, and preparatory means, it becomes the very essence of our effòrt, made revolutionary by the ethical motive that inspires it.

I have undoubtedly said enough for you to see to what extent my conceptions can be called a doctrine of reformism. While Marxism closes its eyes to the reality of the reformist motives that have won the upper hand in the socialism of all advanced countries, I recognize reformism in all its forms—the tendency of the masses toward cultural embourgeoisement, the policy of governmental collaboration, social patriotism, etc.—as a reality, a reality determined by deep and natural causes and which therefore it is necessary to accept. But when I say "accept," I mean to say to accept as a fact in the realm of being, not in the realm of the optative; to accept as a starting point of our action, as an environmental situation conditioning possibilities and methods, but not as an end point, not as a rule of conduct, not as an ultimate goal. Not the goal but the motives are to be changed, to be better inspired thereby, and for that to take place one must begin with existing motives and gradually transform them.

Here I separate myself from the opposition of "youth" that believes that in order to rejuvenate the movement it is enough to assign an extremist goal to existing motives— which are generally only resentments, hatreds, and envies hardly "socialistic" in nature.

Permit me to illustrate this by taking as example the program that de Brouckère has proposed from this same podium. This program includes two master demands: internationalism and democracy. I accept this, all the more since it expresses very well the reality of the present-day tendencies and the needs of the movement. I accept it all the more because de Brouckère has enlarged the meaning of the word "democracy" in such a way as to make it something other than advanced liberalism, by including in it industrial democracy, the organization and administration of production by the producers, this socialization from below without which all socialization from above would be only a deplorable statism, a change from one execrable bureaucracy to a yet more execrable bureaucracy.

However, this "internationalist and democratic" program, if one keeps to its formulation, can appear very modest. One can be a pacifist and a democrat without being a socialist. It is even conservative from one specific and immediate viewpoint: for in present-day circumstances the struggle is above all to conserve peace and to conserve democratic institutions that have been won.

But this program that, by its formulation, *can* be ultramoderate and conservative, *can* also be ultraextremist and radical—in the deepest sense of this word—according to which motivational lever is applied to it. In accordance with its motive, internationalism can consist in that bourgeois and conservative pacifism that simply wants pacific methods of oppression and exploitation and wishes to keep the present peace, having leave to make war or to have it made by others if "national honor" requires it—or, instead, that socialist pacifism for which the struggle for peace is only a particularly urgent aspect of the struggle against all oppression, all injustice, all organized and managed violence, for violence is by definition injustice, the suspension of the rules of law.

For this socialist pacifism there is something other than preventing war; rather, there is above all the organization of peace—a positive task, a psychological task, a social task before everything else. And to tell you all that is in my mind: to carry out this task well requires not only demanding institutional realizations from others but also demanding of oneself that supreme duty to condemn violence, bodily refusing to make war or to participate in its preparation.

This entails indeed something more than official pacifism. This entails notably an ardent and dangerous struggle against the nationalist psychosis. Do you believe that

that is a task for tomorrow? Don't you then see that everywhere there remains for us a tragic heritage of war to liquidate, a heritage of passions, prejudices, fears, and cowardice? Don't you then see that the deadly moral abdication of socialism in the face of nationalism, which has empoisoned the world since 1914, has continued its effects until our days? Don't you see how so many of our own have become incapable of a real psychological resistance against nationalist ideology, and dare no more brave the demonstrations of bourgeois patriotism other than by a shameless outbidding, as if our patriotism prided itself in being of the same kind?

Let us say, let us continue to say, following Jaurès,[10] that internationalism is possible only through the nation, but let us not forget to follow that other example of Jaurès proclaiming, and therewith paying with his life, the truth that there is no longer any internationalism other than that beyond the nation, that the state and the community are not the same thing, that a frontier to the rights of states must be established, that the international unity to be organized presupposes an always greater limitation on their autonomy—yes, I do not hesitate to say it—the gradual liquidation of national statism.

Let us recognize the reality of the nation, but let us make war, a war without fear and without mercy, on the nationalism of states, up to denying them, even in front of the execution squad, the right to dispose of our life or, through us, of the life of another; let us demand as a moral duty of individuals the refusal to make war!

Indeed, we are very far from all that at the present time when so many socialists still turn away from the liquidation of the lie of unilateral responsibility for the World War, hesitate to discover the execrable doctrine according to which there are innocent people and people to be punished, show themselves less energetic in exposing the

[10] As noted above, Jean Jaurès was assassinated on the eve of World War I.

absurdity and the danger of treaties of reparation than
bourgeois economists, less resolved to overthrow the protectionist walls than the free-market bankers! My young
friends, who wish that socialist action would offer a broader
field for your intransigent pugnacity, don't you see that
there are enough present-day tasks for your courage, that
these are not programmatic formulations, that these are
the motives and the acts that count? Enter into those lists
where you will find the unchained forces of the madness of
mobs in panic, where you will have to dare to be alone with
your conscience subject to being proved right only
afterward—and you will see that true radicalism is not in
the extremism of the program but in the present energy of
the deed, not in what we demand of others, not in the mot-
toes of faith, but in the motives that these convictions in-
spire in acting individuals!

I have taken internationalism only by way of example. I
would be able to make an analogous demonstration on the
subject of the problem of democracy, the second point of
de Brouckère's platform. You would then see how futile is
the criticism, which you take so much to heart, of the tactic
of governmental collaboration. You will never prevent a
party, of which the very essence is the will to power, from
exercising this power in the measure in which it can do so.
The real question is not that of participation or nonpartici-
pation. An energetic socialist influence can be exercised in
a coalition government; Belgium demonstrated it in 1919
and 1920. And one can have a soft socialist policy of shilly-
shallying and of opportunistic compromises while in the
opposition; Germany shows that to us at the present time.
The real problem is to energize and activate our policy in
any form in which our acts are realized, and that problem
does not depend on the external attitude of one party with
regard to others, but on the internal question that is the
cardinal problem of all institutions and of all states at the
present time: the psychological organization of resistance
to bureaucratization, the control by the electors over the

elected. This does not consist in the negative organization of blind distrust, but in the positive organization of enlightened and conditional confidence, or, if you prefer terms of distrust, let us say the education, instead of the exploitation, of distrust.

This is what I have wanted to say to youth, with all the more insistence since I sympathize with its feeling of impatience, which I deplore precisely because it is governed by so little insight and thereby is condemned to be futile and even to worsen the evil that it wishes to cure. This gives me all the more right, I think, to say to the elders: take care not to encourage this deviation of youthful energy toward futility, by obliging them, so to speak, to reproach you for a growing divergence between the theory in whose name you speak and the policy that you in practice follow. Show them by example that there is an extremism of action which is worth more than any extremism of doctrinal formulations. And consider that this pragmatic extremism will convince by its sincerity only if it gives up the too facile use of outmoded formulas, with which it can easily dispense.

What is at stake here is something more than doctrinal verities. As was said in Germany, it involves a reformation rather than a revision, the invigoration of new impulsions rather than enriching the movement with new concepts. Oh yes, I know very well that science, theory, can only create these impulsions to a very limited degree, so long as the masses are moved by interests and passions rather than by knowledge. But when a new state of knowledge coincides with modifications that are really in being, when these modifications are blocked by a traditional doctrine impugning them in the eyes of those who feel them, when it is simply a matter of becoming aware through a new doctrinal expression of already developed new desires, of new needs already present, when a new intellectual instrument must be created for certain new responsibilities recognized by everyone, then the work of theory can, if not create, at least promote in a remarkable way the renewal of belief and of will that the socialist movement so greatly needs.

The huge task of today—a task in which I am only a worker in a team charged particularly with the work of preliminary clearing of the site—is to create a new state of consciousness for a new state of will, and thus to make this will more effective and more self-confident, to take away from it the doubt that is paralyzing it at the present time.

In the absence of making this effort, socialism is condemned to fail, to lose along with so many faiths of the past its spiritual vigor just as it consolidates its temporal power. What has made the progress of the socialist idea irresistible for the two preceding generations is the obvious unity of conscience and of will that it incarnates, the dazzling probity of its ideal, which has taken from its very opponents the support of a good conscience. It has brought together, then, the fighting fervor of a crusade, the fervor for sacrifice of religion and the fervor for truth of science. Let us make sure not to lose this fervor and this force, let us show ourselves, while remaining a formidable interest movement, capable of continuing to be an irresistible movement of ideas!

9

Joy in Work

The one aspect of the *Psychology of Socialism* that found nearly universal acclaim was the author's realistic and knowledgeable characterization of the European worker. While there was spirited dispute as to the causes and consequences of the blighted and naive state of the proletariat that was so sympathetically sketched, the concreteness of de Man's presentation appeared in sharp contrast to the crudity with which left-wing polemicists customarily viewed their favored instrument for the overthrow of the historical order.

In fact de Man's analysis was also informed by ideological coloration, namely by that rejection of utilitarianism he had adopted by virtue of a critical rereading of Marx and his epigones in the light of his own personal experience. In the investigation he undertook into the conditions for work satisfaction at the Frankfurt Labor College in the early twenties he emphasized the historically derived and socially structured expectations in terms of which individuals experience and assess the reality of their life. Operating on the basis of a classification of gratifications as direct, instrumental, and moral, he proceeded to discuss the possibility of their fulfillment in terms of both technical and social conditions offered by the work role within the world of industrial capitalism. The following selections, excerpted from his pioneer study in industrial sociology of 1927, reveal his insightful use of social psychology and his personal experience, as well as the reports of his worker-students, to throw entirely new light on the situation of the worker in industrial society, whether capitalist or socialist, and thereby to raise disturbing and heterodox questions about the erstwhile panacea, the socialization of the means of production.

ARBEITSFREUDE[1]

CONSIDERATIONS OF SELF-INTEREST

Sometimes, in the reports, rational considerations of private advantage obtrude themselves in the form of an awareness, that, since a worker cannot live without earning wages, his work has a meaning, and is therefore more tolerable.

We note, however, that such considerations almost always appear in a negative form, inasmuch as we see that a feeling that the wages are too low makes the work disagreeable. It must not be inferred from this that considerations of private advantage (in other words, the acquisitive instinct) are factors of joy in work. One who has gone for a long ramble in the wilds without taking enough food with him, will probably find it difficult to enjoy himself, but this does not mean that the desire to fill his stomach was the primary motive of the excursion.

No doubt under contemporary conditions, the acquisitive instinct, or at any rate, a recognition that the choice lies between work and starvation, is what drives the worker to his work. But it is no less unquestionable, that this motive is not a positive and intrinsic constituent of joy in work. On the contrary, we are entitled to assert that where the acquisitive instinct is predominant there can be no joy in work. The consideration of private advantage is forced upon the worker by extant social conditions. It is foreign to the real aim of the work; it acts as an objective coercion, and therefore exerts a spiritually inhibitive influence. The

[1] *Joy in Work*, translated by Eden and Cedar Paul from *Der Kampf um die Arbeitsfreude*, first published in Jena by Diederichs in 1927; London: Allen & Unwin, 1929, pp. 49-77, 207-222. Reproduction of this translation, the spelling of which has been Americanized, is through the courtesy of Allen & Unwin.

man who takes the greatest delight in his work is the man who, while he is doing it, is able to forget that he must earn his livelihood. Thought about daily bread, thought about earning, kills joy in work.

This applies, of course, only to normal instances, in which the acquisitive instinct is not congenitally excessive or has not been unduly intensified by unhappy experiences. If, after a long period of unemployment or inadequate earning, a worker secures a job which relieves him of his most serious anxieties regarding a livelihood, this improvement in his circumstances will certainly increase his joy in work. But here there has been nothing more than the removal of an external hindrance. The consideration of private advantage will only be a positive element of joy in work when the person concerned suffers from a congenital or acquired hypertrophy of the acquisitive instinct, so that, like a miser, he subordinates everything to the gratification of that instinct. Since among the workers, in view of their restricted earning possibilities, such a mood is necessarily altogether exceptional, the acquisitive instinct will only show itself in them within narrow limits, as one of the external elements of pleasurable feeling. As a rule, it is a hindrance rather than a help; it is a motive for work, but it is not a factor of joy in work. Very instructive, in this connection, is the report of the book printer who says that he enjoyed his work more in his apprentice days than he does now, explaining this on the ground that the apprentice gets no wages, whereas a fully equipped printer "thinks of his work in terms of his wages."

CONSIDERATIONS OF SOCIAL UTILITY

In the reports, we find references to rational considerations of social utility here and there only, as accessory factors of joy in work. When we bear in mind that the writers of the report belong to the more cultivated strata of the working class, and are therefore especially accessible to considerations of the kind, we may infer that, as far as the mass of the workers is concerned, considerations of social utility (or, at any rate, consciousness of the social utility of their work) must be practically inoperative as a factor of joy in work.

Such a consideration is most likely to be influential in cases where the social utility of the work will accrue to a comparatively small community, to one with which, for special reasons, the worker feels himself solidarized. This applies, for instance, to the book printer whose joy in work was increased when he transferred to a socialist printing establishment, and felt that henceforward he would be serving the movement. A worker in a cooperative institution refers in similar terms to his employment, although here the more favorable working conditions are obviously a main cause of the community feeling. Again, the shorthand typist, who worked for a time in a socialist press bureau, reports that she took more pleasure in her work, and explains this on the ground that the work there was more congenial to her. Even the trade-union employee, who lays more stress on the agreeable character of his activities than most of his colleagues are wont to do, tells us that his joy in his work was due rather to the satisfaction of his instincts by his particular technical duties, than to an intellectual awareness of their social significance.

The most usual way in which the community sense manifests itself as a factor of joy in work, is what is known as esprit de corps. Thanks to this feeling, when circumstances are favorable (when the occupation is good, when the wages are satisfactory, when the other conditions are to the worker's taste, and when he can take a pride in what he is doing), we find that the individual seems to identify himself with the enterprise, or with a part of it. It is obvious, however, that in such instances, social instincts, such as the herd instinct and the collective instinct of self-assertion, play a greater part than any superadded considerations of social utility. The general rule is that even in the case of the workers who are most alive, mentally speaking, and are

most keenly interested in the social problem—just as in the
case of their employers—the idea of the social utility of
their work is, at the best, nothing more than an accessory
intellectual factor. It is never an important instinctive element in the production of joy in work.

Here is a lesson for all those social reformers who rely
upon a coming transformation of working motives thanks
to the development of new intellectual aims; for the possibilities of such psychological transformations are extremely restricted. As concerns motive, we are dependent
upon instinctive impulses, upon what will satisfy the individual affects and the group affects of mankind; purely rational considerations, motives overcast with the pale hue
of thought, are of little avail. This brings us to a problem
which is of decisive importance in relation to all plans for
the socialization of industries, though it is one which is apt
to be overlooked by those socialist theoreticians who think
exclusively in terms of economics or of law. The actual
producers' joy in their work, and, consequently, in great
measure their effective productivity, will not be so much
promoted by any centralist reform of the relations of
ownership, as by a local reform of working conditions in
respect of workshop technique and in respect of hierarchi-
cal workshop organization. The essential thing is the formation of a new group consciousness within the individual
enterprises. The touchstone of the effectiveness of any centralist change in property relations will, therefore, always
primarily be the question, how far the change will tend to
awaken this group consciousness on democratic lines, by
arousing a keener sense of responsibility and by promoting
the joys of self-determination. The worker in a bureau-
cratically controlled state enterprise, makes acquaintance
with "reasons of state" only as a form of coercion, which
conflicts with a truly spiritual sense of working community;
and he feels less joy in his work than does the worker in
private capitalist enterprises characterized by more indi-

vidual freedom and self-determination for the worker—
where, in a word, there is more effective industrial democracy. When we come to consider the problem of workshop
discipline, we shall see how important a factor of distaste
for work this bureaucracy is in the case of the workers, employees, and officials in public enterprises. From this outlook, socialization from beneath, socialization on the psychological basis of working solidarity and of a healthy
democratic esprit de corps in the individual enterprise, is
far more important than can be any socialization from
above. But the latter is the easier, because the paper on
which laws and ordinances are written is more patient than
are human beings.

The Sense of Social Obligation

A thoroughgoing analysis of the motive of joy in work must
take into reckoning the fact that there are working habits
for which rational introspection is unable to find any
adequate reason, either in respect of an awareness of social
utility, or in respect of a causal explanation in terms of any
specific instinct. As William James said, a good many years
ago, "Man is a bundle of instincts, modified by habits." It is
true that every habit formation presupposes instinctive
motives; but the peculiarity of a habit is that, through the
frequent repetition of an action, this action encounters less
and less inner resistance. Thus the habit, so to say, cuts its
own furrow. It does this by severing the actions from their
motives and rendering them automatic. Thus do actions
become habits, and even needs, for which no other reason
can be found than that "it has always been so," and therefore "it is right and proper." If, as in the case of work, the
habit formation has been sanctioned for thousands of years
by custom, religion, and law, then, in the end, it becomes
an ethical norm. When that has happened, the manifold
streamlets originating at one time or another from the

most various sources of motive, will be found to have coalesced into the slowly flowing stream of "normal feeling" whose existence seems its own justification.

Psychology enlisted in the service of social science must, therefore, primarily content itself with recognizing the norm, the standard, the rule, the custom, as a motive in itself, severed from its individual historical factors, whose study is the task of folk psychology and cultural psychology working in accordance with the historical method.

This latter task is extraordinarily difficult, extraordinarily complicated, and science has scarcely begun to grapple with it. Insofar as a history of civilization can as yet be said to exist (insofar, at any rate, as there exists a history of civilization based upon the study of collective psychology), it has not dug below the surface of social life. It is true that since, a century and a half ago, critical philosophy broke the spell of the Aristotelian conceptual realism, there have been a number of preliminary attempts at a psychology of thought; it is true, that students of the history of religion and of the history of art are tending more and more to find the root of ethical and aesthetic sentiment in the social subconsciousness: but these works relate only to the vital manifestations of a small and select circle of intellectuals; they are works about intellectuals by intellectuals. They leave almost unconsidered the broad current of mass life; they are scarcely concerned with the far less conspicuous and far more slowly changing daily customs of the millions. For a thousand books on Kant, we have scarcely one dealing with what the common people of Kant's day believed and did, despite the fact that the outstanding achievements of isolated great philosophers are nothing more than symptoms of a hidden mass reality, and do not become intelligible until they are projected against the mass background of their day. For a thousand books discussing socialist ideas, socialist theories, and socialist politics, there is scarcely one dealing with the origin and the transformation of the popular ethical beliefs, which constitute the foundation of all this thought.

For the nonce, as far as the working experiences of the masses are concerned, descriptive social psychology must be content to show that, in addition to all the motives for work analyzable (as already shown) into specific instincts, there is an as yet unanalyzable and irreducible complex of motives, which confronts us in the masses' effective belief in the duty to work. Pending further study, the facts in this connection may be subsumed under the collective concept of the social sense of an obligation to work. This compromises the whole hereditary quantum of motives which (no matter how they may have originated individually, or how much they may have been modified in the course of transmission from generation to generation) from the outlook of the average worker, lead an independent existence as impulses to work and to enjoy working; and whose only motivation is that of every custom, a relation to an accepted standard of mass behavior.

The mere fact that the standard is valid for the community which constitutes the human environment of the person concerned, suffices to give the impulse toward an adaptation to that standard the higher form of a demand of conscience. This explains the remarkable phenomenon that the sense of a duty to labor can simultaneously be as vague as it is in its rationalist motivation for the individual, and as powerful as it is in its effect upon his emotions. The force of an ethical standard, of a sense of moral obligation (even though it may only arise unconsciously, out of the conviction that a particular line of conduct is customary) may be so powerful, as to overcome, not merely conflicting rational considerations, but even conflicting individual instincts.

Something of this kind was experienced by many of the soldiers in the Great War, by persons whose political views and reasoned considerations led them to regard themselves as "forced" into the fight, but who, as a rule, acted in a way that disclosed instinctive impulses overriding all such considerations. Alike in the daily round of military duties, and when the fight was actually raging, there were both antimilitarists and men whose attitude toward the war was one of indifference, who, instead of doing as little as possible (which would have been accordant with the attitude of their conscious mind), did as much as they could, and even went so far as to offer up their lives in obedience to instinctive impulses of whose true nature they were scarcely aware. In my book on my own war experiences, *The Remaking of a Mind*,[2] I defined the most elementary and most general form of this impulse as "the desire not to disappoint others who expect something of you."

Intellectually, each one of us may have an idea as to his relation toward society and toward the community in which he lives, but his conduct toward society and the community is far from being determined by the intellectual content of that idea. Whenever (as happens to soldiers in wartime) we are exposed to the contagious influence of mass passion, and whenever (like the worker at his daily work) we feel ourselves permanently associated with a working community of any kind, what we believe that others expect of us becomes a no less important motive of our actions than are the demands which, as reasoning beings, we make of ourselves. What others expect of us will influence our conduct whether we regard these expectations as rationally justified or no. We shall generally try to fulfill such expectations to a much greater extent than we are actually compelled. Normally—apart, that is to say, from exceptional instances, when both for logical and moral reasons, a man is in revolt against some generally recognized social standard—our instinct of self-assertion is subordinated to the social and moral standards of those among whom we are living, so that we find it impossible to

[2] New York: Scribner's, 1919.

escape the compulsion to act in such a way that others will
not regard us with contempt. A soldier may find few reasons or none in favor of the war in which he is engaged,
and he may have the best reasons in the world against participating in it, but he will nonetheless be loath to act in
such a way as will make his fellow soldiers and superior
officers look upon him as a coward. In like manner, no
worker, however much he may detest the work on which
he is engaged, will (altogether apart from considerations of
self-interest) want to act in a way that will make his workmates and those set in authority over him regard him as incompetent or lazy. Very few persons are endowed with so
vigorous an independence of mind that they are able, in actual practice, to revalue all values in a way that will enable
them to disregard those social standards which become
operative for us all as universally valid traditions in days
before we have begun to think critically as individuals.

It is in accordance with such a traditional standard that
the worker comes to look upon his work as a social obligation, at any rate as far as concerns the environment with
which he is directly associated in his daily life: those who
are dependent on his earnings; his workmates; and those
who pay him and direct his activities.

No less traditional than the worker's sense of the social
obligation to work, and closely associated therewith, is his
sense of social subordination. For thousands of years, those
who were less well to do, those who were socially dependent, and those who were politically weak (no matter
whether as slaves, as serfs, or as wageworkers), were accustomed to look up toward those set in authority over them
with the feeling that subordination to the great ones of the
earth was a duty, and not a mere obligation imposed by
force. The subordinate's critical reason may revolt against
the acceptance of this duty; but customary practice, which
gives direction and content to the thousandfold and mainly
unconscious actions and attitudes of daily life, will never
wholly transcend the fact that the ethic of the communal tie

underlies the *contractual* nature of the relation between the worker and the person for whom he works. Every contract implies reciprocal good faith. The normal individual, the ordinary member of the masses, feels that to disregard this tie would be fraudulent, and therefore immoral.

Even were it otherwise, even were the worker's relation to his employer one imposed solely by force, like the soldier's subordination to the army command, it would still carry with it ethical implications, inasmuch as the employer's superiority of power is reinforced by the psychological prestige of social custom, and is often sustained by religious sanctions as well. This prestige works out in a twofold way. First of all, the underdog regards the position of the top dog as an enviable one; and therefore the underdog cannot free his mind from the suggestive influence of the social and moral standards created and observed by the top dog. Furthermore, since the top dog (at any rate) regards it as the underdog's duty to work for him, the underdog's failure to fulfill his duty satisfactorily, the underdog's refusal to fulfill the obligation, entered into by accepting the labor contract, implies the evasion of an implicit understanding and therefore bears the stigma of fraud.

The cumulative effect of the social prestige of the ruling class and of the standards of that class—the cumulative effect of tradition on the habits of work and subordination, on the one hand, and the influence of the worker's need to gratify his sense of self-esteem by doing his work well, on the other—is so powerful that today no anticapitalist ideology is able to destroy the masses' feeling that for them work is a matter of social obligation. Conversely, as the example of Communist Russia shows, it is no less difficult to influence the traditional habits of work and subordination by political and ideological considerations, to influence them in such a way that the quality and intensity of mass production are notably increased. Beyond question, ideas can affect habits; but ideas can be changed so much more

rapidly than habits can be modified, that decades or centuries are requisite before a change in habits can follow
upon a change in ideas. Fresh tools, new machinery, different ways of paying wages, changes in the personnel of
superiors, will affect working habits far more rapidly than
any change in the form of the state, any revolution, can affect them. For practical purposes, the condition of the subconscious, the habits of the masses, and social and ethical
standards, are almost constant, as contrasted with the varying ideology of social criticism. If in the world of sociopsychological reality, the capitalist system depended so exclusively upon economic and political compulsion as the
Marxists claim, in formulating their sociological specula-
tions and in their theory of the class struggle, it would have
collapsed long ago. The masses would not continue to work
for the capitalists unless they believed in capitalism, at least
in this sense, that they regard the lot of the capitalists as a
higher one than their own, as more enviable than their
own; and that they look upon their work, not only as a
need, but also as a duty. The very socialists among the
workers continue to retain so lively a faith in the social and
ethical value of work, that when they want to reproach the
persons whom they have themselves raised into responsible
positions in the labor movement and whose relatively comfortable position they envy, they cannot find any harsher
expression of criticism than that these officials "have become slackers" now that they cease to work for a capitalist
employer.

These considerations explain why it is that not even the
socialists among the workers have as yet been influenced to
a notable extent, either negatively or positively, by the
ideology of activity on behalf of social advantage that is
propagated by the theoreticians of socialism. In this connection, "society" is but a pale concept. Only a worker's
immediate associates in his work place or in his trade-union
branch, are sufficiently real, sufficiently concrete, to influence him in the direction of habit formation; and in such

habit formation, rational considerations are far less effective than vague feelings, than the slow and subconscious
transfer of traditional sentiments to new concrete institutions. Between the higher, rationally based considerations
of an intellectual elite, and the obscure feeling of the
masses in favor of the performance of a duty sanctioned by
habit, there does not yet exist any psychological bridge, any
sort of interconnection which can be expected to have a socially educative influence. This much, at least, is clear: if
one wishes to build such a bridge, one must not start from a
pillar erected upon the farther bank, upon the bank of a
speculative and rationally conceived future. The bridge
building must start from pillars on this side, from pillars
whose foundations are established on customs that are centuries old, that are instinctive, and deeply rooted in the
strata of feeling. We have no need, here, to seek for new
joys in work; it will suffice to free the old joys in work from
the bonds which now encumber them, and to make them
serviceable to the social aims of a new leadership.

What applies to the socialist rationalization of the idea of
an obligation to work, applies yet more strongly to the
ideology of Christian labor ethics. Here, too, "principles"
deliberately inculcated can have an effect only upon exceptional individuals, and but a small effect even on them. As
far as the masses are concerned, what operates is the un-
critical adoption of a habit which has become a standard.
Four of the reports were sent in by students at the
Frankfurt Labor College, who were members of Christian
trade unions, and ardent Catholics. It is very remarkable
how small a part religious faith plays in these reports.
Catholicism has scarcely affected the writers' attitude toward individual labor problems.

When we compare the reports from these four Catholics
with the others (who are almost all agnostics), we see that in
only one of them (a countinghouse clerk) does religious
faith play any notable part; and even here, religion scarcely
affects the writer's attitude toward his work. Essentially, all

we learn is that religion furnishes "consolation" for spiritual troubles—which are precisely identical with those of socialist workers who belong to no church.

Even more strikingly was this likeness of the mentality of "Christian" and "non-Christian" workers, manifest in the utterances of members of my audience at the Labor College. During the discussions that followed my lectures, I did my best to induce those who belonged to the Christian trade-union movement to formulate their religious philosophy as plainly as possible, expecting that this would have a stimulating influence upon the socialist members of the audience, whose attention I wished to draw to the importance of ethical considerations. But I was invariably disappointed to find that, even among the workers who were professed Christians, the doctrines of the Church (so far as they were known and understood) were little more than a sort of Sunday-go-to-meeting clothes, without any vital bearing on daily experience. As workers, the Christians felt exactly like the infidel socialists whose material conditions of life they shared. The few among them who had adopted some of the terminology of Thomist and other Catholic doctrines concerning labor and happiness, used these only for the purpose of philosophical and political literary flourishes; and it was obvious that where the questions of practical life were concerned, the doctrines had no influence whatever. When I discussed this matter with a man who is actively engaged in promoting the Catholic education of the working class, he confirmed my impression with the words, "Yes, they are all workers first, and human beings afterward; their destinies as exploited persons, the destinies they share with other members of their class, mean far more to them than the ties of a general human kinship, such as is preached by the Church."

The conclusion we must draw from this is, first and foremost, that insofar as the Church has thought out and formulated any ethic of labor, this ethic has even less influence upon the working experience of the masses than has the socialist ideology of communal welfare. Insofar as the Christian ideology of the obligation to labor has a strong influence, that influence is only indirect and unconscious, and is operative only to the extent to which it is incorporated in traditional habits and institutions. When thus incorporated, moreover, it is effective in virtue of a community of lot which embraces all workers without distinction of creed. As far as the working habits of the masses are concerned, what is decisive is this community of lot, and not a community of ideas, which latter is only effective upon the lives of an inconspicuously small minority. I am not contesting the importance of a community of ideas as promoting every kind of progressive development; but we must not hesitate to admit that such a community of ideas can only influence general standards of conduct insofar as it becomes institutionally embodied in a community of lot.

Thus our main problem is to discover how the new aims consciously formulated by a small minority can be brought into effect by way of transforming the customary motives of the masses. The answer obviously is that this cannot be achieved by mere propaganda, by simply "preaching" new principles, but only by the active realization of these principles in institutions and traditions. Whereas, for instance, the new labor code[3] is symbolical of the growing power of a hitherto oppressed class, and is the embodiment of formulas which were originally voiced by a minority of persons who shaped these formulas in a rational way, the subsequent mass process was worked out in accordance with the principle that a new code generates a new sense of right. This may sound extremely undemocratic—for those democrats who have not yet learned that we are talking romanticist fiction when we regard the masses as consisting of absolutely free and equal persons endowed with the

---

[3] In the original "*das neue Arbeitsrecht*." The reference is not to a labor code specifically passing by that name, but to recent laws that deal with collective bargaining, legalize trade-union activities, and provide for the organization of workers' councils [translators' note].

power of self-determination. In the opening phase of the struggle for democracy, the phase of agitation and propaganda, this fiction might certainly provide an aim; but it no longer has the value even of a working hypothesis when the time has come for the constructive realization of democracy. In our days, the establishment of a sound democratic system is dependent on the understanding of the complicated psychological laws controlling the interactions between leaders and led, of the demands of the masses and what those who voiced the demands can do to further them, of sentiment and interest, of the ideas of the few that form tradition and of the customs of the many that are formed by tradition.

If I lay so much stress on mooting the problem as to whether it is possible to transform or reawaken the motive to work in connection with the sense of the duty to work, it is because I am guided by the conviction that the solution of the problem of joy in work depends, in the last resort, upon the diffusion of a new ethic of labor, whose basis must be the idea that work is a debt to the community. Not to mince matters, I contend that the problem of joy in work is insoluble unless the moral duty of work for the common weal is given precedence of every other motive to work. In the absence of this motive the attempt to make work a pure delight would be an attempt to square the circle.

All work is at one and the same time the fulfillment of instinctive wishes, and the inhibition of other wishes that are no less instinctive. Every kind of working activity contains elements which may make it a delight, but it also contains elements which may make it a torment. In every language, the word "work," or its equivalent, contains etymological constituents whose emotional coloration implies the notion of an evil, a vexation, a humiliation. As examples I may mention: the Greek πόνος and the Latin *labor* (still alive in the French expressions *homme de peine* for a handyman, and *laboureur* for a peasant); the Old High German *arabeit*; the Slav *rabota*; the French word *travail* connected with the medieval Latin *tripalium* (carrying with it the idea of work done under compulsion), and also *besogne* derived from *besoin* (need). This is not merely a legacy from the days when the social subordination of the worker made work degrading. Just as in the legend of the Fall, work is a symbol for punishment, so it lies in the nature of things that all work is felt to be coercive. Even the worker who is free in the social sense, the peasant or the handicraftsman, feels this compulsion, were it only because, while he is at work, his activities are dominated and determined by the aim of his work, by the idea of a willed or necessary creation. Work inevitably signifies subordination of the worker to remoter aims, felt to be necessary, and therefore involving a renunciation of the freedoms and the enjoyments of the present for the sake of a future advantage. When the aim is voluntarily chosen by the worker, this renunciation is symbolically regarded as a sacrifice; and when the aim is imposed upon the worker by another, it is symbolically regarded as a punishment. Every worker is simultaneously creator and slave. He is the latter, even if he be the happiest of creators, for he is the slave of his own creation. Freedom of creation and compulsion of performance, ruling and being ruled, command and obedience, functioning as subject and functioning as object—these are the poles of a tension which is immanent in the very nature of work.

It is thus psychologically absurd to suppose that work divorced from its social aim can ever be exclusively pleasurable, simply in virtue of the fact that it is the gratification of an instinct. On the contrary, the ultimate and most difficult problem of joy in labor is to ascertain how all the pleasurable feelings that may arise in connection with work can be intensified and integrated to produce real happiness by being crowned with the greatest of all joys, the joy of fulfilling a duty.

In facing up to this problem we are not led outside the domain of motives, which can be analyzed psychologically.

It is not, indeed, the business of psychology to supply a foundation for ethics; but the recognition that ethical aims and valuations are causes of human behavior, does not put these aims and valuations beyond the scope of psychological observation. Psychology has nothing to do with the genesis of an aim which determines a sacrifice made for ethical reasons; but such action involves the discharge of particular affects, and this phenomenon can be studied by the customary psychological methods. We then discover that the pleasurable feeling of enhanced self-esteem that accompanies the performance of an action regarded as a moral duty, differs in two important points from the pleasurable feelings that accompany the gratification of ordinary instincts.

First of all, the enhanced sense of self-esteem is not (as is the ordinary social instinct of self-assertion) measured merely in accordance with the scale of values of the concrete human environment; for here the standard of values has the consecration of eschatological transcendency, and is in the truest sense of the word a religious ego ideal. Thus the pleasurable sense of the fulfillment of duty acquires a peculiar qualitative intensity, whereby, in the general view, it wins an absolutely higher rank over all other pleasurable feelings, including the social instinct of self-assertion. There is only one gratification which can raise us to disregard the disapproval of our fellows, and that is the gratification of our own conscience by the fulfillment of a moral duty.

In the second place, the pleasurable feeling attendant on a sacrifice made for moral reasons undergoes spontaneous intensification proportionally with the recognition of the magnitude of the sacrifice. It feeds, so to say, on the unpleasurable feelings that are induced by the need for inhibiting certain "lower" instincts. Thanks to the alert consciousness of an aim, a consciousness which is a necessary part of every decision which we regard as a moral choice, the unpleasurable bodily or other elementary sensations

are transmuted into the idea of a sacrifice whereby the
value of the action can be estimated, and the pleasure in
our victory becomes intensified by suggestion. Thus,
thanks to the qualitative difference in virtue of which the
pleasurable feeling that accompanies moral activity stands
on an altogether higher plane than the pleasurable feeling
of a purely instinctive gratification, a miracle takes place.
Pain is transmuted into pleasure, sorrow is transformed
to joy, and simultaneously the intensity of the feeling
grows.

Of course all this applies only to extreme instances (very
rare in daily life) of deliberate and fully conscious moral
choice. Nevertheless, in daily life there is a persistent, a customary, conflict between certain instinctive promptings on
the one hand and a certain moral habit on the other. In this
connection phenomena occur which are like in kind,
though less extreme in degree. Such a moral habit is the
masses' obscure sense of the duty to work. Here, likewise, it
is psychologically possible to solve every conflict of motive
that manifests itself as a struggle between joy in work and
distaste for work, by strengthening the subjective motive of
duty so that joy in work gets the upper hand. In like manner, all distaste for work that is the outcome of bodily suffering and of instinctive inhibition can be transmuted into
the higher form of joy in work when the work comes to be
regarded as the fulfillment of duty bringing happiness in
its train.

We are naturally led to ask why, if these things be so, we
should trouble to investigate the instinctive foundations of
joy in work. Would it not be better to renounce from the
first any attempt to make work easier and more agreeable,
and to concentrate upon developing, by the moral coercion
of education, and in case of need by the institutional coercion of social authority, the psychological mechanism
thanks to which every one would, without qualification, regard work as his duty?

The question is of the first importance. It must not be

dismissed as having purely academic interest, for its underlying purpose does actually guide a considerable proportion of the attempts made by employers to increase the intensity of labor. The ill success of endeavors to use the
"coercive force of education" to promote this end, may
well, however, give us pause to think before answering the
question in the affirmative.

In the first place we must remember that everything said
about a connection between joy in work and a sense of the
duty to work, stands or falls with the existence of a subjective belief in the ethical character of the demand that we
should work for the community. This is a faith which cannot be inculcated by force. Among the workers, it is far less
widely prevalent today than it was in the precapitalist era.
There are objective reasons for the change. In the precapitalist era, it was easier for the actual producer to believe that he was working for the community (or, as it was
often phrased, for the greater glory of God). There was
then a comparatively small severance between producers
and consumers; and, more important still, the free producer was technically and socially independent: hence the
community had a readily perceptible reality. Today, on the
other hand, the worker produces for the "world market,"
and this, from the outlook of the motive for production, is
nothing more than a vague general formula for the acquisitive instinct of an anonymous, soulless, and irresponsible capitalist power. From his own outlook, the industrial
worker no longer works for the greater glory of God and
for the service of the community, but to escape the lash of
hunger and to create dividends for a joint-stock company.

Of course, I am not writing here about the conceptual
community, or about communities whose needs might be
philosophically regarded as furnishing an aim for production. It is easy enough for political economists to prove that
"humanity," "society," the "world market," cannot exist unless work is done on their behalf. But it is a far cry from the
acceptance of such a principle to the practical inference

that the individual worker X or Y ought therefore, as a matter of duty, to work harder and longer than is absolutely requisite for the satisfaction of his own immediate needs and wishes. The very fact that the existence of such communities must remain a matter of preliminary logical demonstration, suffices to show that they are too remote from the daily experience of the individual to be able to function as the goal of his instinctive and customary activities. The notion of the common welfare of mankind may have been plain enough and near enough to the theoreticians of natural philosophy, to the economists of the Manchester school, to the enthusiasts of utopian socialism; but it cannot be classed among the realities with which the industrial worker under capitalism comes into contact in the course of his daily life.

Political zeal, the religious injunction to love one's neighbor as oneself, humanitarian sympathy with victims of some mass disaster, will only in rare instances expand the average man's horizon to a worldwide visual angle. The hard economic experiences of daily life exercise an inevitably narrowing influence. The realities of the world market can do little to promote the conviction that we are all members of a universal brotherhood. The worker's lot makes him more familiar with crises of overproduction and with the cutthroat competition of rival world empires, than with the vaunted solidarity of all producers and consumers.

The greatest communities within the mental grasp of the average contemporary man are those of religion and nationality. As regards the Church, however, there are no obvious economic facts to corroborate its claim to catholicity, to universal influence. Only the state, as the embodiment of the nation, is live enough, and near enough to everyday life, to arouse complexes of feeling and passion sufficiently powerful to influence habits of life and work. The extraordinary intensification of national sentiment among the masses of the population at the very time when the world market had become established, and when inter-

national intercourse had assumed such extensive propor-
tions, has other reasons besides the obvious political and
economic ones. The ultimate explanation is psychological.
The development of the capitalist system has destroyed the
old communal ties; has made an end of local patriotism,
rural neighborliness, the organized estates of the realm,
the guilds, etc. The disappearance of these has left a va-
cancy, an aching need for compensation; and in 1914 the
unfulfilled emotion found explosive outlets in a frenzy of
national sentiment. The new social ties which the workers
had created in the shape of their political and industrial
organizations were still too young, too void of tradition, too
anemic, too markedly wanting the support of general ethical sentiment, to cope with the violent discharge of the in-
hibited herd instinct in the field of nationalism. Bowing
before the storm, the leaders of the working-class organizations accepted the incorporation of these into the machinery of the state, or subordination to the state. The
old-established coercive community of the state, figuring as
protectress of the lives and properties of all, and, with the
aid of the traditional symbols of militarism, becoming the
embodiment of the collective instinct of self-assertion,
gained the victory over the new voluntary community of
the working-class party, which had not as yet rooted itself
so deeply in the soil of the herd instinct.

Thus in all the countries that took part in the World War,
the idea of national interest has been the most comprehensive one to which protagonists of a voluntary intensification
of production could appeal. We may doubt whether, during the postwar period, the result of such appeals has, even
in Germany, been at all comparable to the result of working-class patriotism while the war was in progress. This
much is certain, that in trade-union ideology since the war
the promotion of national welfare has come to play a much
greater part than before—but we have good reason to ask
ourselves whether this may not be a temporary phenomenon expressing the views of the leaders, rather than the

manifestation of changed motives animating the working
masses under the stress of experience. Besides, the passions of the war epoch are still too fresh, and the groupings
of interest in the postwar period are presumably too transient, for it to be likely that the national community will
prove in the end to be the community for whose sake the
masses may be willing to work as a moral duty.

The new "official" trade-union ideology notwithstanding, there are plenty of indications that skepticism is
spreading among the masses, at any rate in Germany. During the war, side by side with nationalist passions, there occurred a spread of intensified feelings of social resentment,
owing to the growth of the conviction that the working
class was having to bear more than its fair share of the sacrifices and burdens. As the outcome of the war, the state
has more than ever assumed the aspect of an oppressive
and coercive organism which is rather to be dreaded than
to be loved, and whose bureaucratic tendencies make it
seem increasingly uncongenial to ordinary folk. Even the
average state official is less ready than he used to be to toil
and moil on behalf of the state. Since the slogan "produce
more" is voiced mainly by employers whose private interests are obviously nearer to their hearts than the national
welfare in whose name they issue their appeals, it is natural
that the workers should regard the unselfishness of such
zeal for the community as open to question.

The contemporary worker, then, has practically no concrete reason for feeling that, in his case, work is a duty he
owes to the community. Almost as effectively in the worker
as in the capitalist, has a system of production for profit
undermined the motive of production for the common
weal. In the mouths of those who reap the advantages of
this system, talk about the "community" is mere sermon
stuff for use on Sundays, mere flat-catching phraseology;
the daily driving force of the actions of persons who utter
such phrases is the desire to put money in their pockets.
The inference is clear. The first requisite for the growth of

a new community sense, is that there should be a new community. No eagerness for work, until there is a working community; no working community, until there is a community of wills and interests; no community of wills, until all have an equal say in the matter; and no community of interests, until all have a right to share in the fruit of production.

Yet this new institutional community, whose genesis has actually begun, can only arise through the operation of a will which issues out of community feeling. Now, community feeling exists independently of extant institutions, as a natural impulse of the moral human being, for it has come down to us in a specific historical form as a cultural heritage from the precapitalist era of Christian Europe. In a minority of persons, it crystallizes into institutional aims and demands. Only in a minority is the moral predisposition strong enough, as yet, to generate a higher joy in work out of a social sense of duty, notwithstanding the elementary inhibitions of socially caused distaste for work. This minority consists of those who, in the communityless world of today, either continue to live psychologically in the community of yesterday, or scent the morning air of the community of tomorrow; on the one hand, persons guided by religious tradition, who unconsciously continue to obey customary rules of work and subordination; and, on the other hand, socialists, whose activities are consciously directed toward a new communal goal. Those who comprise the former part of this minority are gradually diminishing in number, while those who constitute the latter part of it are gradually increasing.

In fine, however (and this is the salient point), we are for the nonce concerned only with a minority, which may point the way for the masses, but does not typify the present-day masses. When we are considering the masses, we must take into account the realities of mass psychology no less than the possibilities of individual psychology. In each individual it is possible that the sense of duty to work may be in-

tensified to the pitch of joy in work regardless of technical
and social obstacles. But in the realities of mass life, these
obstacles are so formidable that they cannot be overcome
without more vigorous ethical motives than are at the disposal of the average man. Just as our experiences of pleasure and happiness can be graded, so, as a matter of psychological actuality, can we grade human beings according to
the aptitude or the power which they respectively possess
for the enjoyment of varying kinds of pleasure or happiness. There are Don Quixotes and Sancho Panzas; Uylen-
spiegels and Lamme Goedzaks; bohemians and philistines;
leaders and led; geniuses and—normal human beings.
Normal human beings only find access to higher pleasures
when they have had enough of lower ones. Besides, ecstasy
is not an everyday enjoyment; and the ecstasy of sacrifice
on behalf of an ethical obligation is something better fitted
to help us to endure an hour on the rack, than to enable us
to bear up against the weariness and the depression of the
daily round of toil. If we wish to make it possible for the
masses to enjoy the higher pleasure induced by work that is
done for the fulfillment of duty, there is only one way of
doing this. We must first secure for them the maximum
amount of ordinary joy in work, or at the very least we
must see to it that they are not debarred from such ordinary joy more than is absolutely essential in the interests of
the community.

The wearing of a crown of thorns can, indeed, be a joy;
or, rather, a happiness. But is that a reason why we should
wish others such a happiness, or should refuse to relieve
them from a suffering which they find intolerable? Not
even one who himself wears a crown of thorns has any such
right—to say nothing of one who lies on a bed of roses.
Agreed that no happiness can be greater than that of one
who enjoys the ecstasy of sacrifice, of one who has learned
that out of suffering cometh joy. But one who is to have this
experience, must be powerful enough for it; he and none

other can show that he possesses this power, and he must gain it by a voluntary act. We may demand it of ourselves, but we have no right to demand it of another. One who would demand it of another, lays himself open to the suspicion that he would rather see others suffer than suffer himself.

Before we wish others to taste the pain-fraught joys which can only be joyful to those who have spontaneously sought them out, we should try to facilitate access to those joys which are accessible to all. Especially should we do this if we are among the fortunate persons who are in a position to enjoy these more elementary pleasures. Before one of my readers ventures to preach morality and duty as a means for overcoming the industrial worker's distaste for work, it would be well if such a reader were to make himself personally acquainted with the suffering he is so lightheartedly willing to counsel others to bear—the "ordinary" frustration of the "elementary" instincts which I am now about to discuss. Or are we to suppose that the "spiritually minded" man, for the simple reason that he is acquainted with higher happiness, need not concern himself about the "paltry" troubles of the millions, for whom every struggle for happiness is primarily a struggle for bread? Who is entitled to speak in such a way, as long as he owes his own happiness to the labor of these same millions, without whom he himself would be but a human beast, naked, cold, hungry, a prey to all the basest material cares? . . .

Extraoccupational Social Hindrances
and Inhibitions

. . . The psychological difficulties of industrial life do not all originate within the framework of the industry. The relation of the worker to his work cannot be fully understood unless we take into account all the circumstances which determine a worker's psychological reactions. But a worker

does not live only in the workshop. What he is there, depends largely upon influences that have acted on him
elsewhere.

The frequently quoted example of the United States
shows that, in cases where workshop conditions may seem
to be very much the same, the reaction of the worker to
these conditions may vary in accordance with general differences in class relations. To take one instance only, if the
social conditions are of such a kind that the worker (no
matter whether on account of economic realities or on account of sociopsychological traditions) does not regard
himself as permanently condemned to a proletarian existence, his attitude toward his work will naturally be modified by this circumstance. He will lack the spur of resentment that arises out of the sense of being permanently
relegated to a lower class. An American enterprise may
seem as like to a European as you please, and the man who
works in it may be ruthlessly exploited, nevertheless he will
react in a very different way from the European worker if (as
happens especially in the western, more recently colonized
parts of America) he regards his employer as a social equal.
For all that anyone can tell, the two may change places tomorrow. The worker is not distinguished from the boss
either by origin, or by speech, or by the conventions of social life. No sense of strangeness is aroused when the two sit
down together at the same table and converse with one
another on equal terms. At school, the children of both sit
at the same bench; and at the university they join in the
same organizations. When the worker travels by train, he
sits beside the boss, for here too there are no class distinctions. He can make love to the boss's daughter without
being cursed as an "impudent dog." It would never occur
to him to take off his hat to the boss—or, for that matter, to
any other mortal man. Naturally the American worker to
whom this applies, has very different feelings from those
which animate his European classmate. For the latter, the
employer is a man belonging to a class apart, a class with

well-marked social privileges; the employer's arrogant supremacy is decked out with and supported by the plunder in the hands of a quasi-feudal hierarchy of "birth and breeding."

To put the matter in other words, the social inferiority complex of the working class (which practically means the same thing that Marxian socialists usually describe with a more positive emphasis as proletarian class consciousness) colors the whole attitude of the worker to his work, but cannot be regarded as primarily or exclusively derived from workshop conditions. Three other factors have mainly to be taken into consideration: (1) his permanent allocation to a lower class; (2) the insecurity of his livelihood; (3) the conventional disparagement of manual labor.

Permanent allocation to a lower class, namely the proletariat, acts as a subjective mental state in contributing to produce the inferiority complex. It does not matter, in this connection, how great may be the chances for an individual worker to climb into a higher class; it does not matter what percentage of the workers can actually achieve this climb. In Europe, at any rate, the fact is that the average worker does not entertain thoughts of the possibility of such an ascent. The mental attitude is what is psychologically determinative.

The individual worker's belief that he has no chance of ever becoming anything else, produces a feeling of inferiority that is as a rule all the stronger because it is supplemented by a conviction that his children will necessarily inherit this status. Very few European working-class parents can venture to hope that their children will succeed in achieving an independent position. The great number of the children, the cost of higher education, the need that young people should begin to contribute to the family earnings as soon as they leave the elementary school, the fact that the liberal professions rarely enable those who enter them to earn an adequate income until some years after the period of training has been completed, the social disadvantages suffered by those who lack "breeding" and the help of influential relatives, the absence of culturally stimulating factors in the domestic atmosphere of a working-class family, the difficulties attendant on mental work under bad housing conditions, and the perpetual pinching that is needed to pay for books and other necessaries for study—these are among the obstacles which, despite all theoretical recognition of the principle of equality of opportunity and of an open career for the talented, subject those born in the working class to a crushing handicap in the race for social ascent by way of higher education.

The barriers on other routes are even more formidable. An attempt to start an independent business career without special training and special facilities, is almost always shipwrecked by the lack of capital. The natural and obvious line of ascent for the worker would, of course, be by promotion within the industry at which he works. In the early days of capitalism, a considerable number of talented industrial workers were able, in this way, to become independent employers, for the reason that, in those times, there was much more scope for the development of small-scale enterprises. Those times are over and done with. Large-scale enterprises, joint-stock companies, under the aegis of financial capital, are dominant. The occupational hierarchy has been militarized. The management of enterprises has been bureaucratized, and itself subjected to the division of labor, so that a specialized theoretical training is demanded from applicants as an essential preliminary. Thus the possible road to promotion for the worker is usually barricaded just beyond the most subordinate posts of the occupational hierarchy; we find in industry, no less than in the army, that the gulf between the sergeant and the lieutenant is far less easy to bridge than the gulf between the private and the noncommissioned officer. Furthermore, those who occupy subordinate posts in the occupational hierarchy are most likely to come into frictional contact with the manual worker in the enterprise, so that

on them will generally be concentrated the class resentment of the latter. In many of the workers who might
otherwise be qualified for subaltern posts on the staff, this
induces an almost insuperable spiritual inhibition; especially in view of the fact that these same subalterns, being
largely responsible for the discipline of the enterprise, are
themselves subjected to an especially severe and direct
pressure from above. In the previous chapter we learned
how the principle of selection works out in appointment to
such posts; how, in these underlings, authoritarian qualities are considered more important than occupational
competence. Naturally, then, the most efficient among the
workers will often be little inclined to earn more (and not
very much more) at the cost of taking up a post which
would involve cringing before superiors and being trucu-
lent toward inferiors.

The upshot is that there is only one important possibility
of ascent, the transition from a manual to a more or less
intellectual occupation as a clerk or some similar kind of
salaried employee. That is the usual road which aspiring
working-class parents endeavor to open for their children,
above all because they think it will make the livelihood of
these more secure. But the number of working-class aspir-
ants for such posts is so large as to frustrate, generally
speaking, the prospect of social ascent, and this for two
reasons. Compared with the life of a clerk, the existence of
the manual worker is comparatively free, comparatively
adventurous and strenuous, and for this reason it is not the
persons endowed with the most intelligence or strength of
character who are likely to prefer the former to the latter.
The mediocrity of the results of this "natural selection" is
therefore usually conformable to the mediocrity of the as-
pirants' aims. In addition, this rush for places at office
desks and behind shop counters depresses the standard of
life of the black-coated proletariat to a level below that of
many industrial workers. The bureaucratic principle of
promotion by seniority, and the barbed-wire entanglement

of a system hedged in by examinations and testimonials, make it still harder for the black-coated worker to lift himself above the level of a proletarian existence.

The result of all this is that for a considerable and growing number of workers, among whom are many of the most intelligent and most energetic of their class, the winning of positions in the service of the labor movement is the best and shortest way of escaping proletarian life. From the point of view of industrial enterprise, this skims the cream off the working class; and from the outlook of the working class, it leads to the formation of a stratum which is superior in the sociological sense. The social and psychological consequences of these remarkable developments are too complicated to be discussed here. At least this much is plain, that they have no tendency to undermine class consciousness.

Passing now to consider the insecurity of the worker's livelihood, which takes the form of a perpetual risk of unemployment, we see that it is primarily rooted in general social conditions which are independent of the will of the managers of individual enterprises. Nevertheless it induces a sense of chronic anxiety and impotence, which has an unfavorable effect on the worker's attitude toward his occupational environment, and more especially toward the actual work he has to do. Devotion to a particular kind of work, the entering into a close spiritual relationship with that work, presents itself, therefore, to the worker as a dangerous temptation. The more effectually he withstands that temptation, the less will he suffer when the next crisis throws him out on to the pavement. Insofar as he is dominated by such a feeling (and anxiety as to the possibility of unemployment is always lurking somewhere in his subconscious), he will avoid getting too much attached to his work. He will behave like a man of nomadic habits who has already been made wise by experience, and carefully avoids becoming too fond of environing persons and things, for he knows he will not be able to take them with him next time he makes a move.

Thus the system which refuses the worker the opportunity of exerting any decisive influence on the permanency of his relations to a particular task and a particular working environment, thwarts his natural tendency to joy in work. I knew a cabinetmaker, a master in a small way of business, who was given notice to quit his workshop, and hanged himself in it on the last day of his tenancy. The wageworker knows that from day to day or from week to week he may be given the key of the street. That is why, under stress of a natural impulse toward spiritual self-protection, many of the promptings that would otherwise make him love his work and find delight in it, are transformed into a distaste and even a loathing for his occupation.

Finally there has to be considered as an accessory social cause of the industrial workers' distaste for their work, the conventional disparagement of manual labor. This disparagement influences the worker by suggestion, and tends to inhibit the instinct of self-assertion which seeks gratification in working activity. Such a general attitude toward manual labor is the sociopsychological expression of the fact that the performance of such labor is enforced by poverty, implies a position that is economically disadvantageous, and is the occupation of a class which for centuries was deprived of political rights, and which is down to this day looked upon as being of inferior social status. The consequences of this disparagement of manual labor have been discussed seriatim in the foregoing pages.

It would be futile to follow the example of those well-meaning philanthropists in various countries who carry on "propaganda" on behalf of a higher valuation of manual labor. No such simple method will suffice. Little will be achieved by dictating to children in the elementary schools essays about the beauty and dignity of manual labor, or by ornamenting our public squares with the sculptures by Constantin Meunier[4] romantically portraying the heroism of the workers' lives. Reality, sarcastically underlining the contrast between these artificial valuations and the actual

[4] 1831-1905, the distinguished Belgian sculptor, painter, and etcher.

judgments regarding manual labor that underlie our whole social order, is too near to those for whom such flattering unction is provided for them to be willing to close their eyes to the facts. They reject the proffered opiate.

There are concrete, institutional causes for the disparagement of manual labor and of those who perform it. Industrial work actually is burdensome, when it is done under stress of need, when it is enforced on social inferiors by social superiors; its performance actually is a mark of social inferiority when it is done by persons who may stand at the lowest grade of culture and intelligence without being unfitted for it; it actually is less intelligent than mental work when it is nothing more than the work of semi-automatized machine slaves; the lot of the manual worker actually is one little to be envied when his work can provide him with nothing more than the barest subsistence, and when it leaves him the minimum of freedom and pleasure; it actually is debasing when it compels a man, under the lash of hunger, to obey a master in the choice of whom he has had no say, and over whose decision he has no influence; it is certainly anything but beautiful when it has to be carried on in hideous, gloomy, prisonlike factories; it certainly is unhygienic when it exposes those who perform it to the risks of overfatigue, occupational disease, and avoidable accidents; it unquestionably is dirty when the workers have to go home from their daily rounds blackened with grime, powdered with dust, or smeared with oil. In a word, manual labor reserved for a class occupying an inferior social status is, beyond question, disparaged.

As long as these things are so, propaganda of the before-mentioned kind is about as likely to be effective as would attempts to deprive the Negroes in the United States of their sense of racial inferiority by distributing among them tracts assuring them that they had white skins. Social reality holds up before the blackavized proletarian a mirror in which he can see his own face clearly enough. His sense of social inferiority can only disappear in proportion as the concrete causes of that inferiority disappear. Insofar as such a process occurs (thanks to improvement in technique, to the workers' increased will to power, and to the consequent growth of a keener sense of social responsibility among the employers), the workers win more self-respect, grow more fully aware of their human dignity, and have a livelier inclination toward pride in their work. What has to be done to promote the further course of this evolution toward its natural end, is plainly disclosed by the analysis of the causes of the proletarian's inferiority complex.

To what extent is the worker's attitude toward his work influenced by the social aggressiveness resulting from the class consciousness that is awakened by the realization of this inferiority of status? How far can class consciousness promote, and how far is it likely to hinder, joy in work?

If the social inferiority resulting from the propertyless condition of the worker seems to the latter to be the inevitable and permanent lot of his class, then the sense of inferiority lacks the normal and obvious compensation of a belief in the possibility of a personal escape from such a situation. In that case, the unsatisfied sense of self-esteem seeks another outlet. The class on which an inferior status is forced by those who rule under the present system, then comes to identify its own cause with a struggle for human dignity and social justice. The worker is thus able to esteem himself more highly by thinking more highly of his class. By "class consciousness," part of the social aggressiveness arising out of direct conflict of wills and interests, is transferred from concrete individual determinants and concrete individual beings to an impersonal whole, the "system," the social organization in general.

In some of the workers whose mentality is tinged by this class ideology, the transference of affect just described has remarkable psychological influences upon their attitude toward their work, their occupational environment, and those set in authority over them in the enterprise. Such modifications become most obvious when we compare the mentality of the German workers who are strongly influenced by Marxism with that of the American trade unionists who have not "become class conscious."

In ordinary circumstances, the American worker has very little social aggressiveness. His subjective attitude toward his employer is akin to that of one man of business toward another. He is aware, of course, that there is a conflict of interests between the buyer and the seller of labor power; but as a rule, for him, that conflict is held in check by the predominant interest both parties have in the prosperity of the enterprise. But when a wage struggle is in progress, when the American workers' instincts of social pugnacity become active, there is apt to be a vigorous moralization of affects and aims, for the dispute usually turns on questions of contractual obligations in which the notion of "fairness" is involved. The ethical principles to which an American worker appeals in such instances are not colored by any class ideology; they are part of the traditional heritage of the nation, and find expression in biblical texts, popular maxims, and quotations from the famous spokesmen of the national democracy. When an American worker believes that his adversary in the social struggle is behaving "unfairly," he is inspired by an even fiercer hatred than is felt by a German worker in similar circumstances; for in the United States the "unfair" employer is not excused as being representative of a "system," and his responsibility cannot be shifted on to the shoulders of any "class." Precisely because the American worker distinguishes sharply between "good" and "bad" employers, he shows exceptional strenuousness in his fight against the bad ones.

This ethic of the "ordinary man" likewise colors the permanent attitude of the American worker toward the problems of his daily environment. In comparison with the German worker, he has a much opener mind and a much sounder judgment as regards the personal merits and defects of his superiors, whom he looks on as individuals, and not as representatives of a system. This by no means signifies that he judges them less harshly. For the very reason that "superiors" and "inferiors" in industrial enterprise are in their personal relationships considered to be social equals, the American worker, though "not class conscious," takes exception to a great many things which a German worker swallows without winking. American workers who come to the continent of Europe and gain direct experience of working conditions there, are always astonished at the actual "subserviency" of the workers in the very countries where, as far as numbers are concerned, the labor movement is strongest, and where Marxian "class consciousness" is developed to an extreme. No American, for instance, would understand . . . the simple-hearted delight of the joiner when his employer cordially clapped him on the shoulder. One who, like the average German worker, considers on principle that all employers are bad, simply does not know what to make of it when he meets an employer who shows him a good side. "Class consciousness" easily induces a condition of rationalized hypertension, in which a relation to the concrete conditions of working-class life are lost. Under the promptings of unsophisticated instinct, the worker then often feels in a way very different from that which would correspond to his theoretical views. The naive readiness with which he is won over by a kindly gesture and with which he sheds tears on hearing a friendly word, the ease with which he ignores the contradiction between his social aggressiveness as far as theory is concerned and the humanitarian sentimentalism of his relations toward his social adversary, show to how great an extent the Marxism of the German worker is an intellectual construction, an edifice built up in the imagination as compensation for an inferiority complex, and how little it is an effective motive of individual practice. In the mouths of learned professors, in philosophical discussions, in theoretical literature, and (even at this late day) in the phraseology of political agitation, Marxism may still play its part; but in the atmosphere of actual working conditions it is unreal and anemic, deriving as it does, historically, from an atmosphere so very different from that of the workshop.

These considerations explain why, in the reports, the attitude of the socialist workers toward their work is so much less influenced by Marxian class consciousness than might have been expected. Fifty-seven percent of them declare that they find joy in their work, and only 19 percent that a feeling of distaste for work predominates! They are persons whose theoretical condemnation of the capitalist ordering of the world is unqualified in its harshness; and yet when there is some trifling break in the monotony of their labor, some pitiful embellishment of their working environment, some slight alleviation of the pressure of workshop discipline, some inconspicuous hint of a feeling of human kindliness on the part of one of their chiefs—this fitful ray of the pale sunshine makes their whole inner world glow with happiness! They are fanatical advocates of a class consciousness which shall be common to all proletarians without distinction of craft, and yet when we read between the lines there peeps out everywhere a repressed inclination to occupational pride, and they seize at the first chance of telling us we are not to suppose their occupation to be less skilled than their neighbor's! They are irreconcilable champions of the class struggle, but they crave for opportunities to subordinate themselves to just and efficient superiors! They are orthodox believers in historical materialism, and yet they bubble over with gratification when their employer says a word or two to show them that he looks upon them as human beings like himself!

I can say with good conscience that the facts disclosed in my investigation fill me with joy and hope. My interest in the problem of the industrial workers' distaste for their occupation is the outcome of an ardent desire to find some way by which toiling humanity can be freed from the doom of unmeaning and unpleasurable labor. I entered upon the study without preconceived opinions, but not without an aim—and my aim was rooted in the world of feeling. It was naturally an agreeable surprise to me to find that this investigation confirmed, nay emphasized, most of the theoretical views previously expressed by me in my book *The Psychology of Socialism* (the rooting of the problem in the domain of the psychology of instinct; the importance of the instinct of self-assertion and of moral feeling; the increasingly skilled character of much modern machine minding; etc.). I was even more pleased with the confirmation of my prognosis than with that of my diagnosis. For I had already been inclined to believe that none of the problems of the industrial workers' distaste for their occupation can be confined within the iron framework of the antinomy "man versus machine"; and that the acceptance of technical advance need not involve the renunciation of joy in work. I had been optimistic enough to expect that a favorable solution could be found, before I was in a position to see what that solution would be. I did not set out to prove a theory; and, indeed, the main purpose of my earlier books has been to discount the undue prestige of theoretical systematization. I was animated by the wish to serve the cause of human beings with whom I feel united by sympathy and by a common longing for a better future.

Such being my attitude, the reader will readily understand that I was more pleased than not to find how comparatively small are unsatisfied needs of the masses, with what amazing ease their working instincts can be modified in order to be fitted to new working tasks, the tenacity with which they cling to the vestiges of their aforetime joy in work, and the adaptability they show in the search for new possibilities of gratification. It is easy for an intellectual, for one who regards himself as a person of culture, to look down with sarcastic superiority on those who seem to him too easily satisfied. But side by side with the perennially urgent question, how the "damnable unexactingness" of the masses can be overcome, there is a yet more urgent ques-

tion, namely, how the extant needs can be better satisfied
with the means actually available. If close examination
shows that this latter problem is easier to solve than we had
supposed, not only because the available means are ampler
but also because the needs are less extensive than we had
supposed, we ought to be pleased because our fellows can
win happiness more easily than had seemed likely, rather
than disappointed because our own ideals remain unfulfilled. Besides, the fuller satisfaction of existing needs will
take us a considerable step on the way toward the more distant goal of an increase in cultural needs; for it is an essential feature of mass psychology that higher needs can only
arise when more elementary ones have been satisfied.

The main question is, not how we can make a homun-
culus, equipped with new qualities appropriate to our utmost desires. It is, rather, how to treat living human beings
in such a way that their qualities will be enabled to develop
as freely as possible in the way best calculated to promote
their own happiness and the general welfare. The deeper
we descend into the purgatory of capitalist industry, and
the more keenly we become aware of the torment of joyless
labor, the better pleased shall we be when we discover that
there is a means of relieving these torments, that there is a
way of escaping from this purgatory. But the path which
leads out of it is only accessible to those who wish to tread
that path; consequently, not our will, but theirs, must determine its course.

A study of the direction of this will, shows us that the social aspirations of the workers, even of the socialist workers, cannot be exhaustively summed up under the catchword "anticapitalism." The old struggle for the rights of
man, taking on a new form as a struggle for joy in work,
has shifted the problem to some extent. In one sense the
aim of this struggle falls short of the abolition of capitalism;
in another sense, it is much more than this. It is less, insofar
as many of the worst causes of the workers' distaste for
their work can be done away with even without an abolition

of the capitalist profit-making economy; it is more, insofar
as there are other causes, deeper causes, rooted rather in
industrialism than in capitalism, and the task of overcoming these would still face an industrial socialist society.
Thus the workers, as well as the employers, have still a
good many problems of which they dream little in their
present philosophy to solve—problems toward whose solution I have tried to give pointers.

Nothing more need be said to those who understand the
significance of the questions discussed in this book. Those
who lack a sympathetic understanding, will not be helped
by the formulation of the most detailed program in the
world. Understanding is the first and last requisite. I do not
mean to imply that there will necessarily be complete
agreement of outlooks and wills among those who do understand. Such agreement is neither possible nor desirable,
seeing that only from a conflict of thoughts and wills can
arise the tension that makes life worth living, and enables
us to believe that it has a purpose and undergoes a significant progress. But this tension can only be fruitful in proportion as its meaning is understood. Even in these days of
overwhelming aggregate suffering and of enormously
complicated social problems, life can, therefore, be worth
living if only we can regard every problem which the epoch
sets us, as setting us also a task to perform. How each one
of us should devote himself to these tasks, is a matter for
his individual capacities, and to be determined by the opportunities provided by his particular environment. But to
each one of us who is able to understand, there is at least
vouchsafed a possibility of enjoying the greatest happiness
man can know—that of working to promote the happiness
of others.

10

Embourgeoisement of the Proletariat

"When I became aware how impossible it is for the working masses to attain more prosperity without undergoing embourgeoisement, I suffered one of the most grievous disappointments of my life."[1] This statement of 1926 reveals as much about Hendrik de Man as it does about the experience of the European labor movement within its twentieth-century capitalist environment. For to de Man the socialist movement, sustained by its providential instrument, the proletariat, represented salvation from what he experienced as the sordid, grasping, vulgar world of capitalist efflorescence, and he was ever on the alert to detect signs of contamination in the movement, discovering time and again that its leaders had feet of clay, painfully aware that the idealized version of the proletariat presented in Marxist clichés was far from spotty reality. Nevertheless he managed to preserve his faith in its historical mission by adopting a Manichaean (or perhaps "dialectical") interpretation of the process of embourgeoisement, which allowed both for recognition of the workers' imperfections and for the prospect of their perfectibility. His anguish in detecting signs of a falling off from the heroic struggles of yesteryear was a major impetus to his attempt to develop a new and more adequate ideology to guide the socialist movement. For in large part de Man laid the responsibility for the development of reformist accommodation on what he diagnosed as the implicit but effective sanction given by Marxism to the pursuit of interests. To be

[1] *Psychology of Socialism*, p. 469 (translation modified).

sure, he notes below that the fact that there is "widespread evidence of embourgeoisement in countries of non-Marxist socialism" indicates that this phenomenon is a "sociologically conditioned (and therefore only in part ideologically produced) concomitant of the present phase of improvement in the living condition of the proletariat."[2] But he goes on to state that this form of embourgeoisement is only an "epiphenomenon, which does not belong to the essence of the matter,"[3] and he resorts to the thesis that the very satiation of material needs afforded by participation in the capitalist world order would enable the masses to culti-vate a disinterested commitment to demands for the crea-tion of a just society. The process by which class grievances are sublimated into such universalistic appeals is analyzed in his 1931 article on "Capitalism and Socialism," reprinted as the next chapter of this volume.

A second major theme enunciated in the present article—representing indeed the "dialectical" basis for his continued faith in the revolutionary mission of the prole-tariat—was to lay emphasis on the *bourgeois* origins of the socialist tradition. In his major work of 1933, *Die sozialisti-sche Idee*, de Man was to attempt a detailed, historical deri-vation of contemporary socialism from leading sources of the Western tradition—the rationalist heritage of antiquity, the ethics of Christianity, medieval communal democracy, and, embodying them all, that apotheosis of labor, that reconciliation of man and nature, that he found most strik-ingly represented by Thomistic philosophy, Gothic ar-chitecture, and guild democracy of the early Middle Ages. But in a long, slow process marked by successive phases in the modes of production, the working bourgeoisie of those early days was, he argued, gradually converted into the propertied bourgeoisie of the industrial capitalist era, a class that utilized the universalistic justifications of its glori-ous past for the defense of privilege resting upon exploita-tion of the masses and the usurpation of prestige. Thus it

[2] See below, p. 231.   [3] Ibid.

had fallen to these masses, unknowingly imbued with the same Western heritage but unburdened by the special pleading of the privileged, to implement these values in the circumstances of full industrial development, to become thereby the "testamentary executor" of the forefathers of the exploitative bourgeoisie of the present day.

VERBÜRGERLICHUNG DES PROLETARIATS?[4]

Misunderstanding on Right and Left

Until a few years ago, astonishment still reigned if one spoke of the "embourgeoisement of the proletariat." The idea was as good as taboo in the literature of Marxist socialism. To be sure, there was no lack of left-Marxist criticism of persons and of particular events; the careerism of leaders, the philistinism of many incidents of party life, "petty-bourgeois weakening" were deplored. But the criticism was really a weapon of intraparty infighting. People refused to see that the proletariat—including the active class-conscious proletariat—more and more showed a tendency to follow the model of the bourgeois or petty-bourgeois style of life in the nonpolitical areas of everyday living. Any attempt to observe this tendency as a mass phenomenon, the causal interpretation of which should be assessed on the basis of a sociological approach, was eschewed. General interpretation of this widespread phenomenon was denied in order to avoid recognizing a development that did not fit into the model of the growth of socialism out of class interest.

It is perhaps the clearest sign of the spiritual exhaustion of recent Marxism that it does not attempt to support its fight against reformist opportunism with a scientific analysis of the mass phenomena of embourgeoisement. The fact that it has left this task to its opponents cannot be changed. The struggle of Marxist radicalism against the degeneration of socialism has thereby lost in effect; for this struggle remains as shadowboxing within an area—that of decisions about party tactics—where only symptoms, not deeper causes, are to be found.

Hence it is easily understood why my own attempt at a scientific explanation of the tendencies toward cultural embourgeoisement (in my book, the *Psychology of Socialism*, 1926) shocked precisely the left Marxists the most. Both the so-called radical social democrats of Germany and the Russian Communists attempted to make their followers immune against my ideas by falsely presenting me as a defender of reformist opportunism and of embourgeoisement. Because I analyzed these developments as sociologically and social-psychologically conditioned, I am reckoned as their advocate, despite my explicitly critical observations.

But my presentation led to truly remarkable results also from the "right," bourgeois side. Here the catchwords "embourgeoisement of the proletariat" have been suffused by a certain refined snobbishness, in order to justify an emotional rejection of the proletarian class struggle.

Just as I rejoice should this paradox lead to the recognition of truth, so am I distressed when it is used as a cliché to disguise antiproletarian antipathy. It is not my aim to help ladies and gentlemen in evening clothes digest their opulent meals by means of witty mockery of proletarians, who are always depicted as philistines. The intention—generally only unconsciously adopted—is clear. People are reluctant to attribute their social superiority to property alone. *They* are cultivated, and look down on the philistine, for whom ideal existence is summed up by assured material circumstances and by the punctilious maintenance of a socially appropriate style of life. Silk scorns plush, not at all because it is cheaper, but because it is tasteless. But it must not be forgotten that the worst tastelessness in a time of mass poverty and mass unemployment is luxury, that is, ostentation for the purpose of social effect.

No, Mr. Chairman of the Board, the fact that the worker

finds a few pennies more important than you find your dividends, or that he values his reproduction as much as you
do your Cézanne does not mean that he is a greater philistine than you; that would only be indicated if in *his* material
and spiritual conditions of deprivation *you* valued these
things differently from the way in which you do now with
the riches that make it easier for you to be blasé.

And also you, Madame, have no right to reproach the
worker's wife because of her clumsy imitation of your fash-
ions of cultural debasement and of philistinism. Isn't your
whole life a striving for the realization of a style of life that
comes down to symbolizing social prestige, and whose law
is fashion—fashion even unto spiritual life? Your expensive fur coat may be more elegant than the cheap cloth
garment of the store clerk, but it fulfills exactly the same
sociological function, with the sole difference that in the
case of the worker's daughter it comprises a personal
treasure won through her own efforts, whereas for you it is
a symbol of class dominance based on payment by the labor
of others.

I have had the experience that ladies of "society" have
asked me if I didn't regard the shortening of the workday
in industry as a drawback because the greater free time of
the workers would encourage cultural vulgarization. This
concern for the soul of the proletarians obviously expresses
a particularly subtle relationship between a feeling of social
guilt vis-à-vis the workers and a feeling of responsibility
via-à-vis culture. I must observe that a century ago pious
reactionary wives of manufacturers justified the twelve-
hour day on the basis that one should not give the workers
so much time as to get themselves drunk in the tavern and
so ruin their families, and I cannot repress the comment
that whoever still regards class guardianship in this way
would do better to educate himself with Karl Marx than to
take up his present-day critics.

Other matters might be mentioned. I am reminded of an
asinine argumentum ad hominem that I must repeat: that

if the workers were victorious, ladies with unearned income would be condemned to eight- or nine-hour factory work so that they would not "embourgeoisify." The "frivolous distractions of the irresponsible and the thoughtlessness of the humble" so excoriated by Lassalle, which mark the evening and holiday distractions of the tired worker, are less bourgeois than the potential utilization of "culture" for sensual gratification and for the advertisement of one's social superiority. There is more true culture in the raw, unformed thrust of the proletariat for leisure time as an escape from the industrial juggernaut than in all the drive for "cultivation" of the ever-so-educated and refined upper class.

These instances nevertheless serve to demonstrate how much a far-going elucidation of the expression "embourgeoisement of the proletariat" is needed. All the more so, since the misunderstandings arise not so much from self-interest as from the exaggeration of class determination of ideas on the part of the left Marxists, and from the denial of the reality of classes on the part of the salon socialists. Moreover, there are countless and worthy socialists for whom this problem is so new that out of uncertainty they have become caught in all sorts of contradictions. Many socialist workers have already asked me: "How can you reproach us for absorbing bourgeois culture, since there is no other culture at the present time?" And, on the other hand, others ask: "How can you so unperturbably observe the cultural embourgeoisement of the proletariat as if it were an unavoidable stage on the way to socialism, whereas in fact it is the greatest danger for socialism?"

Improvement in Living Conditions

For the solution of this apparent contradiction it is first necessary that two things, which are all too often confused, be distinguished: the improvement in living conditions of the proletariat, and its embourgeoisement.

The two phenomena are, according to all experience, interwoven in many ways. The last fifty years have been at once the time of the improvement in the living conditions of the workers and the time of their absorption into bourgeois culture. Here as elsewhere the phenomena are made up of an interlacing of cause and effect in mutual dependence; scientific analysis, however, can and must identify without ambiguity different types of patterns of dependence. A single example shows that such variation is not just hypothetical: thus since 1919 cultural embourgeoisement has been found not only in those countries where, in comparison to prewar times, the proletariat has experienced an improvement in conditions (as, for instance, in Belgium) but also in those where its position has declined (as, for instance, in Germany).

Embourgeoisement refers to qualitative changes, improvement in living conditions to quantitative ones. The improvement in the conditions of the proletariat can be assessed by outward measures: an increase in real wages, shortening of the workday, an increase in security and rights through protective legislation, social insurance, and labor law, an increase of power through strengthening of organization and of political representation, etc. Embourgeoisement, however, can be understood only as qualitative changes in wants and needs, which gives a distinct configuration to the drive for improvement, namely, definition in terms of an "ideal" style of life. There is a question here of psychological composition or of physiognomy. A class experiences embourgeoisement to the degree that the concrete contents of the style of life for which it strives are the same as those that are realized or striven for by the dominant bourgeoisie. The embourgeoisement of the nobility shows that this is a phenomenon that can be accompanied both by increase and by decrease in material circumstances.

The improvement in living conditions of a stratum reflects the degree to which it finds that the needs it experiences are generally satisfied through an increase in its affluence and power. Here what is important is the degree of satisfaction, not the type of need. Better conditions without embourgeoisement are indeed conceivable: for instance, the Russian Revolution was supported by a striving for better conditions that did not at all take the style of life of the possessing classes as a model; neither the proletariat nor the peasantry wanted to become bourgeois. A similar relationship existed between the upward thrust of the bourgeoisie and the life style of the aristocracy at the time of the French Revolution. That afterward it turned out quite otherwise there, and in the case of contemporary Russia as well, is another story. The fact is that motives of a very different cultural derivation can lie behind the quantitative embodiment of improved conditions. And in the case of the will to betterment of the socialist proletariat of Europe there are many elements that have nothing to do with bourgeois life style, but on the contrary arise from a rejection of bourgeois tinsel.

The real nature of the relationship between the improvement in conditions and the embourgeoisement of the European proletariat becomes clear if one asks what form this improvement has taken since the beginnings of the labor movement.

Aside from various anomalies arising out of particular circumstances, in general the following characteristics of this improvement can be set forth:

1. The shortening of the workday. Without exaggeration it can be said that for the great part of the European industrial work force this has brought about a reduction of two to three hours per day in the course of the last generation alone. This is a revolution in the conditions of life of millions such as world history even in its most revolutionary periods has never before experienced in this magnitude and with this speed. The benefits of these changes have in part been lessened through other conditions of work (especially through the more intensive exploitation of labor power); nevertheless the fact remains that every single

newly won hour of leisure time remains a newly won hour of leisure. How the worker uses this time is not the point—which is that he can make up his own mind as to its use; the decision arises from his own free will and not from an imposed factory discipline. The expansion of freely chosen conditions of living is a value in itself that has nothing to do with embourgeoisement; it holds for the capitalist as for the peasant, for the scholar as for the hod carrier.

2. The rise in material standard of living. The extremely intricate question of social statistics as to whether and to what degree a rise in real wages has taken place is not the point. It simply cannot be denied that a very significant rise in the purchasing power of a great part of the European labor force has been visible for a century. Worker and pauper are no longer interchangeable expressions, as they once were. To be sure, embourgeoisement can take place if the increase in income is used to imitate the bourgeois style of life, but it is not requisite that the increase be so used. In reality the increase in the standard is in large part used otherwise. Before anything else: freedom from the worst poverty, that is from the situation in which wages are not enough to take care of the satisfaction of even the most urgent biological needs. But subsequently: an opportunity to satisfy those needs that go beyond this minimum for physical existence. Here arises the possibility of embourgeoisement, but here also is the possibility to satisfy those general human needs that have nothing to do with embourgeoisement.

It is an improvement in itself if it is no longer necessary to endure hunger, or if it is possible to buy enough coal and warm clothing for winter. Roomy, healthy, airy dwellings; a better, variegated diet; a greater opportunity for outdoor recreation; enough clean clothing and bedding, soap for washing; the means for reducing heavy, dirty, and monotonous housework (running water instead of a pump, electric lighting instead of candles or gas, etc.)—these and a thousand other material improvements (unfortunately not

yet sufficiently implemented) have as much cultural worth
as health itself, or as the realization of the economic principle of the avoidance of unnecessary effort. If this is embourgeoisement, then one must say: long live embourgeoisement!

3. Improvement of moral life and legal assurances. The
same goes for the less material indications of improvement
of the living conditions of the workingman. I note only a
few: (a) the lessening of alcoholism as a class-typed concomitant of poverty, arising from bodily exhaustion, too
long hours of labor, and the hopelessness of the worker's
existence prior to the modern labor movement; (b) the rising personal self-esteem that is linked to the emergence of
the labor movement and to its struggle for political and
economic democracy; (c) the conquest of civil equality and
of participation in the determination of working conditions, etc. All these achievements of the last decades are
implementations of values having the same validity for all
classes. But dedication to the dignity of man is no
bourgeois failing—otherwise the workers would not have
had to wrest what they have in fact realized of man's dignity against the opposition of the bourgeoisie.

The Crucial Motive

This last circumstance shows that the fight of the workers
for the realization of their rights must be carried on as a
class struggle against the positions of property and power
of the bourgeois class. Thus the values at issue are from the
standpoint of the bourgeoisie class values, but from the
standpoint of the workers they are universal values.

Hence the inclination of the bourgeoisie to see tendencies toward embourgeoisement where they do not exist.
Their own motives are attributed to others. The bourgeoisie can and will not understand that the struggle of the
workers for a living wage has a cultural significance other
than its own striving for profit and ease. Hence also the

mistaken equivalence of "improvement" in living conditions and of embourgeoisement.

A ludicrous mistake indeed—for nothing is more ludicrous than when one thinks he sees a strange, ugly face in the mirror, and in truth it is his own. A very instructive mistake, however, for it exposes the moral outlook of the bourgeoisie as a class, if their most sophisticated representatives use, in the name of culture, as the ultimate argument against the rising workers' movement the contention that it will make the workers bourgeois.

The mistake is also instructive for the workers' movement. For within that movement is found an ideology—Marxist or at least vulgar-Marxist—that supports this misconstruction of the motives of its own adherents and enemies. Partly responsible for this is the justification of class struggle on the basis of class interest, which in turn is understood as the interest of both sides in one and the same object (the Marxist error) out of one and the same motive (the vulgar-Marxist error). A good part of the spiritual weakness of Marxist radicalism in its fight against embourgeoisement arises from this false proposition, from its lack of understanding of the noncapitalist origin of existing socialist motives out of fear of recognition of a moral ranking of these motives, out of a mistaken respect for the slag of bourgeois materialism in the Marxist philosophy of history and social theory.

It is a paradox, significant for theory as for practice, that the class that fights for the goals of mankind justifies its demands with egoistical class interests, whereas the class that in reality is concerned only with egoistic assertion of its own interests brings into play the rejection of the "materialistic" class struggle. The slender support that Marxist socialism attacks outside the industrial proletariat, in comparison with Western and especially English socialism, is doubtless linked with the fact that Marxism, which has brought justified criticism to the hypocritical moralism with which the class struggle is conducted from above, is given to exaggeration to the point of refusing to recognize the ethical and universalistic basis of its own volition. It thereby helps its opponents to picture the workers' movement as more materialistic and self-interested, and thus in the end, as more "bourgeois," than it is, for the movement itself presents itself in this way. And this is also a form of embourgeoisement, and indeed an especially dangerous one, because it is hidden away where one does not expect to find it.

But that, as Kipling says, is another story. The widespread evidence of embourgeoisement in the countries of non-Marxist socialism as well is a sociologically conditioned (and therefore only in part ideologically produced) concomitant of the present phase of improvement in the living condition of the proletariat. But only a concomitant, that is, an epiphenomenon, which does not belong to the essence of the matter. The actual function of the improvement in circumstances is to give the proletariat opportunity for the development of its own life style. Embourgeoisement depends on whether this way of life shall pattern itself on the model of the upper classes or on different values stemming from socialist conviction.

Embourgeoisement thus does not lie in the fact that things are sought that are in the possession of the bourgeoisie and that must be wrested away from them in conflict: leisure time, income, privileges, positions of power, etc. Indeed the most materialistic of these things can be fought for out of motives that have nothing to do with the materialistic outlook of their sated possessors. The struggle for bread means a struggle for universalistic, ideal values if lack of bread brings denial of liberty, if—in other words—poverty is experienced as injury to the dignity of man in the form of degrading worry, social dependence, economic exploitation, and class oppression. And vice versa, panhuman ideal values—such as religious precepts or ideals of justice—can be used as a pretext in striving for things that are sought (as with the present-day bourgeoisie) only because they belong to the distinctive style of life of an upper class.

In the end, the embourgeoisement of the proletariat is a matter not of the object of its desires but of its motives. Embourgeoisement is present when the motive for the wished-for advance is to realize a bourgeois style of life. Style of life is, however, not determined through level of well-being. It is found in a distinctive pattern of meaning that obtains as a norm for the whole class, with its own hierarchy of social and ethical values, its own type of needs, its own way of thinking, its own manners, its own symbols for collective self-esteem.

The lessening of social distance between a rising and an upper class by means of an increase in well-being and an improvement in legal position by no means necessarily involves similarity of style of life. For instance, there are striking differences in style of life among those of identical incomes within the lower strata—compare the industrial worker with the peasant, the clerk, the artisan, and the retailer of the same income bracket.

The decisive concrete index of embourgeoisement is hence the question of whether there is an attitude that includes a taking over of values that underlie the "manners" of the bourgeoisie. It is this that I have called the embourgeoisement of the proletariat. In my opinion it is a relatively easily established and very powerful tendency, which must be considered if the cultural situation of the workers or the substitution of revolutionary by reformist motives are to be understood. Historically, this tendency goes together with improvement in the condition of the workers, for on the one hand it is one of the motives for this change, and on the other it is itself encouraged by the change. But it is not identical with this change. It first appeared relatively late in the development of the workers' movement, after the inception of this movement had developed out of entirely different motives—out of a drive for freedom, out of moral revulsion, indignation with injustice, rebellion against class oppression, etc. And today there are still found two types of motives in the workers' movement—I have called them the capitalist and socialist soul of the workers—and out of this circumstance arises a tension between two forces.

Since there is tension here, the expression "embourgeoisement" refers to a tendency rather than to a condition. In reality the worker is no bourgeois, not even a petty bourgeois. Even when he has a petty-bourgeois income, other characteristics of his class position—in the first place his socially dependent work role—prevent him from becoming petty bourgeois. He is missing just that agreement between style of life and social experience that has given its stamp to the settled form of life of petty-bourgeois tradition. The real cultural condition of the proletariat is hence a hybrid, a mixture of forms of culture both "true" (corresponding on the one hand to the workers' work experience, on the other to socialist convictions) and "false" (sought as substitute for, or as outward expression of, a feeling of inferiority).

The result is chaos. Unfortunately—and thank God. Unfortunately, because the workers are subjected to the experience of the stylelessness of an epoch of cultural degeneration, and because a greater part of their vital expression has hence become empty of meaning. Thank God, because the search for another pattern of meaning to life is prompted by this chaotic circumstance, because the tension between rising and declining forces creates an unstable equilibrium from which anything may develop.

Embourgeoisement or Philistinism?

Another misunderstanding which should be cleared up here stems from the double meaning of the word "embourgeoisement." This arises from the fact that the expression "bourgeois culture" is applied to two separate phenomena. In the one case one is referring to the cultural characteristics of the present-day bourgeoisie—to approximately what I have previously called the bourgeois style of life. In the other case bourgeois culture is used to refer to the entire cultural heritage of the bourgeois historical epoch—which, in accordance with whether burghers, the bourgeoisie, or industrial capitalism is meant, begins with the founding of cities in the eleventh century, with the Renaissance, or with the steam engine. Of course there are as many different things involved here, as in the case of the ethic of Christianity and the actual morality of contemporary churchgoers.

For a somewhat more adequate clarification it is appropriate further to distinguish, on the one hand, between culture and civilization, cultural development and decay, cultural ideals and the popular norms of civilization; and on the other hand, among burghers, bourgeoisie, and capitalist class. But these last distinctions are not at all necessary to establish that socialism has a completely different relationship to class culture (that is, to the "state of civilization" of the present-day bourgeoisie) than it has to the historical culture (that is, to the cultural creations of the medieval burghers). The first relationship is negative, for socialism rejects not only the capitalist social order but also the "civilization" of the contemporary bourgeoisie. The second relationship is positive, for this rebellion of socialism rests on cultural, legal, and moral values, each and every one of which has its origin in the spiritual world of the bourgeois cultural epoch.

Modern socialism itself belongs to this epoch. Not a single one of the ideas alive in it but comes from the spiritual heritage of bourgeois culture—in its creative, revolutionizing period of growth, and the historical writing of the coming century will have as much right to name our socialism bourgeois socialism as we to call Plato's socialism the socialism of antiquity.

Socialism as an idea is precisely as much a product of the distinctive dialectical development (self-fulfillment, the younger Marx would say) of the spiritual forces that formed bourgeois culture as the pursuit of interests of the proletariat is a dialectical epiphenomenon of contemporary capitalism. Just as industrial capitalism has produced its own gravedigger in the proletariat, so bourgeois culture has produced its spiritual gravedigger in the process of dialectical self-development; in the name of cultural ideals, in the name of self-determination of the individual and of the worth of labor, it produces ideas that will sentence, bury, and—perhaps—overcome the "civilization" of the present-day bourgeoisie. And socialism, which seeks this victory, can identify itself as the testamentary executor of the spiritual originators of bourgeois culture, and can say of itself, "I am not come to destroy, but to fulfill, the law and the prophets."

In my opinion, then, the expression "embourgeoisement" means something quite different from the relationship to bourgeois culture in general; it involves only the style of life of the contemporary bourgeoisie. Completely aside from that is the relationship of socialism to those cultural values that are still finding expression as key creative attainments of science and art, to be sure in part without visible or conscious relationship with the urge for socialism—but in any case based on impulsions that are directed to the realization of completely spiritual values.

This continuation of cultural development in the time of "civilization" is a problem in itself, and indeed one that gives socialist theory a hard nut to crack. But it is on an entirely different plane from the problem of embourgeoisement. For these attainments either leave the style of life of the bourgeoisie entirely undisturbed because of the abstract nature of thought involved (as in the new physical theory), or (as in the new architecture) they have effect, on the basis of their close relationship with social life, as a part of that creative rebellion of which socialism is simply the political and social component. The intellectuals, the scholars, poets and artists, in short, spiritual man, for whom the highest values of life are of culture and not "civilization" (truth, beauty, virtue; not money and class prestige) brought the word "bourgeois" into disrepute long before the proletariat learned to say it with hatred. Even Marx had scourged the philistines and vulgarians among the bourgeois before he knew anything of capitalists.

In order to avoid misunderstanding in this matter it has been proposed to describe what I have called embourgeoisement of the proletariat as "philistinism," or "the making of a petty-bourgeois mentality." In favor of this proposal is the fact that the cultural world from which the proletarian masses experience the influence of the capitalistic environment is really not that of the burghers nor of the bourgeoisie but that of the petty bourgeoisie, the directly contiguous stratum. Yet in favor of the expression "embourgeoisement" let it be said that with the growth of cultural decadence the style of life of the upper class is the model that in fact is used. The intermediate strata act only as means of transmission. In this respect especially suggestive are the tendencies to imitate made possible by one of the most effective of all means for the transmittal of "civilization," the cinema: the working public is interested not in the life of the petty bourgeois but in that of the well-to-do.

Hardly less telling for the recognition of embourgeoisement is material acquisition as the paramount ideal, as a valuation legitimizing behavior—which is, it should be said, just as "bourgeois" as is the kind of social order that receives its stamp from domination by the bourgeoisie. But it is all the same whether it is called embourgeoisement proper, permeation by a petty-bourgeois spirit, or philistinism—what is decisive is to recognize the phenomenon itself, however it is called.

Once this situation is properly recognized it also becomes clear why its significance cannot be weakened by reference to the intensification of the class struggle. It is not important whether it is the aggravation of methods of conflict or the (much less problematical) increasing economic disparity of need and satisfaction among the workers—increased intensity of the class struggle and embourgeoisement are compatible. Intensity of the conflict is not the question; granted exactly the same intensity, it is the psychological character of motives and goals that determines cultural import. Class conflict is doubtless much stronger today than it was a half-century ago, but it turns around completely different matters, and in large part quite different motives are at work. Russia shows that the purest proletarian revolution from a Marxist standpoint can with time turn to embourgeoisement; just think of the NEP,[5] of the fad for American methods, of the bureaucratization, in short of everything that has turned so many disappointed revolutionaries into oppositionists or cynics.

From the standpoint of embourgeoisement the only decisive question remains the motives of individuals or, if one wishes, of the behavior of different types of typical men. Of course no answer to this problem is hereby given, but if the question is put in the right way much has already been won. And this is the question that more than anything else will decide the future relationship between the workers' movement and socialism.

[5] Lenin's New Economic Policy of 1921 reversing the leveling impact of War Communism by acknowledging the tenure and right to trade of peasants and artisans and legitimizing wage differentials in industry.

11

Capitalism and Socialism

De Man held that the philosophical limitations of Marxism, diagnosed and criticized in the *Psychology of Socialism*, were paralleled by its empirical inadequacy to account for the rise of the socialist movement in the West. This fact had been, however, disguised by the perspicacity with which Marx had unmasked the play of interests heretofore screened by the self-serving sentimental rationalizations of ruling classes, especially in his brilliant and insightful analysis of the historical flowering of capitalism in nineteenth-century Europe. But this very narrowing of focus to what was regarded as a universally valid model of historical development enabled Marx to deny the efficacy of noneconomic elements of action, to demonstrate that the distribution of interests revealed by his analysis sufficed to account for the pattern of historical development—specifically to account for the rise of the socialist movement in terms of reactions by the proletariat to capitalist exploitation.

The most conspicuous exception to this pattern was of course the failure of the United States to develop in accordance with Marxist expectations. The classical ex post facto explanation was Werner Sombart's 1905 essay,[1] which, after recounting the exceptional circumstances surrounding the inception of American capitalism, argued

[1] Werner Sombart, "Warum gibt es in den Vereinigten Staaten keinen Sozialismus?" Revised reprint of vol. 21, *Archiv für Sozialwissenschaft und Sozialpolitik*, Tübingen: J.C.B. Mohr (Paul Siebeck), 1906. De Man had, perhaps independently, taken much the same line in his "Lettre d'Amérique: l'Handicap Europe-Amérique," *Le Peuple*, 2 October 1920, p. 1.

that it was only a matter of time before the inexorable operation of the laws of capitalist development would bring about the domination of a propertied bourgeoisie that would learn to differentiate itself from the common man and thereby to engender a socialist opposition. De Man wavered between this alternative and a more sophisticated position, originating in his personal experience in America and gradually assimilated into his theoretical outlook, that admitted permanent distinctiveness of historical development to entities with similar economic systems. But in propounding this viewpoint he subjected himself to systematic misunderstanding on the part of many critics who did not realize that he found "the Marxist analysis of capitalism closer to the truth than that of his antagonists;"[2] it was Marx's derivation of socialism directly from that capitalist environment that he found inadequate and therefore misleading. In the pages below de Man specifies both his positive and negative appreciation of Marx's singular contributions in these respects.

Rather than being only a reaction to the one-sided distribution of interests within capitalism, the socialist movement, de Man insisted, transcended that environment with respect to both its historical impetus and its institutional objectives. Indeed, he argued that to the extent to which this was not so, the movement lost its raison d'être, both existential and moral, for, in contrast to the conventional wisdom of his time, he contended that capitalism *could* satisfy the material demands of the proletariat, and thus it was the success rather than the failure of capitalism that appalled him. In contrast to Europe, the American example showed that a basically identical distribution of interests—the capitalist environment—was compatible with a conspicuously different, i.e., democratic, social structure and thereby engendered what indeed might possibly be called a strikingly

<hr>

[2] "Le Capitalisme libéral," *Bulletin d'Information et de Documentation de la Banque Nationale de Belgique*, VIe année, vol. 1, no. 8, 25 April 1931, p. 270.

successful labor movement "but no political class struggle according to Marxist prognosis."[3] Accordingly, with respect to the European movement it must be said that "the socialist critique of economic organization in general only symbolizes a rebellion that stems from the actual effects of class stratification,"[4] for in Europe in contrast to America, "the new order that was established on the ruins of the absolutistic and feudal *ancien régime* did not have an individualized and atomized society as a starting point, but rather an economic, political, and social hierarchy, the heritage of the system of hereditary estates."[5] This new social order, which justified itself in the name of the universalistic goals of the French Revolution, contradicted these same goals by its system of invidious social distinction resting on a foundation of privilege and systematic exploitation—and thereby prompted its moral rejection by those who were its victims. This rejection encompassed thus not only matters of relative income but more importantly the dignity of man, which was attainted by the European social order. Hence the movement was oriented to the institutional implementation of the entire gamut of values arising in the central Western historical tradition. Moreover, the perspective that there was *systematic* denial of these rights of man led to the sublimation of individual indignation into a communal mission for the redemption of mankind. The proletariat was not uniquely called to this mission, but by virtue of its victimized position it was induced, "earlier, more generally, and more decisively than the other members of the working community . . . to make the demands of socialism its own."[6] The fight for interests was thereby converted into a crusade for the benefit of the members of society in general, and in view of the infinite variety of goals subsumed under this formulation of socialism, reali-

---

[3] See below, p. 245.   [4] See below, p. 245.
[5] "Le Capitalisme autoritaire," *Bulletin d'Information et de Documentation de la Banque Nationale de Belgique*, VIe année, vol. 1, no. 2, 25 January 1931, pp. 1-2.
[6] *Die sozialistische Idee*, Jena: Diederichs, 1933, p. 231.

zation could only be asymptotic—in sharp contrast to the eschatological assumptions involved in the Marxist "day of revolution." On the contrary (and as he had already indicated in *Joy in Work*), the struggle for the implementation of socialism was already possible to a significant degree within the capitalist regime and at the same time would by no means be guaranteed of success by the socialist conquest of power—a prospect both exhilarating and sobering for the responsible militant. It might be noted that couching his interpretation in these terms also made it possible for de Man to preserve faith in the eternal redemptory mission of the socialist movement within the world of the flesh.

KAPITALISMUS UND SOZIALISMUS[7]

Introductory Remarks

The placing of the matter here treated within the general pattern of organization [of the book of which it forms a part] requires that only those aspects of socialism be treated that make it the antithesis of capitalism. But socialism is more than anticapitalism. For my essay I must hence insist upon noting the restriction, indeed the warning: to relate socialism to a contemporary social and economic order assures the advantage of a nearby, easily reached intellectual locus, but if one thereby encompasses socialism at the point where it is linked with the present, one does not encompass it in its entirety.

Two examples should suffice to show how great is the area left out by the equating of socialism with anticapitalism. In the first place, socialism existed long before capitalism. And secondly, in the contemporary socialist movement are to be found very important impulses that are directed not so much against capitalistic characteristics of the economy as against social, political, and ideological

[7] In Bernard Harmes, ed., *Kapital und Kapitalismus*, Berlin: Hobbing, 1931, pp. 53-74.

concomitants that stem from a precapitalist inheritance. Thus in the socialist movement much that appears as anticapitalism in reality is antifeudalism or antiabsolutism.

I do not wish to tarry here with consideration of the first phenomenon, that is, with the problem of precapitalistic socialism. The danger is too great that with a superficial treatment, without detailed analysis of specific events in their respective historical contexts, we will end only with a quarrel over words and definitions. May we put forth only the following as unchallenged fact: all historians of socialism apply this label—although it is scarcely a century old—to theories and movements that belong to precapitalistic periods, for instance, to antiquity, to the European Middle Ages, and to modern history prior to the so-called industrial revolution. They shared some common characteristics: first of all, the striving for a just social order, that is, the application of an ethical principle of justice in the demand for a social order corresponding to this principle; in the second place, addressing this demand to economic, social, and political socialization, that is, to an order that rests on cooperation rather than on domination—in other words, on community of possession of the basic means of production appropriate to the cooperative provision of labor, instead of on a property-based superiority of individuals or of groups.

This also has its practical significance from the standpoint of modern socialism, for the present-day class movement has inherited from its precapitalistic forerunners on the one side standards of social-ethical values, on the other side images of ideal goals. In this connection it is particularly instructive to see how Marxist socialism, for instance, which has moreover set itself as most resolutely opposed to precapitalistic socialism, has tacitly and with hardly any modification taken over these ethical propositions and goals.

It is thus apparent that present-day, anticapitalistic socialism also includes a principle that is more than simply an inversion of capitalistic principles. For my part I would be tempted to express it this way: in all socialism there lives a drive, a striving for a just social order, that is eternal insofar as it is addressed to the then existing order, as is every unfulfilled effort at perfection with respect to the always imperfect reality. Contemporary socialism is anticapitalist in that the social reality against which it rebels is capitalist. "In that" means both "because" and "insofar." The "because" is self-explanatory. "Insofar" is understandable if one asks the second question here put forth, namely the question of the extent to which contemporary socialism is not anticapitalist.

This question as to the *not anticapitalistic* elements in contemporary socialism is especially instructive if one looks to socialism as a mass movement rather than to socialist doctrines. Doctrines are true expressions of the real motives just as little as our own experiences of consciousness are true expressions of our essential, largely unconscious motives. For instance Marxism, the anticapitalist doctrine par excellence, in reality often fulfills the function that Marx himself described as ideological: it often serves for the justification or the disguise of motives that in reality have a quite different character. Thus in the prewar years the orthodox party Marxism of German social democracy was in many respects such an ideology. A theory of anticapitalistic revolution acted as a declaration of faith for a mass movement that in the end was a movement of discontent subordinates. The Marxist theory of revolution was frequently only the emotionally satisfying symbol of a stand that called on the half-feudal authoritarian state for the recognition of civil rights and for the social reforms of better living conditions and security—a movement truly proletarian in its membership and Marxist in its ideology, but largely liberal and democratic in its real motives.

Another especially instructive example of the discrepancy between ideology and the impulsion of a mass movement, which I intentionally take from Marxism, is shown by contemporary Russian communism. One has only to apply the Marxist method and to ask how this movement stands vis-à-vis the degree of development of capitalistic forces of production, in order to recognize the difference between appearance and reality. In a country with such weakly developed capitalism the revolution means something entirely different from what it should according to an ideology imported from the capitalistic West by a leadership trained in exile. The deepest impulsions are directed not so much against the hardly existing capitalistic economic order as against the undeniably real absolutistic social and political order. This discrepancy between anticapitalistic class ideology and the rejection of precapitalistic estates reveals the real problem of Russian communism, which appears in the burning questions of the land hunger of the peasants, the inheritance of bureaucratic methods of government, the continual need of the masses for a mystique to replace religion, unweakened nationalism, the Asiatic drive for power, etc.

However, the most illuminating example of the difference between economic organization and social content is provided by the United States of America. It is well known that there is no mass proletarian socialism despite the most highly developed capitalism. This presents for Marxism a really perplexing—and moreover unsolved—problem. According to a famous sentence of *Das Kapital*, "the industrially developed country shows the less developed only the picture of its own future" with respect also to the matter of class conflict. The only way out of the dilemma that emerges from this contradiction between prediction and reality consists in saying—and it has been said for fifty years—"Just wait, this is only an exception that proves the rule, a delay in a natural line of development."

But this delay has its causes. In general there is little disagreement as to the nature of these causes. The most important are: natural resources remaining unexhausted for many years; a rather high level of productivity; the long-preserved possibility of internal colonization, that is, an industrial development without territorial limitations; no feudal past; no traditions of class differentiation taken over from the estate society; no debasement of physical labor in social estimation; a greater ease of upward mobility—in former days especially through the autonomy of economic development, still today through the lack of educational privileges and of social class-prejudices; a state that has never been authoritarian; an ethical-religious atmosphere in which profit is regarded as proof of diligence, etc. In short, despite all economic conflicts between rich and poor, up until now the social and psychological conditions were lacking for the mass of the American workers to regard themselves as a class, that is, destined for permanent, inescapable social inferiority. Hence there was indeed a union interest movement and an intellectuals' socialism, but no political class struggle according to Marxist prognosis.

If now the question is asked, as I have for a number of years, from the American vantage point—why is there socialism in Europe?—light breaks through. For then it can be recognized that the real mass impulsion to proletarian socialism in Europe is in reality directed at a social, political, and cultural structure that has emerged out of the particular conditions of the origin and development of European capitalism. This does not mean that socialism is not anticapitalist, for the economic underpinning of this structure is indeed capitalistic. But this means that the existing specific makeup of socialism cannot be explained by an abstract and formal characterization of capitalism; it must be related to the existing objective makeup of a given capitalistic social structure in a given phase of development. The socialist critique of economic organization in general only symbolizes a rebellion that stems from the actual effects of class stratification.

The Psychological Components of the Anticapitalistic Mass Movement

In reality one fights only against circumstances; the fight against a system is an intellectualization, just as is the system itself. Anticapitalism is only real to the degree that anticapitalistic ideas are effective as motives for action. Fluctuations in wages, changes in the hours of work, in the type of work, the methods of payment, prices, housing conditions, the legal situation, the relations of powers, etc.—in short, the circumstances and the men against which one fights are facts, but capitalism is a construction—whereby it is not said that it does not exist but rather that it exists on another level of being. For its part, socialism is not only a system of concepts but in the first place the name of a movement.

It is perhaps not superfluous to recall these epistemological truisms before asking how socialism, on the one side as an intellectual system, on the other as a movement, is related to capitalism—viewed here both as a social phenomenon and as an economic system.

The understanding of these mutually entangled relationships will be facilitated by taking up the two forms of socialism that are characteristic for the current situation: the practice of the proletarian mass movement, and the doctrine of Marxism, which in fact is the most notable theoretical expression of this movement.

It was with Marx that socialism became, out of a general striving for a just and classless society, an anticapitalistic mass movement, but at the same time it was legitimated— the meaning of this expression will be explained below—as a movement within capitalism. Just as every movement results from tensions, so this movement arises from the tensions between given social expectations and given social gratifications. Two types of motives contribute to the formation of these expectations, motives that are linked together in the most variegated complexes but that must be clearly separated in order for their nature to be understood. I would like to call them needs and convictions.

NEEDS

The fundamental difference between need and conviction lies in the fact that needs are always addressed to a currently available object, thus to a value that belongs among the existing range of values. In this sense we speak, for instance, of economic needs when it is a question of a lack, or a desire, whose satisfaction can be assured by the acquisition of economic goods. Such needs are, for instance, the desire of workers for higher wages, more leisure time, protection against unemployment, etc. But there are also needs outside the economic area, such as those of the state for power, social needs for respect, etc. The common characteristic of these motives lies in the fact that they are always oriented to values that are recognized as such by the society of that time, and which are striven for because they are valued just as much by competitors. In this—that is, concerning such matters as money, hours of work, and power—it is largely a question of distribution.

To the extent that socialism arises from the nonfulfillment of needs of the sort that can be satisfied through goods or values belonging to the existing scale of values, it is in reality a movement within capitalism. To this extent it does not overstep the border of the existing order; in fact, to a certain degree it delivers a tacit confirmation to this order in that it recognizes its scale of values as valid.

Another psychological characteristic of needs is that they can be satisfied through an appropriate change of circumstances of individuals who experience a need. For this to take place it is not necessary to change the social order in general, but only that individuals or groups change in social location within a given order.

CONVICTIONS

Convictions act as motives in a completely different way. What is really anticapitalistic in modern socialism does not lie in a demand for a different distribution of values but in the fact that capitalism is viewed and judged as an economic and social system. Here the question is not the distribution, but the evaluation, of values. The scale of values itself is subject to question and judged according to criteria that lie outside and above the social order itself. It does not matter whether this judgment rests on ethical norms such as justice or on scientific norms such as the correct understanding of the laws of development: a social order is judged as such, because it is in contradiction to a postulated scale of values. To the extent that it rests upon this motive, socialism is a movement against capitalism, thus oriented not to the capitalistic scale of values but to a completely different, even opposed, social order. Here is found the eschatological principle in socialism, because reality is judged by a self-transcending conception of what should be, and is absolute or is taken for absolute.

With reference to the motivational side, what is essential is that here there is striving for an overthrow of a whole order, and not just for private advantage, as with needs. The new order, the just order, should be for the benefit of all men. The motives that are active here are similar to those of religious chiliasm, which expects the salvation of everyone to take place in a new kingdom. Parallels with the phenomena of religious psychology as to the role of willingness to sacrifice as a source of enthusiasm and of strength are justified on this basis.

UTOPIA

Here we come upon the utopian element in socialism. I need hardly say that by the expression "utopia" is meant the strictly scientific meaning of the image of a wish located in time or space, without the vulgar addition of an unrealizable idea. One should be careful to avoid this pejorative use, for it takes only a little knowledge of technical discoveries and of political revolutions to understand that we live literally in the midst of utopias that have been realized. The radio, aviation, and the democratic republic were yesterday's utopias, as the utilization of atomic energy and classless societies are today's.

Social utopia is nothing but the idea, projected into an

imaginary future, of a social order fulfilling certain ideal requirements. But in their specific content these requirements are neither eternal nor absolute, nor do they arise accidentally. The history of social utopias shows that ideal images are always in a determinate relationship to the social environment of the time, or rather to the idea and evaluation made therefrom. They are really mirror images of reality, arising from the psychological process called compensation. Just as the tired and hungry dream of the land of Cockaigne, so the utopian projects his unsatisfied wishes and aspirations into a dream image that turns the hated aspects of the present into their opposite. The ideal image corresponds to the image of reality as a photographic positive to a negative.

It has often been noted that this psychological origin of socialist utopias is revealed by the manner in which they generally proceed by negations. The most effective expressions are negatively defined, such as the classless society, the expropriation of the expropriators, the abolition of private ownership of the means of production, the overthrow of the class state, liberation from exploitation and oppression, etc. When he is called upon to describe his future state, the revolutionary feels exactly as uncomfortable as the conservative when he must extol the existing order. Only that which is not wanted is really clearly expressed. Hence descriptions of socialist society have little scientific value as soon as they extend beyond the formulation of principles of opposition. Thus it is clear what is meant by the classless society to the degree that this idea is applied to the present-day reality of class stratification. But what is meant by socialization is much less clear. For no indication is thereby given as to the social means for socialization, but really only that a kind of property is wanted that puts an end to the present separation between the possessors of the basic means of production and the propertyless wage workers.

What utopia is to the final goal, myth is to the means: words as symbols of wishes and of commitments. There are students of Marx, such as the French syndicalist Georges Sorel,[8] who have had the scientific courage to interpret ideas such as "social revolution" or the revolutionary "general strike" by religious psychology and to present them openly as myths whose psychological function is the same as the religious myths of sacrifice and salvation. It is hardly necessary to say that no depreciation of worth is entailed in bringing forth this view from the standpoint of psychological function. On the contrary: myth has proved itself up until now the most potent force in history in its capacity to create culture and to shape reality—much more potent than the rational products of philosophical thought, which have become effective in mass psychology only as they have been crystallized in utopias and myths.

Utopias must not be confused with grievances nor with projected actions. They are summit panoramas, not climbing paths. Their real effectiveness depends on whether they point the way for an already existing wish to climb on the part of the masses, adequately sustaining a given collective volition. In other words, utopias and the myths that envelop them are always effective forces for the masses when the image that they paint corresponds to the frustrated needs and the resentments and convictions arising from the unrealized aspirations of the masses.

It seems perhaps odd that I here name needs and convictions in one breath, whereas I have taken pains to clarify the distinction between the two types of motives. The reason therefor is that in the practice of mass movements there is a continuous interlacing of motives. To be sure, the different motives must first be distinguished in order to understand this process, but once their differences have been recognized it is possible to understand rightly the relationship of the one kind of motives to the other.

[8] 1847-1922; most noted for his *Reflections on Violence*, first published in 1908.

INTEREST AND IDEA

The history of socialism shows a continual and reciprocal influence of needs and convictions, or, if the expression is preferred, of interest and idea. Just as every emotion has a tendency to evoke ideas, and every idea to produce emotions, so needs and interest on the one side, convictions and ideas on the other, stand in a permanent dynamic relationship.

Sociological and social-psychological consideration of economic problems is indispensable, because without this the quantitative and qualitative dependence of the economic needs of the masses on noneconomic facts cannot be understood. For instance, the whole problem of Asiatic capitalism depends on the question of the formation of needs on the part of workers and consumers, on the question of the work ethic and the work habits of the workers, on the business ethic of the entrepreneurs and the merchants. However, these are social-psychological phenomena, which are decisively influenced by religious ideas and cultural traditions. In Europe it is also evident how the needs of the masses were formed through ideas that in earlier times were largely religious, later largely those of political and social equality. The perfected techniques of transportation and of communication, schooling, the press, advertising, the cinema, and the radio have effects in this context hardly different from the ideas—utopias and myths, as far as I am concerned—that, first from the bourgeois revolutions, then from socialism, have formed mass needs. It is known that capitalism is the only economic system the inner dynamics of which are bound up with the dynamics of the universal and boundless expansion of needs, and this process takes place in large part by the instigation of new ideas. The American myth that a happy life consists of the possession of a single-family house, a car, and a radio, has the same effect in this respect as the old bourgeois myth of "freedom, equality, and fraternity" as the rights of man, or the new socialist myth, which has

turned the ideas of political democracy into the catchword
of the struggle for social emancipation.

But for the relationship between needs engendered by
capitalism and convictions sustained against capitalism, it is
even more essential to understand the process that leads
from the frustrated need to the judgment of the system—
or, if one wishes, from interest to idea. This process is so
complicated in its specific and historical expression that I
must restrict myself here to only a few suggestive headings.
Those who are interested in the course of the argument
may refer to my book *The Psychology of Socialism*. There I
have attempted to analyze the different elements of the
state of feeling of the workers, the essence of which I can
only tersely sketch here.

The essential drive of the working masses is expressed in
needs that, despite an increase in the absolute level of satisfaction, can only in part be satisfied. The balance of unsatisfied needs shows a tendency, relative to the needs that
are or can be satisfied, to grow. Moreover they in part include needs that in principle are not capable of satiation,
because they are formed by eschatological expectations
that originate in the cultural heritage of the Christian,
bourgeois-humanistic, and democratic environment.
These needs require (beyond any satisfaction of a desire
for gain) a degree of economic security, autonomy with respect to working and living conditions, social respect and a
right to participate in the organization of the society, which
perhaps is compatible with the capitalistic economic system—America has long made this plausible—but which is
in any case not compatible with the present-day social
structure of European capitalism. For this structure is that
of a hierarchy of upper and lower classes resting upon a
debasement of physical work.

This class stratification provokes among the lower classes
with a growing consciousness of reality a feeling of humiliation, a *social inferiority complex*, hence a class indignation,
hence a striving for compensation. According to the extent

and kind of frustration of need, this striving can take forms that appear as a movement within capitalism or a movement against capitalism. The relationship of the two tendencies—which can be called revolutionary and reformist in their political aspect—is complementary within any given situation. It is always conditioned by the relation of two psychological components of emotion, each one of which can increase only at the expense of the other. Everyday language gives the best names to these fundamental components: they are hope, and despair.

Hope dominates when the social rise of the individual and of his descendants—from a subjective viewpoint, that is, the overcoming of the inferiority complex—appears possible by virtue of change of circumstance in the existing environment. For this belief to take root it is enough in general to have the feeling that the chances at hand are growing; consideration of their absolute magnitude is of little significance. On the other hand, despair sets in when the feeling is dominant that the chances for mobility are receding. Then the striving for compensation moves from the personal to the general, then needs lead to the process of judgment, then social indignation is addressed to the economic system and to the social order, then a revolutionary will develop out of the will for reform.

And then that conceptualization of socialism that, like Marxism, represents anticapitalism most radically, appears as the closest compensation for the class feeling of inferiority. The thought of a total reversal of the existing relations of power, of a principled overthrow of the economic system, releases psychic forces of communal moral sentiments—solidarity, readiness to sacrifice, the ecstatic feeling of being the executor of the world's decree and the pioneer of a new manhood. This feeling plays the same role with regard to class inferiority as do feelings of identification with others in the cure of the neurosis of individuals. The inferiority complex is resolved and thereby put on a moral basis by shifting blame from what is personal to the system as a whole. The thought of the class mission of the revolutionary liberation of man creates a redemption similar to the beatitude concerning the poor and the suffering in the Sermon on the Mount: ye are the salt of the earth, the light of the world.

Perhaps Russian communism most strikingly shows with what monstrous effectiveness this alchemy of feelings can work. Indignation born on the one hand out of social and political humiliation, on the other out of truly religious feelings of the ecstasy of sacrifice, have here reached their highest intensity. The same men whose lust for revenge against class or party enemies knows no moral bounds have engaged themselves by the mystique of the revolution as enthusiasts ready for any sacrifice, glad to be able to serve as "cultural compost" for the making of the future. I hold this quasi-religious, prophetic function of Marxism, more than any scientific accomplishment it may have, to be the secret of its powerful historical role and the most realistic criterion for any judgment concerning it.

The Relationship of Marxist Theory to Capitalist Reality

Of course scientific criticism cannot avoid the question of how far Marxist prophecy agrees with an objective analysis of the development of capitalist society, especially since Marx's day. The prophecy in fact rests on the hypothesis that this development follows immanent laws that work out in such a way that the satisfaction of mass needs cannot increase but must always be less, so that the movement within capitalism must always become more a movement against capitalism.

THE FORECAST OF TRANSFORMATION

I depart here from Marx in that I hold as superseded the method on which this thesis rests. I believe that to establish such laws a priori, on the basis of a deductive analysis from an ideally constructed capitalism, has the serious weakness of leaving essential phenomena of the social environment out of consideration. In the first place among these phenomena I place the organized countervailing force of the labor movement itself, of which Marx of course could experience only the beginnings. If this historical event is treated a posteriori and inductively, it turns out that despite his remarkable insight into the essence of the capitalist economic system and its immanent trends of development, the neglect of many elements transcendent to this pattern of development led Marx to false anticipations.

I note here only the most important of these. The "historical and moral" component in the determination of the costs of reproduction of labor power, that is, the so-called indispensable needs, which Marx recognized but treated as inconsequential for this thesis, have in reality exhibited consequential variations. These are sufficient to call into question the thesis of the unavoidable growing impoverishment and degradation of the working class as a hypothesis expressing an ineluctable principle. The mechanization of production on the other hand has not led to the expected general and progressive reduction in skills of the working force, but to a growing differentiation of types of work between unskilled machine tenders on the one hand, and upgraded machinists on the other. Changes in the internal structuring of occupations have contributed still more to this growing differentiation of the workers' circumstances, especially with respect to their economic security. And finally, the institutional realization of the labor movement, growth of its power in the polity, legal reform of working conditions, recognition of a certain degree of participation in managerial authority on the part of unions, the development of the organizations themselves, and, not least, the formation of an official cadre, have called forth inner psychological changes and changes in motivation that in their essential characteristics do not fit at all into the social and political outcomes foreseen by Marx.

The Marxist thesis of the necessary transformation of

the movement within capitalism into a movement against capitalism is, to put it conservatively, at least made very problematical, at least in the sense that a growing number of socialists recognize that the unity of interest and idea, the postulate and the presumption on which the thesis of the causal series—capitalism, class interest, class struggle—rests, is not a phenomenon inherent to the economic system but rather a postulate referring to what should be realized. The growing unity of the workers' interests does not stem from the compulsion of economic laws at all; on the contrary, the economic tendency seems rather to add to the fourth estate of relatively well-off workers at least freed from despair, a fifth estate of the chronically unemployed and of serfs to the machine, for whom alone now obtain the words that in 1848 held for all the proletarians: you have nothing to lose but your chains. But the other groups still anticipate that working within capitalism will lead them in the direction of a gradual transformation into socialism.

I must content myself with this fleeting reference to the present situation of the reform-or-revolution problem, which indeed up to a point is also the problem of the split of Marxism into a social-democratic and a Communist branch. These references should suffice to show that the Marxist way of thinking has not for a long time been able to qualify as the expression of all the real impulses in the socialist labor movement. In my eyes what remains living in Marxist anticapitalism is the following:

1. A causal theory of the proletarian class struggle, which has the extraordinary merit of viewing capitalism as a *social* system and of placing the origin of the class struggle in the process of production.

2. The preparation of a program for international socialism that definitively puts an end to all utopian and moralizing cant and draws attention to the central cause of social exploitation and oppression: the ownership of the basic means of production by monopolistic private capitalists.

3. An effective critique of the old romantic-reactionary socialism, by demonstrating the necessity for the development of the capitalist means of production as a precondition for the realization of socialism.

4. A theory of capitalism and of its development that despite all revisions and emendations maintains the impetus of a pioneering scientific innovation.

THE THEORY OF CAPITALISM

It is particularly instructive to ask as to the reason for the extraordinary fact that Marx was at the same time the prophet of anticapitalism and the theoretician of capitalism. In this connection it is not without interest to point out that the expressions "the capitalist," "capitalistic," and "capitalism" are of socialist origin. They were first used by socialist economic theoreticians, to be sure with the disparaging emphasis that arises from the association of naked possession and unrestricted desire for profit with the pretension to political privilege, social superiority, and cultural prestige. This disparagement meant just about what is meant by the famous phrase: you speak of God, and you mean cotton. Or: you speak of culture, and you mean capitalism; you speak of freedom, and you mean profit; you speak of the eternal, natural laws of the economy, and you mean only the present interests of capital.

What was originally meant only as invective was worked up by Marx into a systematic and objective philosophical conception. The conceptualization of capitalism as a method of production in course of development, and thereby as the organizing principle for the social order and culture in general, was indeed first made possible by Marx. The pre-Marxist political economists furnished a structural analysis of capitalism but no analysis of social development.

It is thus very understandable on psychological grounds that official political economy and sociology, bourgeois according to a Marxist approach, for many years refused to take over this form of expression out of rejection of the

Marxist conceptual world. I must imagine that, if Karl
Marx were still living, he would have given a half-satisfied,
half-bitter laugh at the knowledge that in the year 1930 the
German Association for Instruction in Political Science[9] is
making its theme the study of "capital and capitalism." In
fact there is an important *mutatio rerum* reflected in this
fact. When I myself was studying political economy in a
German university about twenty-five years ago,[10] it was un-
acceptable for reasons of career for either students or professors to use expressions such as "capitalism" and "'capitalistic." There was only on one side the economy—national or world economy—and on the other, "socialist fallacies." Only a few academic socialists, led by Werner Sombart,[11] dared to use the expression "capitalism." Although
Marxism was already a half-century old, the original smell
of sulphur had not been completely eliminated. The
Handwörterbuch der Staatswissenschaften, if I remember correctly, used the term "capitalism" for the first time in its
first postwar edition. German academic scholarship is,
thanks to Sombart especially, still in the lead. The English
Dictionary of Political Economy still finds the central concept
of today's economics taboo, and the Anglo-American *Ency-
clopaedia Britannica* has for the first time (after a timid try in
1922) provided capitalism the honor of a special article in
the new edition of 1926.

These inhibitions are naturally not only of a philological
nature. There would be little stress laid upon the use of an
expression borrowed from Marx if one did not see in the
naturalization of the expression the symbol of the naturalization of a way of thinking. Indeed, the earlier repug-
nance for the term had its deepest origin in the repug-
nance for the recognition of its viewpoint as evolutionary,
hence dialectical, and hence critical. I am decried as a
heretic by orthodox Marxists for enough reasons to be

[9] The sponsor of the symposium giving rise to the present article,
among others.
[10] The University of Leipzig, 1905-1910.
[11] See, e.g., his *Quintessence of Capitalism*, London: T. S. Unwin, 1915.

able to say without suspicion of blind admiration of the master that present-day social and economic scholarship would stand a half-century behind if one were to take the name of Marx out of its history—note well that I have said scholarship in general, for I am also no orthodox Marxist in that I do not recognize any class limits to the validity of scientific truth.

Marx is to be thanked for considering the economy from the historical-development perspective on the one hand, from a sociological perspective on the other—by reason of which the modern economic order has for the first time been able to appear to us as "capitalism," instead of being, as with the pre-Marxist economists, the autonomous operation of quantitative laws of the market, simply an "exchange of goods." Indeed, despite the danger of exaggeration, I would like to say that nothing of what is today possible in the systematic and dynamic analysis of the capitalist system would have been possible without Marx.

To be sure, in this whole outcome I do not want to ignore pre-Marxist, non-Marxist, and post-Marxist elements, nor the so-called bourgeois criticism of Marx, such as the historical school, academic socialism, the theory of marginal utility, cultural sociology, cultural morphology, etc. It should also not be overlooked that other socialist theoreticians, precursors or contemporaries, have also made contributions to the theory of capitalism. I cite here only Saint-Simon and Proudhon[12] as the two greatest of those who are all too often undervalued—especially from the Marxist side, for in Marxism also there is an academic conservatism. Nevertheless the commanding significance of Marx's achievement is that he was the first to see capitalism (or the capitalist mode of production, in his own and better expression) within the general framework formed by conceptualizing a delimited historical and evolutionary social order, out of which the idea of an economic system could

[12] Claude Henri, comte de Saint-Simon, 1760-1825; Pierre-Joseph Proudhon, 1809-1865.

first arise. It is thanks to Marx that the idea of the economy as connecting not things but processes, especially those of the relations between men and classes, was legitimized in scholarship. It is only since Marx that capital appears, as in the *Communist Manifesto* of 1848, no more as a personal but as a "social" force, economic activity and the interests arising therefrom as the "effect of the social mechanism, of which the capitalist is only the driving wheel," and the development of the economy as conditioned through tendencies that lie within its mode of production. The sentence already enunciated by Marx in 1847, that "the relations of production of every society form a whole," is the key to understanding capitalism as a complex of social phenomena. Marx was the first, at least the first systematically, to see society as a process always undergoing change, the dialectical development of which takes place through the conflict of interests that arises out of the class-typed division of men in the process of production. Hence the conceptualization characteristic of his theory of the fundamental connection of the modes of production and social organization.

However opposed one may be to the particular conclusions that in part Marx himself, in part his followers, drew—and I myself reject most of them—yet one must acknowledge that it was Marx himself who first of all shaped the materials in terms of which the rejection can take place. The fundamental significance of the Marxist achievement for all general and systematic consideration of capitalism is illuminated by the fact that today, forty-seven years after his death, almost all debate on the principles of capitalism must take the form of a discussion with Marx.

And now we come back to the question: how is it and how can it be explained that the most incisive critic of capitalism, the most powerful prophet of its collapse, was at the same time its most revealing and insightful theoretician?

I believe that that is first of all derived from the fact that one can only understand a phenomenon completely from an external vantage point. Marx, who experienced the early period of industrial capitalism, found his perspective in the world of values in which he spiritually lived—that is, the world of ideas of classical German philosophy—the postulated values of which were in sharpest opposition to the scale of values of the real world by which he was surrounded. He understood capitalism to the degree that he hated it. All understanding is an act of passion, and everyone knows that there is an insight of hatred comparable to the insight of love.

At the same time love or hate can make one blind. That depends on the moral nature of its instigation and on its intellectual level. Only he who loves can effectively hate, he whose hate arises from injured love as Marx's hate from his injured love for mankind. And passion can only haltingly comprehend what the spirit of analysis succeeds in correctly perceiving. When these three conditions—moral grandeur, extraordinary insight, and demonic passion—are met, the rare combination of hostility and understanding can be realized. No one understood Israel better than Jeremiah; the Roman Empire better than Augustine; the Middle Ages better than Luther; the French Revolution better than Napoleon; capitalism better than Marx.

But if opposition can lead to understanding, understanding in its turn can change the original feeling of hatred into a spiritual passion in which there can be detected that remarkable undertone that psychologists call ambivalence of feeling. Every lasting passionate interest brings about to some degree an identification and changes hate into love-hate, as it can transform love into hate-love. The emotional ambivalence of interest that Marx brought to capitalism had, moreover, an additional base. The whole problem of the change from Hegelian idealism to a realistic conception of the social dialectic, the problem, that is, that necessarily arose from Marx's philosophical point of departure and led him step by step to dialectical materialism, consists in fact in demonstrating the evolution of mankind in the direction of socialism as the outcome of a historical necessity that worked itself out in the laws of development of productive forces and of modes of production. The chain of ideas with which Marx tried to prove that socialism must arise from the growing contradictions of capitalism—the theory of the contradiction of productive forces and the relations of production, of the reserve army of labor, of the falling rate of profit, of crises, impoverishment, and the class struggle in general—these things are so well known that I need only cite them here. What is here interesting is only that in his extreme reaction against utopianism Marx was led to leave out, or at least to conceal, the ethical values that had in fact determined his own interest.

From all this results that almost disquieting objectivity that made it possible for the *Communist Manifesto*, for instance, to include one of the most sparkling and impressive apologias for the marvels of the capitalist economy that has ever been written. An objectivity that stems not from coolness of feeling but from the tension between hatred of capitalism as a system for exploitation and oppression, and love for capitalism as an economic pacemaker for social production. For the laws of necessity from which Marx expected the realization of socialism are—and this is the essential idea of the whole Marxist conception—none other than economic laws, which prescribe the fate of the evolution of capitalism; growing accumulation, concentration, and expropriation; growing susceptibility to crisis up to the point of collapse; growing proletarianization; sharpened class opposition up until the sudden transformation of quantity into quality—up to the social revolution.

*The Relation of the Socialist Movement
to Capitalist Reality*

At this point we are led to the chief problem of the antinomy of capitalism and socialism, to the change, postulated but not conclusively demonstrated by Marx, of the movement within capitalism into a movement against capitalism. If it were only a, so to speak, metaphysical and formal conundrum, then the solution would of course be easy enough to find. For the Hegelian dialectic so beloved by Marx is rich in methods with which to cut some Gordian knots with the sword of logic. For instance, one can say: the movement within capitalism is a part of the movement of capitalism, which is continually changing itself until from self-development alone it becomes the opposite to that which it originally was.

Such general statements sound, to be sure, very fine, and can be supported as indeed plausible in a debate among metaphysicians, but I fear that they do not advance us one step to the solution of any real social questions nor to the specific understanding of today's situation. I believe that one comes somewhat further if first of all a simply descriptive analysis of the situation, freed from all ideology, is tried, and if one simply and modestly asks: how has socialism as a movement acted in relation to capitalism as a reality?

In my opinion, then, three areas come into question: (1) where the evolutionary tendencies of socialism tend to coincide with such tendencies of capitalism; (2) where socialist demands or realizations influence the development of capitalism, without really setting themselves in opposition to it; and (3) where socialism represents ideas or demands that are incompatible with the nature of capitalism.

COINCIDENCE

The first area, that of real coincidence, is speedily described. In Marx's words, it is the area of the development of productive forces; in today's everyday speech, it is technical development. Completely independent of all ideologies there are always real interests, which for instance impel the unions also to approve all means for technical mechanization and rationalization, if only they do not

injure the social position of the workers, for which it is sufficient to view things from the standpoint that the economy
is for the sake of man, rather than vice versa. With that
part of the working class influenced by Marxism these reasons find themselves reinforced by Marxist ideas such as
the development of productive forces as an instigation for
the development of capitalism into socialism, the ideal of
the liberation from burdensome work through the machine, the political necessity of the growth of the industrial
proletariat, etc. The power of these ideas is especially evident in the efforts toward industrialization, electrification,
and rationalization within Russian communism. But already before the World War they had lifted from the German workers the traditional opposition to technical progress, which has been entrenched much longer in the
Anglo-Saxon and Latin countries.

It is hardly an exaggeration when Heinz Marr[13] writes in
connection with the "belief in technology of German
socialism" and "Bebel's giant factory" that Marxist
prophecy "was the bridge over which millions have passed
with dry feet from an agrarian to an industrialized Germany." In an investigation of my own[14] I have countless
indications that the hostility against the machine that is so
widely found among the intellectuals scarcely finds echo
among the elite of the socialist workers. Socialism and
capitalism have both (to put an old image in modern form)
built the motor of technical progress into their cars.

In addition to this coincidence, largely of principle, as to
a constant direction of development, there is a pragmatic
coincidence with respect to the temporary solution of problems of crises. That holds at least for the non-Communist
labor movement. It is apparent that in depressions the
pressure of growing unemployment makes labor organizations concentrate all their efforts on the goal of the restora-

[13] [1876-1940], *Ford und Wir*, pp. 78-79 [de Man].
[14] H. de Man, *Der Kampf um die Arbeitsfreude. Eine Untersuchung auf
Grund der Aussagen von 78 Industriearbeitern und Angestellten.* Jena, 1927 [de
Man].

tion of economic activity. What temporarily is demonstrated in a very clear fashion is, however, a disposition that permanently dominates the policy of the non-Communist labor parties and unions. Only the Communists speculate on the decline and collapse of capitalism; the other socialists speculate on its rise, on growing productivity and prosperity—just as in politics the one speculates on war, the other on peace. There are solid grounds for the charge of the Communists that the socialist movement of Europe helped the capitalist economy onto its feet after the war. One has to think only of the currency stabilization, the displacement of the demands for socialization by the program for economic democracy, etc. The same thing goes for the opposite charge addressed to the Communists, who would have clung to a wreck and sacrificed the economic conditions necessary for a really socialist economy for the sake of the rapid conquest of political power. It is possible that in this controversy there is really only the difference of situation between agrarian and industrial states. In any case it is the fact that the non-Communist labor movement nowadays follows only the goal of avoiding collapse and therewith the revolution; it has completely committed itself to the parallelism of the slow institutional realization of socialism and the slow changeover from the profit economy to a managed economy.

The facts on which this optimistic and prudent conception rests are well known. They characteristically coincide, on the side of productive technology, with many late-capitalistic tendencies that belong to the chapter on the rationalization of production; on the other side, that of social economics, with certain tendencies directed against late-capitalistic monopolization on the basis of early-capitalistic ideas of the competitive market. I cannot here spend more time on these extremely interesting problems; I refer only to Heimann's[15] thoughts in his social theory of capitalism,

[15] Eduard Heimann, 1889-1967, whose essay was also included in the volume of which this article was a part.

which I can all the more easily do since I share his view-points. I will bring forth as especially important only the fact that certain internal structural changes of the capitalist firm bring with them certain psychological changes that belong to the preconditions for a socialist planned economy. I will refer to them with a catchword: the gradual replacement of the profit motive by the work motive within the growing stratum whose activity is decisive for the management of production. In place of the capitalistic entrepreneur appears more and more the salaried employee, an almost anonymous cooperation in the division of labor and of groups in economic management. It is thus that there is developing a generation of captains of industry who are learning to work for the sake of production, for the sake of work, perhaps also really for the sake of service. Thus a change in the spirit of capitalism is prepared, which in its turn is creating again a decisive psychological precondition for the structural change of institutions themselves.

MODIFICATION

With this we come to the place where socialism acts as a force modifying capitalism. In the first place there are the economic consequences of the fact that the labor movement has increased the price of labor through raising the level of needs and by organizing the supply of labor. Doubtless this is, on the one hand, a stimulating force, for certain aspects of capitalistic development, such as the mechanization of work processes, while, for other aspects, such as the accumulation of capital, it is, at least temporarily, a depressing force. In connection with contracts, factory councils, provisions for the mediation of disputes, etc., in general one can speak of a socially stabilizing effect. This is especially true for social insurance, above all unemployment insurance, although here a certain weight of the social burden has the tendency to slow down entrepreneurial activity. I refer only in passing to the monstrous and much disputed complex of problems that are connected with the increase of inner needs through the rise in the buying power of the working masses. The socialist consumers' cooperatives, producers' cooperatives, and workers' banks should also be mentioned, as should the successful interventions of the state, largely under socialist pressure, in economic activity, directly through governmental enterprises, indirectly through management of the economy. Thus one begins to get an idea of the variability of the effects of modification that arise in the most diverse ways from the socialist movement.

Of course capitalism does not endure all these interferences like a lifeless body on which one can try out any social remedy one wants. It has and retains its own dynamics, oriented in the last analysis to the motives of gain, power, and work of the entrepreneurs. And here the forecast of Marx continues to be valid, to the degree that Marx by and large rightly predicted how capitalism would continue to develop by virtue of its immanent tendencies, as if there were only these tendencies. What Marx described (to the degree that it is not simply a historical description of the industrial revolution and of early capitalism) rests on the abstraction of an ideal-typical economic form, obedient to its own economic laws alone. We know how far living reality departs from this schematized progression. But we also know that this schema is not a figment of imagination but in all essential things founded on real trends, actually observed by Marx in action during the heady days of their early development. The decisive charge against Marx in this regard is only that—completely in the style of his classical predecessors—he saw laws of necessity where, according to scientific method, are only trends that can themselves change or be overcome by other trends.

Certainly it is in the nature of such tendencies for unbridled capitalism, on the basis of the economic drive to monopolization on the part of the huge firms—and on the basis of the union of propertied superiority with social power—to develop in the direction of the organization of social domination. As soon as it can, it does just this—with the help of the state where that is available, against the state if it cannot be done otherwise.

The catchword of high capitalistic feudalism is no empty expression. Capitalism is not only a complex of market events; it is also a system of social dependence and hence of relations of authority. It has only replaced military and political by economic fear as a means of domination. The worker is subordinated to it because he must obey the entrepreneurial authority whose *ultima ratio* is deprivation of bread through dismissal. The consumer becomes more and more dependent to the degree that the determination of prices is made by monopolies and cartels in place of free competition. It is obvious that these tendencies would be carried through with brutal strength to their last neofeudal consequences if it were not for the countervailing raw force of human, and above all proletarian, opposition.

This opposition—I hope I have made it clear—is, in the consciousness of those affected, directed against the economic system only to the extent that the class division generated by this system, with the standard of living, leisure time, economic security, personal autonomy, dignity of labor, and social respect accorded to the inferior strata, is found to be *intolerable*. But tolerability does not mean here, I repeat, agreement with a conviction of absolute justice and dignity. Such an agreement cannot be reached by man, either in an economic system or in a political structure. Tolerability means here only that the masses have the feeling that they need not despair, that their situation can improve without their having fearfully to place all their hope on a given outcome since any risk is preferable to endless fear.

CONTRADICTION

To the degree that hope in a gradual improvement disappears, the third possibility appears in which the socialist volition is oriented to the most direct overthrow of the social and political relations of power, so that the working class can build an order that is the mirror image of the present order, namely, a classless society in which all the basic means of production and of exchange will be socialized, and their activity regulated according to need and by planning.

What is utopia for the movement within capitalism—the symbolization of a system of values and a goal to which gradual reformist activity is oriented—then becomes the direct demand that is to be realized by the violent political means of revolution. This is a perspective that is associated with a risk that appears too heavy for most European socialists. Bitter experiences have shown that other, less easily realizable conditions belong to the overthrow of the economic order than the conquest of political power. The capacity of new economic forms to produce can be demonstrated only by experience, and the most certain experimental method known up until now is still proving and improving through competition. It is for this reason that the conviction has become more and more widespread that the best economic way to socialization is to introduce planned, public-law enterprises into economic competition. And in a narrower sense, the workers on whose revolutionary indignation the revolutionary strategy rests, do not at all possess the knowledge and abilities that belong to the direction of an economy in an industrial state; but the indispensable collaboration of the technicians and the intellectuals is seriously endangered when it must be coerced by revolutionary violence. And finally the Russian example shows that in a world of national states any political overthrow by a social-revolutionary program interrupts the network of economic relations in a way that brings completely different difficulties and dangers from the evolutionary way that proceeds step by step. These and still other reasons mean that the great socialist parties of Central and West Europe count more and more on the contradictory tendencies at work in the present order and plainly seek to avoid catastrophe.

This is not to say that that will not happen. What follows

from all this, from the psychological reactions of hope and despair of the masses, is—what are the social and economic conditions for avoiding it? The intensity and the forms of capitalist oppression determine the intensity and form of proletarian counterpressure, decide as to the direction of reform or revolution. It is this that is at stake in the struggle outlined as to the tendencies of capitalism to develop. It is a grave, a tragic struggle in which no decision can be postponed without cost—how could one feel otherwise at a moment when millions of men are unemployed and in growing despair not because the economy produces too little but because it produces too much?

I do not believe that it is appropriate for the scholar to phophesy. I cannot say how the problem of capitalism-socialism will be solved, because I do not know. Scholarship can only state problems and show possible solutions. The solution itself is a matter of political action, which has sources other than simply the knowledge of what exists.

12

The Socialist Idea

A positive formulation of both a conceptual basis for the understanding of social action and the nature of and tasks before the socialist movement, was provided by de Man in his *Sozialistische Idee*, published in Germany just before the Nazi seizure of power. Indeed his book was to be banned and burned, and he himself to return to Belgium, where he entered upon an entirely new political phase of his career. In the new historical circumstances of the time, and in view of the fact that the book did not appear in French translation until 1935, the work did not compare in its public reception to the critique of Marxism with which he had made his reputation seven years before, despite the fact that it could be regarded as essentially a companion volume answering the questions he had himself opened up.

In its long and tightly packed pages, he attempted a thoroughgoing documentation of his basic contention that the socialist movement was a product of the collision between the basic value complex that was the precipitate of the historical experience of the West, and the contradictory institutions of industrial capitalism. Using insights gained from his familiarity with workers' education, his university studies in European economic and cultural history, his firsthand and deep exploration of the ineradicable significance of national differences, his wartime experience of mass psychology both in the trenches and in the manipulation of public opinion, and his basic identity as an heir of the Flemish golden age, he prepared a massive formulation of the origins, mission, and prospects of the socialist movement, a formulation based on an understanding of the nature of human action alternative to that of classical

Marxism. The theoretical outlook underlying the volume is perhaps most clearly reflected in the following excerpts.

INTERESSEN UND IDEEN[1]

Lutheranism, Calvinism, and Anglo-American Puritanism mark the major stages in the decreasing importance of estate status and in the increasing importance of individual freedom of conscience. Considered together, these stages correspond to the social background of the various Protestant movements in the sixteenth and seventeenth centuries, in that an antifeudal and individualistic tendency is realized to the degree that the social distinction between the ruling and ruled strata of the bourgeoisie is slight, and the role in this movement of those strata with little or no property is large.

Of course this does not mean that the social situation has become the cause and the religious doctrine the effect. On the contrary, in each instance it can be seen that the religious currents themselves have significantly contributed, helping or hindering, to rearranging the social order in given ways. Protestantism, notably Calvinism, can hardly be viewed as simply the ideal superstructure of a socioeconomic distribution of interests, since the conceptual unity of its fundamental outlook contrasts with a generally heterogeneous "economic substructure." The same faith united rich bourgeois of Dutch maritime cities, free peasants from the Swiss mountain valleys, bonded crofters in Scotland, and later also the colonial pioneers in the American forests. In this case one can speak of a common interest at best only in the sense of a spiritual interest that bound together all those who looked for the realization of their wishes to a new type of order, freed in spirit from feudal fetters.

The continuation of the spiritual currents that have so

[1] *Die sozialistische Idee*, Jena: Diederichs, 1933, pp. 102-108, 253-255, 258-263.

arisen through the variable phases of later economic and spiritual development also speaks in favor of this autonomous effect. The differences of social structure that still exist today among German, French, English, and American capitalism would not be what they are if it were simply a question of differences of tempo in the development of economic systems progressing in the same direction. They are also conditioned through and through by differences in economic ethic, which can be traced to differences of spiritual origins that go back several centuries.

Even if these differences were originally nothing but the reflections of various economic and social conditions (which however does not mean the same as economic class interests), nevertheless the fact remains that since then in the most varied types of situations they have exercised an influence for change in a direction that was determined by this original impulsion and not by the new situations. The capitalistic social order found in Germany today contrasts with that of West Europe and of North America by traits that correspond precisely to the difference between the half-feudal character of Lutheran Protestantism and the antifeudal character of Calvinism and Puritanism. If a liberal academic such as M. J. Bonn can characterize the social structure and ethic of capitalism in contemporary Germany as authoritarian in contrast to the liberal capitalism of the West, that cannot be understood without reference to the opposition between authoritarian and liberal Protestantism of four hundred years ago.[2]

In all this it is not at all possible to unravel economic causes and spiritual effects, spiritual causes and economic effects. Differences in the rates of expansion of productive forces and of development of the modes of production do not offer any explanation that is ultimately adequate. It is

[2] For a fuller treatment of the ideas of the German economist M. J. Bonn, see de Man's "Le Capitalisme autoritaire" and "Le Capitalisme libéral," *Bulletin d'Information et de Documentation de la Banque Nationale de Belgique*, VIe année, vol. 1, no. 2, 25 January 1931, and no. 8, 25 April 1931, respectively.

doubtless correct that, in comparison with England or France, the maintenance of feudal traits in modern Germany is connected with Germany's later development of industrial capitalism, but this explanation does not suffice to explain the delay in development itself, for it founders upon the fact that there is no question of such a differential development at the beginning of the seventeenth century. It is certainly not the Thirty Years' War alone that is responsible for the fact that since then the development of the German bourgeoisie in the direction of capitalism has been hindered; the outlook founded on Lutheranism itself has also contributed. Until very recently the German bourgeoisie accommodated itself to a subordinate position in an authoritarian state, whereas the religious or philosophical defeudalization of the outlook of the English or French bourgeoisie led to the destruction of the feudal system. When—with notable delay—industrial capitalism arose in Germany on a still half-feudal base, Lutheranism furnished for the bourgeoisie the ideological foundation for its good conscience as a class ruling over subordinate classes and for its lowly submission and political passivity with respect to the governing feudal and monarchical powers, while at the same time it put at its disposition a working class described as "docile and patient" by Troeltsch.[3]

The influence of the various spiritual forces originating four centuries ago is visible, moreover, not only in the social content of capitalism but also in the spiritual content of socialistic anticapitalism. In comparing German and West European socialism it is not difficult to set forth differences between liberal and authoritarian socialism similar to those that M. J. Bonn detected with respect to capitalism. The exaggerated emphasis upon the concept of class in German vulgar Marxism, the undervaluation of the significance of the individual in its political practice, its tendency toward bureaucratic solutions and state socialism that involve only

[3] Ernst Troeltsch, 1865-1923, the German sociologist.

a change in function in the tasks of the formerly feudal-monarchistic state, its trust in the efficacy of administrative regulation of the economy, its denial of the autonomy of moral considerations in the face of a given distribution of power—all these are characteristics that distinguish it from West European socialism exactly as in precapitalistic times Lutheranism was distinguished from Calvinism. Jaurès[4] was undoubtedly right in his famous work concerning the spiritual origins of German socialism to begin not with Germany's idealistic philosophy but with Luther. Similar ideological effects are apparent in the comparison between the two most important forms of West European socialism, the English and the French. The conceptual world of English socialism is just as obviously founded in the evangelical morality of the nonconformist Protestant sects as French socialism is in the rational morality of the anticlerical Enlightenment, which in this country, less indelibly affected by Protestantism, turned the spiritual opposition of the liberal bourgeoisie to feudalism into the form of an opposition of secular thought to Catholic clericalism.

But it matters little how one interprets these differences and similarities in detail; the development leading to industrial capitalism is codetermined in its direction, tempo, and forms through the formation of an economic ethic that can be characterized as the spirit of capitalism, and Protestantism had contributed to this formation long before there was any industrial capitalist system.

Nevertheless it would be just as one-sided and false to see in the formation of the spirit of capitalism "the" cause of the formation of capitalism, as vice versa. The two phenomena are not to be separated; they mutually condition one another in every phase of development. Capitalism would not have been able to expand if events belonging to spiritual history had not created the indispensable impulsions to its development and overcome the obstacles standing in its way. But this spiritual development is in its turn

[4] See note 14, chapter 4.

and at the same time impelled by the change of institutions and of interests associated with them. Neither Protestantism—as has been concluded from the works of Max Weber, perhaps unjustly but not without some degree of responsibility on the part of the author[5]—nor Judaism, as Werner Sombart has at times declared[6]—has created capitalism out of the "spirit of capitalism." Forces working in the direction of capitalism on the basis of the new possibilities of profit offered by the free market and the new life goals proposed by Western thought were already at work long before the appearance of Protestantism and were active on a much broader front than Jewish capital ever controlled, and the ideological repercussions of these forces had already made themselves felt in Catholicism before the Reformation. But undoubtedly the various forms in which since the Middle Ages religions have attempted pragmatically to resolve the tension between the original idea and what later became ideology—in order of their "chemical affinity" for capitalism: Judaism, Calvinism, Lutheranism, and Catholicism—these forms have influenced the direction of capitalist development, as well as of the corresponding political and spiritual structures in the life of nations, in a way impossible to view simply as the spiritual effect of economic causes.

Considered as a whole, Protestantism shows a double face, because it answers to a phase in the evolution of bourgeois culture in which the bourgeoisie was on the one hand still in conflict with the powers of the feudal past, but on the other hand felt itself already emerging as the ruling class. This is apparent also in the two-sidedness, at first sight rather paradoxical, of the religious and cultural effects of the Reformation.

On the one side Protestantism engendered a swell of in-

---

[5] Notably in his *Protestant Ethic and the Spirit of Capitalism*, New York: Scribner's, 1930; first published in German in 1905.

[6] *The Jews and Modern Capitalism*, Glencoe, Ill.: Free Press, 1951; first published in German in 1911.

tensified religiosity. It demanded that one take seriously
the teachings of Christ and especially the commandments
of evangelical morality; it justified its struggle against the
worldliness of the Catholic Church on the basis that the latter had betrayed its original inspiration; it showed itself
backward looking insofar as it proclaimed its determination to give back to this faith its original meaning and
strength and for that reason to return to the sources found
in the texts of the ancient Holy Scriptures.

On the other side, however, Protestantism decisively
contributed to that process that found its parallel in the
secular humanism of the Renaissance and its further development in the lay philosophy of the Enlightenment, and
whose most general significance has been characterized not
inaccurately as the "disenchantment of the world."[7]

To call on the biblical texts to counter papal claims
means, to be sure, on the one hand a return to old sources
of faith, but on the other, the road is opened in which
the bond between man and the written word that is given
him is formed by his own understanding and his own
conscience alone. Moreover, the written word became at
this time the printed word—the invention of printing is
just as real a material condition for the success of the Reformation as the contents of the Bible a spiritual presupposition of Protestant thought. Henceforth science can be
presented as the knowledge of the things of this world just
as theology is the knowledge of divine things; henceforth
the road is open for a shaping of life arising from the play
of individual understandings and interests instead of from
obedience to the Church as representative of the community; and these understandings and interests arise within
the autonomous man from "nature" and "reason."

To be sure, the ascetic Protestantism of the north laid a
completely different value on these concepts than did the
more confident secular humanism of the south; for the

---

[7] A phrase taken from Schiller which found a pivotal use in the thought
of Max Weber.

former, human nature and human reason are parts of a sinful world, to which man is delivered because he himself is a sinful being. In contrast, these words have for secular humanism a much happier sound in accordance with the tradition of antiquity living within it; it believed that man could feel himself at home in nature, if he would only use his reason correctly. But as for the end effect, it all came to much the same thing: it mattered little whether God was excluded from the world in reverently placing him above it or in impiously banning him from it; the conception of the world is profane, the values that can be realized within it are worldly values, contained in nature and attainable by reason.

This applied also to the social-economic conceptualization of the world, in which labor as the creation of value, and wealth as the possession of values, are treated henceforth more and more clearly as objective values, whose measure lies in utility and method of measurement in the process of exchange on a free market.

This process opened up by the Protestant economic ethic was carried out in the centuries that preceded the industrial revolution. It became clearer and clearer that the connection of labor to the working person was replaced by its connection to the utility of the product; it became more and more visible that the idea of property as an office or as a duty gave way to its conception as an acquired right.

Thereby the idea of work became farther and farther removed from its scholastic foundations. Its justification became more and more secular. Francis Bacon (1561-1626), who with the claim that all knowledge and all action should increase the power of man over nature represents the transition from humanism to the Enlightenment, still declared in one breath, "Man should work for the glory of God and for the improvement of man's condition"; with Locke (1623-1704) one already finds the idea that God has commanded man to "subjugate" the earth through labor—and hence property acquired by labor is inviolate.

The indissoluble unity, founded on social utility, of life and labor on the one hand, of labor and property on the other, became in the eighteenth century the very kernel of the secular bourgeois economic ethic, most outspokenly with Adam Smith. When Sieyès wrote the famous declaration of the French Revolution: "What is the Third Estate? Everyone!" he justified it by saying that the Third Estate represented the working producers, while the two superior estates were on the contrary only idle consumers. It is very symptomatic for the transformation of bourgeois principles into socialist implications that Karl Marx founded his entire critique of capitalism on the labor theory of value of Ricardo, the last of the great successors to Adam Smith. The spiritual weapon with which Marx delivered a lethal blow to capitalistic exploitation had been forged by bourgeois learning in its own struggle with unearned income. . . .

The proposition that "spiritual conditions reflect only material conditions," ideas only interests, is completely untenable. It hinders correct understanding of the bourgeois culture of the past just as it does the correct grasping of the socialist culture of the future. The problem of the relations of idea and interest must be attacked again as the young Marx put it, when he came to the understanding that the idea is powerless without interest, that consequently the socialist idea also cannot be realized unless it is rooted in interests that arise from the destiny of the masses and hence incorporate a social necessity. This way of asking things was correct, but in that which Marxism has since provided by way of answer there is much that is incorrect.

The first step toward the overcoming of these mistakes is to recognize that—at least as a rule in the case of classes and mass social movements—there is no such thing as an unambiguous interest determined through the economic situation. An interest is any cathectic fixation of the attention upon an object that appears in a positive respect as a means for the satisfaction of a need. From the subjective conditioning of this valuation it is already evident that interests cannot be determined only by the environment but by the way in which men behave vis-à-vis this environment. Just as this behavior is linked to the environment, so it is likewise linked to existing needs and to aspirations, which in their turn are influenced by traditional or suggested convictions of value, sentiments of justice, reasonings, and ideas.

The class interest of the proletariat in the realization of its socialist demands contains something entirely different from the economic interest of the sellers of labor power in the most favorable possible conditions of sale. It requires a choice between interests as special and general, closer and more distant, higher and lower, and this choice can only be decided by motives of conviction—that is, by value judgments and feelings. As an interest divided by no occupational or political boundary but whose unity has yet to be demonstrated in concrete action, the class interest of the proletariat is in reality crisscrossed by the most diverse differences and oppositions of interests for gain. It is unified only through an interest in bringing class domination to an end. But this interest is not in something already existing, like those objects to the attainment of which economic interests are oriented, but an anticipated goal. Proletarians must indeed be ready to sacrifice strong and urgent economic interests for the sake of this goal, and only under this condition can socialism make their class interest into its own.

In reality there are many interpretations of proletarian interests based directly on the circumstances of the proletariat that nevertheless can hardly thereby be called socialistic. For instance, this happens when shipyard workers support the rearmament propaganda of the naval shipbuilders in order to improve their chances for work, or when an organized group of skilled workers seeks to improve its situation by union action at the expense of unskilled workers, or when miners obtain an increase in wages with the help of protectionistic or monopolistic policies that work out to the harm of consumers and undermine the international solidarity of the miners themselves, or when the labor movement of a country supports a war from which an improvement in the relative economic power of the country is expected. Only those endeavors oriented to the interest of the proletariat as a whole without distinction as to sector of production or nationality, to the general interest of all workingmen, can be regarded as socialistic—thus a policy that would make the industrial proletariat a class favored at the expense of the agricultural producers would not be socialistic.

But this general interest does not coincide at all with the actual economic interests present; that is, with the needs actually experienced by the working masses. These needs and interests are for the socialist cause only raw material, which must be worked up to furnish a starting point for action, making little by little, on an experimental basis, so to speak, a general interest out of the divergent interests of the proletarian groups.

The valid central idea of the Marxist theory of proletarian class consciousness consists in giving to socialism the task of bringing about this general interest through carrying on the struggle for those interests that are common to all proletarians, making them the real impetus of the movement. The proposition that the general interest of the proletariat coincides with the general interest of mankind is justified only because in the end of this process "interest" is identified with the international realization of a socialist social order.

Accordingly the institutional demands of socialism must simultaneously depart from the interests at hand and be addressed through ideas to goals that are not yet realized, and the entire art of socialist politics, which in the end has to be an education in socialism through the experience of action, lies in building a bridge from interest to idea in

every situation upon proper supports. The direction and
tempo of progressive action are hence to be regulated so
that neither do the feet go other than where the head wills,
nor does the head so hurry ahead of the feet as to bring
about stumbling. In the historical succession of events the
institutional movement thus appears as a gradual approximation of the realization of an idea. To this corresponds
the psychological progression by which action itself
through its effects on the masses gradually illuminates their
consciousness, so that a socialist common interest emerges
from their capitalistic individual and group interests, thus
ultimately ideal motives from interested motives.

It is precisely because in the present situation of the
movement—in contrast to that of Marx's time—interested
opportunism has so strongly won the upper hand that the
fulfilling of the task propounded by Marx demands, even
in politics, a shift of emphasis to the leading, goal-setting
role of ideas. Precisely because of the progressive partition
of the world through nationalism, the further realization
of the common interest of the proletariat and of international class consciousness is not possible without orientation to a goal that goes far beyond any interest stemming
from national vicissitudes.

The unity of social idea and proletarian interest is thus
not a given starting point but rather a goal to be achieved,
proletarian interest not a directing principle but matter to
which the idea must give form. . . .

We can no longer be satisfied with the general question
of the relation of idea to interest. In his efforts to make proletarian interests the means for the realization of the
socialist idea, Marx did not succeed, despite correctly identifying the unity of idea and interest as goal, in arriving at a
psychologically consistent doctrine of motives in theory,
nor in a confirmation of his expectations through the experience of the movement in practice. The explanation for
this lies in the first place in the faultiness of his starting

point. He asked the question in much too abstract a way, as
if it were only a question of *the* idea and *the* interest, without
taking into serious enough consideration the concrete differences of value among different types of interests and
ideas. In his struggle against the reification of ideas by
speculative philosophy he did not free himself sufficiently
from the categorical forms of this reified thinking. His
tendency toward abstraction, so useful to him in the philosophical establishment of his theory as a means of systematic examination, prevented him on the other hand from
doing justice to the variability with which the reciprocal influence between ideas and interests takes place in the real
world.

In his time this fault was in a practical sense not so bad,
because the decisive task, in which Marx excelled, was the
unmasking of capitalistic interests hidden behind ideologies, but unfortunately it induced him during the second
half of his life to view the general problem, at first correctly
recognized, almost exclusively from the standpoint of the
criticism of bourgeois ideologies. That was all the more
evident among his successors who found themselves facing
a new situation in which the development of the labor
movement placed on the agenda on the one hand the problem of the ideological education of the proletariat, as a
consequence of the tendency to reformism and embourgeoisement; on the other hand the problem of the application of socialist ideas, as a consequence of the entrance
into a phase of positive construction of society and culture.

These problems have become urgent from the viewpoint
both of institutional action and of cultural life; they cannot
be solved at all any more by reference to the general question of the causal relation of idea and interest. They now
concern the positive content of the socialist idea, with reference both to the old goal of the transformation of society
and to the new goal of the transformation of life; they concern the relation of this idea to the contradictory interests
and needs that arise for the worker out of his social envi-

ronment and from the situation of the labor movement itself; they concern a series of concrete and particular decisions that should make it possible to assess given interests
on the scale of values of an idea so as to choose among
them which to support and which to combat.

If the unity sought by Marx between interest and idea
remains a pragmatic goal for socialism, this of course does
not prevent socialist theory from asking in its historical
consideration of the past how it came about that all great
social movements that (as most recently with the bourgeoisie) have led to the rise of a new class and to the installation
of a new social order appear as a realization of ideas and
interests at one and the same time. But this has nothing to
do with the general question as to whether ultimate causes
are to be found either with ideas or with interests. To be
sure, it is easy to debate this issue, but this debate does
nothing to advance us one inch toward the understanding
of real, concrete historical relationships. On the contrary,
as the example of Marxism shows, in the long run it makes
us turn our attention away from the real historical and psychological relationships so as—in contradiction to Marx's
intention—to turn the problem over to ways of completely
speculative and deductive thought leading nowhere.

Realistic and inductive consideration of historical events,
such as can, for example, be observed in the development
of the bourgeois period, helps one arrive at pragmatically
important conclusions with respect to the relation between
ideas and interests in modern socialism. The historical facts
show neither ideas nor interests as the ultimate cause of
development. They do not justify any conclusion on this
matter. They show only that those ideas according to which
men try to shape the world surrounding them are conditioned in their development through changes of the environment, just as are the collective interests of the classes
and the masses.

Additionally there is a direct influence of ideas on interests, such as, for example, the influence of the religious

Reformation on the economic ethic of the early capitalist bourgeoisie, or the participation of the socialist idea in the definition of class interest with the awakening proletariat. However, there is also an influencing of ideas through interests, for which by way of example the same periods and the same events can be used. This is not to suggest that in reality there are only mutually opposed relationships. For instance, we can certainly acknowledge those ideas as productive forces and therefore as real causes of events which, through their opposition to existing environmental conditions and paramount interests, appear as autonomous forces, but this always holds only in relation to given ideas and in a causal complex that is limited to a given set of events, so that the endless regression for causes lying further behind the appearance of this complex is excluded. Where the theme of the historian is the birth of a given hen, he may propose a given egg; if it is a question of the background of the egg laying, then he may name the hen as cause; but as to the question of whether the egg or the hen was first, nothing has been said. That is not answerable through a deductive procedure that attempts to trace back from one causal connection to another to the ultimate cause.

If, however, we cannot be satisfied with regarding each concrete group of phenomena in isolation, it follows that we can look at the relation between hens and eggs also from the standpoint of the development of the species. Then the question of who was first is no longer pertinent, nor even how given environmental conditions make the hen act on the egg, or the egg on the hen; then the concern is, rather, with variations in the relation between environmental conditions on the one hand, and given phenomena and properties of hens and eggs on the other. Translated to the problem of interests and ideas, there is then a meaningful and solvable cardinal question, namely, about the cause of the fact that in certain circumstances (which dominate especially in phases of cultural growth) ideas develop in the same direction as the interests incorporated in institutions, whereas in other circumstances (which especially characterize phases of cultural crisis) the production of ideas is dissipated in the opposite direction.

Consideration of the period of bourgeois culture, which has brought us knowledge of the social causes of the disintegration of culture, with its growing opposition between productive spiritual forces that continue to be active and the ideologies of consumption, furnishes an answer the validity of which is not limited to this epoch. Where interests appear as means for the realization of ideas that have already been expressed, ideas may be placed at the beginning of a causal chain of a given set of phenomena, while on the contrary in instances where given ideas can be demonstrably explained as accommodation to a distribution of interests that are already present, interests must be recognized as the cause of the ideologies; in the one case as in the other, however, the respective relation must be explained through conditioning by one and the same environment. And this environment in its turn cannot be understood as simply material nor as simply spiritual but includes material and spiritual "relations" and "productive forces," institutions and a cultural heritage all rooted in the past.

The bond between the development of interests and ideas does not consist only in the logical necessity of admitting common causes lying in the environmental situation. To the commonality of these causes corresponds a commonality of certain effects, which offers a homogeneous basis for the outcome of both ideas and interests. This basis must be sought in the collective unconsciousness.

The formation of both ideas and interests are events of the psychological consciousness that can fundamentally be understood as reactions of subjects to the stimulus of the environment. For a single mind to bring about the realization of ideas via their embodiment in the form of mass interests, it is sufficient for the originator on the one hand accurately to identify the environmental stimuli acting on the masses, and on the other to manifest the sort of patterning of behavior that corresponds to that of the masses in question. When both conditions are fulfilled, the idea appears simply as the conscious form of an evaluation, the interest for the fulfillment of which is experienced as a need. Evaluation and need, however, both presuppose an emotional reaction that takes place as such in the unconscious. In this way attitudes that produce a given pattern of reaction preponderate on the basis of a given human nature and of a given cultural heritage. The shared pattern in a given situation appears as the current content of the collective unconscious.

Shifts in the collective unconscious furnish the lowest common denominator for the formula that expresses the relations of mutual dependence in the pattern of development of interests and ideas. Scholarship assumed the task of their investigation only a few years ago; it is in its very beginnings. Means of understanding necessary to its mastery are at present spread out in the most varied special disciplines, whose different methods and modes of expression impede the finding of common conclusions.

History presents facts—for example, the fact of the acceptance of Christian, humanistic, democratic values by the modern proletariat, under the influence of centuries-old traditions and institutions—but it does not bother with the psychological processes whereby this acceptance takes place. The sociology of knowledge asserts the influence of the social environment on certain specific events of consciousness, but both for lack of psychological methods and at the same time for lack of consideration of the unconscious processes among the masses, it succeeds in most cases only in arriving at dogmatic affirmations as to universal causal relationships without adequate analysis of specific individual events. Depth psychology, which from analytic psychotherapy became attentive, first to the decisive role of the unconscious, then to the collective contents

of this unconscious, is still too much oriented to the etiol-
ogy and care of disturbances to health to be able to apply its
methods with success to the great collective phenomena of
social and spiritual history. Only the psychology of primitive peoples, broken off from so-called ethnic psychology,
has made a somewhat better application of its methods to
its object of investigation, and consequently has achieved
somewhat more satisfactory results, although many of the
conditions for the transition from ethnographic to truly
historical analysis are still lacking. For this reason one
gropes around on all sides, and much of that which is encountered is still most uncertain and unclear. The only
thing that is certain is that there is in this area, still little
known but in principle entirely accessible to scholarship,
the key to the central problem recognized but not solved by
Marx: on what is founded and how is realized corre-
spondence between the forces of historical development
that on the one hand take the form of the dialectical struggle of interests, on the other that of the dialectical struggle
of ideas.

13

The *Plan du Travail*

Despite the fact that he had won his international reputation as a socialist's intellectual, de Man's major preoccupation was never the splitting of ideological hairs but rather the resuscitation of the élan of the movement, which stood in sad contrast to the heroic days of socialism, when it was necessary "to be a hero, an apostle, in order to be a socialist."[1] With the onset of the depression and the rise of rightist totalitarianism, the plight and the morale of the remaining Western socialist parties were worse than ever, all the more in view of the fact that, out of a curious amalgamation of Marxist inevitabilism and classical economics, passive resignation before the political and economic catastrophe seemed to be the only possible policy, however distasteful in its consequences.

Against this defeatist and dreary perspective, de Man now appeared with a positive, activistic, concrete, and comprehensive policy of action for socialists, legitimized in terms of the esoteric ideological reformulation in which he had been engaged these many years. Returning to his homeland with the solicitation of the leadership of the Belgian Labor party, he prepared the famous *Plan du Travail* adopted as the party program at its tumultuous Christmas 1933 congress, during which he was by acclamation elected vice-president, essentially upstaging the grand old titular leader, Emile Vandervelde. In implementation of the *planiste* principles, there soon appeared under de Man's direction a relatively detailed specification of a whole series

[1] "Réalités et illusions du progrès socialiste," stenographic report of the address given by Hendrik de Man at Liège, 13 March 1926, *Education-Recréation*, vol. 8, no. 5, May 1926, p. 67.

of governmental measures to be adopted on both the political and economic fronts.[2]

Perhaps more important than the specific measures, however, was the tremendous recovery in morale that followed the adoption of a plan of action; de Man's essential contribution lay in legitimizing in terms of the ideology of the socialist movement the possibility of undertaking effective and immediate action both to combat mass unemployment and to lay a basis for political action that went far beyond the industrial proletariat, to appeal to all those suffering from the hegemony of monopoly capitalism. In political terms, it might be said that what Roosevelt's New Deal represented pragmatically in America, de Man's *Plan du Travail* represented ideologically in Europe. Its adoption by the socialists in Belgium played an important part both in the partial recovery of the Belgian economy and in de Man's personal career, even though the *Plan* was never implemented as such by the successive Belgian governments with socialist participation that emerged in the mid-thirties.

LE PLAN DU TRAVAIL[3]

The Congress of the Belgian Labor party, convened in Brussels at Christmas 1933, taking into consideration that:

Whereas the struggle of the labor movement to develop the reforms and freedoms hitherto gained, and even to maintain a tolerable standard of living, can, in view of the continuing economic depression, only be effective by undertaking a profound transformation in the economic structure of the country;

Whereas in order to be effective this transformation must bring about the reduction of unemployment by

[2] *L'Exécution du Plan du Travail*, Antwerp: De Sikkel, 1935.

[3] H. de Man, rapporteur, Forty-eighth Congress of the Belgian Labor party, Brussels, 24 and 25 December 1933; Brussels: Lucifer, 1933.

promoting the production and distribution of goods, through an increase in the purchasing power of the population proportionate to the development of productive capacity;

Whereas the chief hindrance to this policy is the private monopoly of credit, which guides economic activity by the pursuit of private gain rather than by the satisfaction of the needs of the collectivity;

Whereas, moreover, the dependence to which this monopolistic power reduces the state paralyzes all efforts to transform political democracy into a real social and economic democracy;

Moves, therefore, to assign as the goal for action of the Belgian Labor party the realization of a plan of economic transformation based on the nationalization of credit, the leading instrumentality to create an economy oriented to the development of the purchasing power of the masses of the population in such a way as to assure everyone useful and gainful work and to increase the general well-being;

Adopts the directives of this plan, as they are described in the attached document entitled *Plan du Travail*.

The Congress instructs the Office of Social Studies to undertake the detailed elaboration of all the measures that its realization entails in collaboration with the executive organs of the Belgian Labor party, the Trade Union Council, and the Office of Cooperatives and Mutual Benefit Societies;

Appeals not only to the working class but also to all classes of the population suffering from the present economic distress, and to all men of good will regardless of party or of faith, for joint action in this direction;

Decides that the Belgian Labor party will immediately undertake an offensive for the conquest of power by all constitutional means in order to realize this plan;

And declares that it will reject participation in any government not advocating the *Plan du Travail* as a program for immediate implementation, but is ready to accept for the winning and exercise of power the support of all groups favoring that program.

Plan du Travail

The goal of this plan is an economic and political transformation of the country, consisting in:

1. The institution of a mixed economic system including, in addition to a private sector, a nationalized sector comprising the control of credit and the principal industries that are already monopolized de facto;
2. The submission of the thereby reorganized national economy to directives of the common welfare looking to the enlargement of the internal market so as to reduce unemployment and to create conditions leading to increased economic prosperity;
3. The realization within the political sphere of a reform of the state and of the parliamentary system in order to create the bases for a true economic and social democracy.

I. NATIONALIZATION OF CREDIT

The legislative power will take the necessary measures to organize the disposal and distribution of credit as a public service.

These measures will include notably:

1. The creation of a State Credit Agency, with the duty of subjecting the operations of lending agencies to the directives of the Plan. An ad hoc legislation will allow for the transfer to this agency of shares the possession of which will be necessary to assure a preponderant influence in the control of the great banking organizations that at the present time jointly exercise a monopoly of credit.

2. The coordination under the guarantee of the state and in conformity with the directives of the Plan of financial activity of the institutions currently under the control of the state, such as the Postal Savings Bank, the Bureau of Postal Checks, the National Society for Credit to Industry, etc.;

3. A revision of the statute for the National Bank permitting this body to adapt its operations of issuance and of discounting to the financial directives of the Plan;

4. The reorganization of the system of social insurance in conformity with these directives;

5. The creation of a Financial Commissariat deriving directly from the legislative power and with the responsibility for the general direction of credit, the monetary system, and changes in the balance of payments.

Thus nationalized, the organization of credit will be oriented to distribute credit in the best way to bring about the adaptation of production to the needs of an enlarged internal market.

The acquisition of shares that may be necessary will be made either by mutual agreement or through expropriation by reason of the public welfare. The liabilities of funding will be charged to the Credit Agency. They will have a form preventing their use for ends harmful to the interest of the new system.

The staffing of the agencies affected by these measures will not be changed at all, provided that the interested parties demonstrate their readiness to give their loyal and devoted support to the reform envisaged by the Plan as a whole.

II. NATIONALIZATION OF BASIC INDUSTRIES

The legislative power will take the necessary measures to organize into public agencies the principal monopolized industries producing raw materials or power.

Within each of these industries there will be created a consortium with the task of integrating policy with the directives of the Plan.

These various industrial consortiums will acquire, by the same procedures already indicated above for the Credit Agency, shares the possession of which will assure them a decisive influence in the management of the enterprises in their respective jurisdictions. Within the consortiums the Credit Agency will exercise the rights of the shares forming part of the portfolio of the nationalized banks.

The industrial consortiums will be subject to the general direction of a Commissariat of Industry deriving from the legislative power.

III. ORGANIZATION OF TRANSPORTATION

In like manner a Commissariat of Transportation will be set up with the general responsibility for public transportation already organized in public agencies.

It will regulate in accordance with the general needs of the Plan the terms of the cooperation and competition among the various types of transportation.

IV. THE PRIVATE SECTOR

All areas of the economy that have not been treated under the preceding titles make up the private sector of the economy.

No change at all will be brought to the property system in this sector. The policy of the state and of the economic institutions governed by it will be guided in this regard by the following principles:

In all areas of economic activity in which the unity of property and of the application of the means of production has been preserved (as among artisans, farmers, small business, etc.), to protect this property.

In all areas of production organized on a capitalistic basis but which do not fall into categories of the monopolies of credit, power production, or of raw materials treated under the preceding titles, to maintain the present system of free competition unhindered by the shackles of monopolistic capitalism.

In this sector the system of competition can be expected to produce all that it is capable of producing from the viewpoint of the development of both the spirit of initiative and invention and the pursuit of increased productivity and profitability.

Individual savings will be considered as a legitimate form of insurance against economic vicissitudes and as a means for participation in the continual reconstitution of the capital necessary for reinvestments that the credit of the state and the development of production require. Savers will remain at liberty to decide as to the investment of their savings.

Legislation on inheritance will bring to the free transmission of goods only those controls necessary to prevent the reconstitution of a hereditary financial oligarchy.

The system of foreign capital invested in Belgium and of Belgian capital invested abroad will be submitted to the same principles: freedom of circulation limited only by necessities of national welfare and of the defense of the national heritage against any attempt at sabotage on the part of those hostile to the regime.

This private economy will nevertheless be a directed economy, because it will be conditioned, just like the nationalized sector, by the general directives indicated in title VI.

V. ECONOMIC COUNCIL

The legislative power will create an Economic Council, which will be associated in a consultative capacity with the financial Commissariats of Industry and of Transportation, with the right of initiative to submit any propositions to these commissariats or to Parliament, and with the right of supervision over the activity of these commissariats and of agencies submitted to the authorities of the latter.

VI. GENERAL GOALS OF THE PLAN

In order to stimulate economic recovery and to create conditions looking to an economic prosperity increased by the enlargement of the internal market, the state and the agencies of economic management will take necessary measures to influence the present situation so as to produce the maximum possible within the national framework.

In this effort there will be notably:

1. A savings policy looking to security of investment and to discouragement of speculative action in the money market;

2. A credit policy especially favoring areas of the economy that are appropriate to develop for the success of the Plan;

3. A price policy discouraging monopolistic exactions and speculation in commodities, and tending toward the stabilization of agricultural, industrial, and commercial profit;

4. A labor policy looking to the reduction of the hours of work and to the standardization of wages by the establishment of a legal contractual system for labor: union recognition, joint commissions, collective contracts, wage minimums;

5. A monetary policy that, while safeguarding the advantages that the amount of its gold reserves and the stability of its money bring to Belgium, allows increase in the purchasing power of the various occupational categories;

6. A commercial policy that, far from tending to autarky, encourages the development of foreign trade while favoring the general interest of consumers in moderate prices as against the private interest of certain producers in high profits, by means notably of the following measures:

   a. The readjustment of commercial treaties in the light

of the conditions created by the economic transformation of the country and by the new methods of international competition;

b. The reduction of measures of defense against the protectionist policy of other countries to the minimum necessary in order to maintain adequate purchasing power on the part of all occupational categories;

c. Recognition of the USSR;

d. The close integration of the Congo with the new national economy;

7. A fiscal policy making use of the budgetary increase created by the recovery of economic activity to lessen, in particular, tax rates that are levied directly on production and commerce;

8. A social policy making use of the budgetary increase to organize a complete system of social insurance based on adequate contributions from the beneficiaries and their employers and increasing the part of the national income going directly into consumption;

9. A policy for rents, tenancy, and mortgage loans lightening the general costs of industrial and agricultural production as well as those unproductive charges on trade that make it bear the heightened burden of rental income; and making the land tax the burden of the owners.

Altogether the application of these measures will be oriented to:

A. A broader satisfaction of the most urgent needs, notably from the viewpoint of mass nutrition and social hygiene;

B. Increase in comfort by the construction of new housing within the framework of urban policy;

C. The improvement of the economic infrastructure, for example by the electrification of the railroads and the construction of a highway network for automobiles;

D. Progress in education, notably in view of an increase in
    the age of schooling, by apprenticeship and reappren-
    ticeship, and by the formation of an elite corps of
    engineers, technicians, doctors, social consultants,
    teachers, etc.;
E. The realization of a comprehensive program for the
    use of leisure.

The Office of Social Studies will study the possibility of
ordering these steps in terms of a five-year plan, in the expectation of an increase in purchasing power within the
internal market of at least 50 percent within three years,
and of 100 percent at the end of the fifth year.

VII. POLITICAL REFORM

In order to reinforce the bases of democracy and to prepare parliamentary institutions for the realization of the
economic transformations that are envisaged, the reform
of the state and of the parliamentary system must satisfy
the following conditions:

1. All powers stem from unadulterated universal suffrage;
2. The exercise of constitutional liberties is fully guaran-
    teed to all citizens;
3. The political and economic system will assure the inde-
    pendence and the authority of the state and of public
    powers in general with regard to the money powers;
4. Legislative power will be exercised by a single chamber,
    all of whose members will be elected by universal suf-
    frage;[4]
5. This chamber, whose methods of work will be simplified
    and adapted to the necessities of modern social organi-
    zation, will be assisted in the working out of laws by con-
    sultative councils, whose members will be chosen in part

---

[4] This provision was the only one officially adopted requiring a constitutional change, but in the elaboration of the *Plan* expressed in *L'Exécution
du Plan du Travail*, all such changes were omitted in the interest of secur-
ing rapid and unproblematic support for the *Plan*.

outside of Parliament in view of their recognized competence;[5]

6. In order to avoid the dangers of statism, Parliament will give to the agencies charged by law with the management of the economy those powers of implementation indispensable to rapidity of action and to the focusing of responsibility.

[5] An expression of de Man's predilection for corporatism, spelled out in his *Corporatisme et Socialisme*, Paris-Brussels: Labor, n.d. [1935]—an attitude rare among Continental socialists but finding some echo in English "guild socialism," as with G.D.H. Cole, who expressed support for *planisme* at this time.

14

The Theses of Pontigny

The ideological rationale of the *Plan* was most graphically set out in a series of propositions put forth by de Man at an international conference called to consider *planisme* in 1934 at the Abbey of Pontigny in France. Here are found the economic and political parameters of the *Plan*, establishing the minimum and maximum dimensions of the program of "structural reforms" to be followed, and later there is an explicit rejection of *ouvriérisme*, or the cultivation of the industrial proletariat as the only feasible basis for the achievement of socialist objectives. Another familiar element of de Man's thought is represented by the explicit recognition of the conceptual and pragmatic separation of ownership and the exercise of control, an insight that eased the political legitimation of a managed economy within a bourgeois society.

At this point the international *retentissement* of *planisme* was still great, although the refusal of the French Socialist party under the leadership of Léon Blum to approve such a program despite its adoption by the Confédération Générale du Travail removed the most important site on the Continent for its application, now that Germany had been taken over by the Nazis. Though Blum's move was couched in esoteric ideological terms, the basis for his action was primarily tactical, namely, to avoid contributing to a split in the party divided particularly between orthodox Marxists and the neo-socialists. Nevertheless, it should be pointed out that *Plans* of vaguely de Manian inspiration were advanced by a dozen or so groups within France, and, furthermore, that the socialist parties of Czechoslovakia, Switzerland, Norway, and Holland all officially adopted

Plans. Lastly, the idea of planning itself, as reflected in attendance at two international conferences succeeding the one reported below, found support among such figures as G.D.H. Cole, Colin Clark, Hugh Gaitskell, Carlo Rosselli, Bertrand de Jouvenel, Georges Gurvitch, to mention only a few names of international significance.[1] The last thesis below, which was added at the conference itself, was soon reflected in the slogan, "The Plan, the whole Plan, and nothing but the Plan," a commitment that proved embarrassing at the time, in spring 1935, of the decision of the Belgian Labor party to enter a tripartite Government of National Renovation pledged not to *planisme* but to reversing the disastrous economic consequences of the deflationary policies of the preceding administrations. De Man served as minister of public works in this government, and subsequently as minister of finances until 1938. The cautious reflationary policies of these governments, aided by a massive program of public works, contributed to a gradual reduction of unemployment, but de Man found himself frustrated by the opposition of the financial community, which was hardly keen to cooperate with a minister whose *Plan* envisaged the nationalization of credit as the indispensable first step to the assertion of social control over the economy.

Under these circumstances, he experienced deep misgiving as to the course of events, for if *planisme* was not integral socialization, participation in bourgeois governments was not even *planisme*. In the desperation of the late thirties, it seemed to de Man that perhaps the last best chance for the achievement of socialism had been effectively foiled by the resistance of the occult powers of finance.

[1] See Henri Brugmans, "Henri de Man et les Pays-Bas," pp. 143-149; Georges Lefranc, "La Diffusion des Idées planistes en France," pp. 151-167; Alain-Gérard Slama, "Henri de Man et Les Néo-traditionalistes français (1933-1936)," pp. 169-188; and, finally, Georges Lefranc, "Les Conférences internationales des Plans et la Commission internationale des Plans," pp. 189-196; all in *Revue européenne des sciences sociales et Cahiers Vilfredo Pareto*, vol. 12, no. 31, 1974.

LES THÈSES DE PONTIGNY[2]

1. The present economic crisis is organic. It results from the fact that, after have been progressive, the evolution of capitalism has entered into a regressive stage.

   This change is visible in three principal dimensions:
   a. Predominance of finance capital in place of industrial capital;
   b. Systematic monopolization in place of competition in the key positions of the economy;
   c. Economic nationalism in place of international expansion in the world market.

2. By virtue of this situation, reformism, which has in practice dominated the labor movement up until now, has become unviable. Distributional reforms have become incapable of realization, save for structural reforms sufficiently radical to influence the course of development noted in section 1.

3. The labor movement must give up its passive attitude with regard to the economic crisis. It should replace its deterministic theory of the business cycle—basically of capitalistic origin—with a voluntaristic policy, the immediate though partial goal of which would be to eliminate unemployment and to overcome the slump.

4. The goals of this policy must be defined so as to be capable of realization by means of action available within the national framework and by the reorganization of the internal market.

5. To define these goals, it is necessary to establish:
   a. A minimal condition, by raising the question of what are the indispensable steps for efficacious action against the slump within the national framework;
   b. A maximal condition, that stems from the question of what can be done, given the present makeup of active social forces, to bring about a political major-

[2] Appendix 1, *l'Idée socialiste*, Paris: Bernard Grasset, 1935.

ity by means of the common interests of a sufficient proportion of the population.

The question of the minimum is economic; the question of the maximum is sociological and political.

6. The solution that answers to this double condition is a mixed economic system (a nationalized and a private sector), which can be considered as transitional between the capitalist and the socialist economies.

7. The principle that can give structure and impetus to such a mixed economy is that of the managed economy, that is, the use of political power to create the economic conditions for the adaptation of consumption to productive capacity.

8. This goal implies a double shift in emphasis in the theory of socialization:

   a. National implementation is no longer to be subordinated to international implementation and takes precedence over it, which means that the present form of socialization can only be nationalization;

   b. The essence of nationalization is less the transfer of ownership than the transfer of authority; or, more exactly, the problem of administration takes precedence over that of possession, and changes in the property system are functions of changes in the system of authority required by the managed economy.

9. So that the extension and reinforcement of the authority of the state stemming from this new economic function may not lead to internal bureaucratization and external imperialism, the new economic state must be differently organized from the former political state: an autonomous corporative organization of firms nationalized or managed by the state, a removal of the processes of administration from parliamentary responsibility, a change in the theory of powers, etc.

In place of the classic theory of bourgeois democracy, which no longer corresponds with present-day realities, one must substitute a new theory based upon a different conception of the separation of powers. The executive is to administer, the representative institutions are to supervise. In this way, within the new economic state now in the course of formation the representative institutions, that is, those based on the exercise of the right of individual suffrage, will have only the right of inspection and supervision; the exercise of the right to administer will be based on the delegation of powers by the executive and through the representation of corporative interests.

10. In fighting for the realization of its goals the socialist movement must give up its "laboristic" prejudices, which have become obsolete since the evolution of capitalism has stopped giving rise to a continuing increase in the number of proletarians. The immediate political goal is the formation of a majority which, beyond the proletariat, includes as large a section as possible of the so-called middle classes, while neither anticipating nor promoting their inclusion within the proletariat, and accepting their will to resist proletarianization.

11. The formation of this alliance implies that it be directed not against capitalism as a whole but rather against that which, within the capitalist system, constitutes the common enemy of the working classes, proletarianized or not: monopoly capitalism and, most of all, finance capitalism.

12. In countries with political democracy, the action to take must be based exclusively on the use of legal and constitutional means for the attainment of a majority through persuasion. This majority is not only a political necessity but above all an economic one, because the functioning of a system of mixed economy presupposes under all circumstances a minimum of con-

sent. The economic majority is at least as indispensable as the political majority.

13. Planning must take the place of programs. The success of any attempt at a managed economy presupposes a complex of measures that are mutually conditioned and which for their successive realization must be staggered and coordinated in time. Moreover, the Plan, in contrast to a program, forms for those whom one wants to attract by propaganda in its favor a strict obligation to use power for a limited goal, the realization of which must begin forthwith and be completed within a limited period.

14. The concentration of all the effort of the labor movement on this goal can bring out its full effects only if the socialist parties make the motto, "all the Plan, nothing but the Plan" the basis of their political strategy, asserting that they are ready to govern with the support of all those who accept the Plan, but that they refuse to enter into a government that does not satisfy this condition.

15

Must One Sacrifice Peace to Freedom?

De Man's participation in World War I was to be fateful in more ways than one. As we have seen, the intellectual and moral necessity of rationalizing his wartime commitment had precipitated the reformulation of socialist ideology, and thereby of the underlying conceptualization of social action, with which he came to make his distinctive contribution in writing of sociological as well as of socialist import. Of course, other elements of his historical setting and experience also deeply influenced his ideas and his conduct. But that searing experience of war remained as a primordial referent for his adoption of basic policy, as the sequel was also to show.

As a pacifist and internationalist, he had volunteered for military service upon the collapse of the International on the basis of a half-conscious identification with the victims of unprovoked aggression and with the conviction that only thereby could he serve those causes—including those of pacifism and internationalism—to which he had resolved to give his life. Hence, the outcome of the war became, as we have seen, a matter of overpowering concern for him, and the intensity of his disillusionment with Versailles and the postwar world of the victors could be summed up simply in the proverb: once bitten, twice shy. Never again would he be taken in with the propaganda of the warmongers whatever their pretentions; never again would he be persuaded to sacrifice his most cherished values on the premise of thereby contributing to their ultimate realization.

With hindsight, the fallacies of the *Munichois* may appear banal, but the moral intensity and historical plausibility of their arguments cannot be gainsaid. As de Man had been a bitter-ender in the war, so he continued in peace, for he remained true to the convictions expressed in the following article even through the first year of the Nazi occupation of Belgium.

FAUT-IL SACRIFIER LA PAIX À LA LIBERTÉ?[1]

Bellicose Pacifism

One of the most dangerous aspects of the present situation in Europe is that a great part of the traditionally peaceful forces are now acting in a way that increases the risks of war. Until very recently those men most impassioned for social justice and political liberty, headed by the socialists, were also the most decided adversaries of any war and of any diplomatic or military policy that could lead to it.

For some time this situation seems to have been deeply changed. This is the outcome of a development that took form after Hitler's triumph in 1933, became pronounced after the reoccupation of the left bank of the Rhine, the Italo-German intervention in Spain, and the *Anschluss* of Austria, and has attained full flower after the Munich Agreement.

At the end of this development there is a belief that liberty can only be saved by a coalition of nonfascist states marshaling their military strength against that of the totalitarian states. Those who hold this position may continue to reject preventive war, the war of liberation, or even the inevitability of war, but it cannot be denied that the logical outcome of their current premises is that to the extent that

---

[1] *L'Oeuvre* (Paris), 27 November 1938; reproduced as part of a pamphlet, *Une Offensive pour la Paix*, Paris and Brussels: Labor, 1938.

they are right in believing that the fascist powers want war,
Europe will not escape it.

One of the most influential representatives of this conviction, Emile Vandervelde, avowed at a recent congress of
the Belgian Labor party that he did not believe in the possibility of making peace with the totalitarian states unless
their governments were to be overthrown by internal revolutions, the which he moreover recognized was improbable
at the present time.

Thus many persons who have always been the most pas-
sionately attached to what they considered as the inseparable cause of peace and liberty have now come to say: rather
liberty without peace than peace without liberty! It is obvious that they no longer believe—as I continue to do, despite everything—that one can choose between liberty and
peace on the one hand, and war and servitude on the
other.

A surprising paradox: while maintaining an attitude that
ineluctably leads to war because it despairs of peace, they
can continue to regard themselves as faithful to their old
pacifist ideal, without being subject to the accusation of bad
faith. For this attitude is derived from an antifascist passion
which is itself nourished by a pacifist passion. And it is supported by the fact that in reality the fascist states have been
the only ones for some years to threaten Europe with war.

Certainly Hitler has declared that Germany has no more
territorial demands in Europe and that the question of col-
onies will not lead to the mobilization of armies. Certainly
he also cannot be unaware of how much the idea of a new
war horrifies his own people. And there are many who, like
me, have often believed the evocation of the frightful
image of war in his speeches to reveal the sincere tone of
the veteran who has not forgotten what that word means.
But all this does not mean that his policy has not implied,
many a time, recourse to force, or at least to the threat of
violence. Munich has shown with fearful clarity that countries with democratic systems obey the *Diktat* of those who

used this threat, and this only confirms a cardinal ideological stance of authoritarian states, practiced as much in Africa and Asia as in Europe.

Let us then recognize, without having to impute to Germany and Italy any present intention of making war, that the recent past has at the very least solidly justified the belief in the division of Europe into two camps: the totalitarian states, which do not shrink from aggression, and the others, which want peace.

It is this that explains how the pacifism of some has been transformed into a latent bellicism, in a neo-Jacobin mode varying the old formula which has so many times already brought war out of the armaments race: *si vis pacem, para bellum*.

So that there may be no mistake: whatever the explanation that can be given to this psychological change, it leads no less surely to a frightening contradiction between its psychological origin—the attachment to peace—and its final pragmatic result: the fatality of war.

War Kills Liberty

This contradiction is found in the most variegated expressions, but they are all equally symptomatic of a fundamental mistake in judgment. First of all, the contradiction between the goal of "liberty" and the means of "war": the traditional enemies of the militaristic *grandes illusions* that led to 1914 cannot have forgotten certain truths in this respect, of which they have been the courageous bearers for such a long time. War resolves nothing. There is no more a "good" war between peoples than there is a "good" murder among individuals. The results of war are always worse than any evil whatsoever that it seeks to avoid. It always leaves behind it only conquered peoples, even in the victorious camp.

And war is always a loss for liberty. For from its beginning it necessitates such a concentration of wills on a single

objective that it automatically brings for all peoples a totalitarian and authoritarian regime, in the fullest sense of
both these words. Even if a modern war were not to bring
about literally the suicide of Europe, it would lead at the
very least to the suicide of liberty. It is already apparent in
the democratic countries that to the degree that the obses-
sion with war becomes more compulsive not only is all social progress halted by the economic and financial consequences of the armament effort, but the accompanying
psychological climate tends likewise to lessen progressively
the difference between the authoritarian countries and
those democratic up until now.

For here now is the second basic contradiction to which
the neo-Jacobins lead: a contradiction not only with the future consequences of what they do but even with the
present-day circumstances to which they want to attune
their action. They strangely undervalue the difference between the Europe of 1792 and that of 1938. They see it as
if it were made up of two homogeneous blocs, the "Western" bloc being identified in their eyes with the cause of
democracy, liberty, and international justice. This is to dis-
tort reality, notably the economic reality that holds that in
Europe there are not only different political systems but
also one bloc of sated, another of ravenous, imperialisms.

This is also to forget that Munich has shown how little
the two principal democratic powers of Europe can be considered the champions *sans peur et sans reproche* of international equity as to the right of small nations to dispose of
themselves, and even of the respect for honorable en-
gagements taken in their regard, either in the form of collective security or in that of military alliances.

Hence, those who see no solution to the present situation
other than the policy of one military bloc against the other,
than an armaments buildup that bleeds people white before sending them to the charnel house, will end up,
whether they wish it or not, in the destruction both of the
peace they wish to defend and of the liberty they wish to
save.

To Make a New Peace

But I know very well that the retort can be made: you who argue that there is no salvation outside of peace and who believe this peace is possible in present-day Europe, are you yourself also not running up against a predicament with no solution? Isn't it obvious that the totalitarian states, precisely because they represent imperialisms hungry for raw materials and territories for settlement, because they are moreover fanaticized by theories of violence, do not want peace, except by an uninterrupted series of capitulations that will end by making them the uncontested masters of Europe?

Most assuredly the organization of peace also involves enormous difficulties and risks of failure. But these difficulties are far from being unsurmountable, and the possibilities of success are incomparably greater than that of a policy that leads to general warfare.

Moreover we must not be deluded: the problem is capable of solution only if it is considered as concerning not the maintenance of the present-day peace at all but the construction of a new peace. This involves a gigantic task, which can be realized only by a series of arduous and tenacious efforts and if one has the courage from the beginning not to refuse new objectives or new methods.

The new objectives will be those of a peace that, drawing all the lessons from the failure of the peace of Versailles and the weakness of the League of Nations, realizes a comprehensive solution in order to eliminate the "causes" of existing antagonisms, instead of acting only on the symptoms.

For my part, I see the dominant traits as follows:

1. The replacement of the treaties of 1919 by new agreements freely accepted;
2. Progressive and simultaneous disarmament;
3. General renunciation of military alliances;
4. The complete reorganization of the League of Nations on these bases;

5. The progressive lowering of economic barriers;
6. The complete revision of the system of colonial pos-
sessions, looking to the rational distribution of raw
materials and to the "open door" for international
commerce and for settlement;
7. The definitive cancellation of all international debts;
8. The abolition of all hindrances to the international
circulation of capital and of persons.

As for the method, I see only one that can give good results, namely, to hand over all new satisfaction of the demands of the totalitarian states to a General Conference of
Peace, bringing together *all* the states for the joint examination of *all* the problems.

I do not think that it will be denied that this solution
would be infinitely preferable not only to war but also to
the repetition of the employment of the procedures of
Munich.

Is it realistic? Who would dare to assume the responsibility of denying it—a frightful responsibility in the face of
the alternative that war constitutes!—before having tried to
do it?

May it then be tried, and without longer waiting. A psychological moment is favorable, since, after the passing
euphoria of Munich, it is sadly evident to the whole world
that we are as far from real peace now as we were two
months ago.

16

Democracy and
the Frustration of Socialism

The tragic climax of de Man's political life was compounded essentially of two ingredients: his fidelity to a pacifist stance rendered absolute by virtue of his experience of World War I and its aftermath; and a growing conviction, emergent from his political experience in Belgium, that a socialist breakthrough could come, not through the devious and irresolute procedures of the parliamentary democracy with which he was tediously familiar, but only through determined and autonomous leadership by a responsible political elite operating within a refurbished constitutional framework. He had now arrived at the reversal of the conclusion, the validation of which had been essential to justify his actions during World War I, that "political democracy—that is, a certain minimum of political rights and laws—is the absolutely indispensable condition for the success of social revolution."[1]

This commitment to democratic political institutions, while real, had always been defined in substantive terms, that is, as an indispensable means for the attainment of socialism, or as meaning self-determination, notably with respect to working conditions. He had never subscribed to a procedural appreciation of democracy as a means for the reconciliation of political differences. Undoubtedly his attitude in this respect reflected his naive belief—in turn the product of the intensity of his convictions—that underneath all the strife of interests and misunderstandings there was a common substratum such that good men,

[1] See above, p. 32.

properly instructed as to the facts, could not but be socialists. "The true Catholic, the true Moslem, the true Buddhist, the true agnostic, inevitably end up not only by meeting on a level superior to their differences but also in resembling one another by virtue of developing a like departure from their original positions."[2]

In the apocalyptic atmosphere of the late thirties and in view of the contrast between the diabolical dynamism of the fascist governments and the torpid inertness of the bourgeois capitalist regimes of the West, de Man called ever more urgently for the creation of strong, "authoritarian" and "national" governments capable of supplying resolute leadership to their peoples. With nothing but personal contempt for the art of political compromise, which he invariably interpreted in terms of personal venality, he came to view the practice of parliamentary democracy as simply furnishing a bastion for the defense of capitalist interests. He borrowed brazenly from the fascist vocabulary in calling for the construction of governments that could carry through bold and imaginative projects against the opposition of special interests, urging the indispensability of corporatist representation to which the activist political elites should be held periodically accountable.

A close examination of the constitutional reforms that he advocated in a series of articles as president of the Belgian Labor party in 1939-1940 reveals, however, that despite his flamboyant vocabulary and provocative ideological heresy, the actual changes discussed were in the direction of establishing a stable executive to replace the current parliamentary practice of a dreary and endless succession of governmental crises dissipating responsibility and vitiating the possibility of executing any coherent and effective long-term policy. Indeed, de Man evinced some degree of respect for the Scandinavian and Anglo-Saxon political sys-

[2] *Cahiers de ma Montagne*, Brussels-Paris: Toison d'Or, 1944, pp. 188-189.

tems on the basis of their relative stability and decisiveness. But for the weak and vacillating systems of Belgium and France, he had nothing but contempt.

HERVORMING VAN DEN STAAT VOORAF![3]

In the previous number of *Leiding* I spelled out why I think that we must henceforth place the reform of the state at the forefront of our immediate demands. I expected that there would be those in the Belgian Labor party who would consider my position as largely heretical, or anyway as at the very least dangerous. I expected caustic reactions, strong admonitions from those who for years have upheld the conservative motto of "the defense of existing democratic institutions" as the only means of salvation against fascism.

To my astonishment I must admit that this reaction has been lacking. On the contrary, since then I have heard a number of leading party members—including Walloons, most certainly not familiar with my article—use the expressions, "the crisis of democracy" and "the indispensable reform of the state," and I was not used to hearing such expressions from these men. And on February 11 the executive committee of the Belgian Labor party voted unanimously, except for one abstention, for a resolution that ended with the following decisive phrase: "The Belgian Labor party is ready to join in any governmental program that is of a nature better to assure the steadfastness and durability of governmental action."

Among the cadres of our party the emphasis has apparently shifted more and more from the *defense* of democracy to the *reforming* of democracy. And this change is to be at-

[3] *Leiding*, vol. 1, no. 2, February 1939, pp. 68-73. It might be noted that, as is reflected in the second paragraph of this article, de Man interpreted his relegation to the editorship of this Flemish Labor party journal in place of that of its officially co-equal *Revue socialiste* as an attempt to sidetrack his influence, in view of the fact that while most Flemings master French, Walloons tend to take pride in their ignorance of Flemish.

tributed much more to the direct influence of events than to the influence of theoretical considerations.

For one must be really afflicted with blindness not to conclude from the events of the last months and weeks in Belgium that we have to deal with a deep, organic crisis of our system of government.

I described the symptoms of the crisis in my last article, as I have learned to know them during the course of three years of participation in government. There I dealt with points that, although they are of decisive importance, have been exposed in their full significance only to the host of men who have had personal experience within governmental service. Some of these points, and not the least of them—such as the influence of extraparliamentary forces, especially of the money powers—are known to public opinion only very vaguely and inadequately. Here we are always dealing with events that by their very nature mostly take place behind the scenes. But now in the recent past enough has taken place on stage visible to everyone to convince an ever growing number of at least the reality and danger of this disease, if not of its whole extent and very deep nature.

What is at present brought about by this pestilence is not so much one or another style of governing, but the paralysis of the entire system of governing. The widespread consciousness of crisis is based less on misgivings as to what the machinery produces than it is on whether it can produce anything at all. It does not work, just as a used-up machine that is falling apart does not work, and every workman knows that in such a case defects must be corrected in the machine itself, and not in its products.

The most splendid programs, the best prepared plans, the finest intentions no longer avail. Governments are perceptibly losing in stability, unity, power, and prestige. The level of parliamentary debate is perceptibly sinking, the Chambers have become discredited through their lack of self-discipline and self-respect, incapable of fulfilling their constitutional functions, capable only of preventing the government and themselves from carrying out their real work. Respect for authority has been destroyed through indiscipline, and with the obliteration of authority the basis of freedom also disappears. The whole thing makes an impression of chaos, in which opposing elements destroy one another as much with rumors as with misconduct, instead of supporting and disciplining one another.

So many people are beginning to understand this, that the most conservative socialists are starting to take up the expression of Spaak[4] in his governmental declaration of May 1938: in order to save democracy we must reform it.

However, this does not mean that there is already enough understanding at hand to bring about a solution. Far from it. The danger threatens rather that a chaotic condition within our party will reflect the chaotic condition in the state, naturally especially in ours, since as the most recent party to participate in government it has not long been weaned from the habits of oppositional irresponsibility.

There is a double danger: increasing indifference and despair among the masses, increasing discord among the leaders. The masses see enough symptoms of decline, in a system in which they decades long have had to cling to hope in order not to surrender to despair—unless a clear, knowing leadership is to give them the feeling that they also are called upon to work for the restoration of better conditions. The leadership labors under a different handicap. They often do not see the forest for the trees, just because they are in the middle of the forest. Everyone is attached one way or another to a specific, partial function,

[4] Paul-Henri Spaak, 1899-1972, Belgian premier at the time of the writing of this article. He had moved from a left-oppositional viewpoint to share de Man's outlook on most issues at this point, as was evident in their joint publication, *Pour un Socialisme nouveau*, Paris-Brussels: Labor, 1937, but the two were to split irrevocably over the appeasement issue. Spaak, of course, enjoyed a distinguished career as a Belgian statesman during the postwar years.

and understandably sees things predominantly from his special vantage point. The parliamentary members complain of the government, the men of government of the Parliament, and party officials complain of both.

One has only to think of what we have had to hear on this topic during the last months in our national party organs and newspapers, such as *Le Peuple*, from de Brouckère, Buset, and Spaak[5]—to mention only three representative viewpoints with three names. None of them denies the crisis, but each one views only one aspect of it and attributes the blame, according to his standpoint, to the party, the government, or Parliament. In this way one gets a fragmentary picture of symptoms but no general insight into the causes of the trouble; bickering, but no solution; confusion, but no enlightenment; a reciprocal thwarting of mutually opposed forces, no parallelogram of forces leading to a resolution giving direction and leadership.

The evil is all the worse in that the problem of the crisis of democracy and the reforming of the state finds our party almost wholly united from a programmatic viewpoint. Its political program—as well as the intellectual background of its older generation of leaders—is still derived from the time when universal suffrage had to be won, and the results of its conquest are thus naturally viewed as the realization of a kind of ideal. And afterward, when it had to be adjusted to the evolving necessities of new responsibilities and new techniques—among others, of new economic responsibilities and new administrative techniques—the new system was even less brought up to date and thought through.

One of the most outstanding instances of this humanly very natural and understandable conservatism is shown by our beloved *patron* Vandervelde. At the time of the struggle for universal suffrage he did splendid work, both in

---

[5] Max Buset, 1896-1959, a member of the *équipe planiste*. Spaak as spokesman for much of the left, de Brouckère for the old guard, have been identified in previous notes.

practical and theoretical terms, but what he has since then written about political problems, as in his *Le Socialisme contre l'Etat* and *L'Alternative*, has yielded little fruit because it was no longer rooted in the soil of present-day reality. Even such a glittering, supple mind has been able to take only a conservatively inclined position of resistance to the new *planiste* conceptualization of government, and he remained completely consistent when later in the Van Zeeland government he defeated attempts to create a special governmental authority for the stabilization of the economy, such as the Office for Economic Recovery and the agencies recommended by the *Plan du Travail*.

The conservative devotion of the leaders of the older socialist generation to the existing parliamentary system as it emerged from the conquest of universal suffrage is one of the main reasons why the *Plan du Travail* has remained something very unfulfilled in the field of political reform. In my previous article I recalled how a gap developed between my personal convictions and the official party decisions, which in the end—in spring 1935—were embodied in a half-hearted compromise between *planiste* political reform and classical parliamentary conservatism. But in that article I made no secret that before my experience in government I myself, despite all alertness, had not yet realized until May 1935[6] the essential, prior significance of political reform, including therewith constitutional reform.

On this point I can completely join the expression of Spaak in his sensational address of December 6 of last year in the Chamber of Representatives: "At one time I thought that it was necessary to begin with economic reforms in the area of structural reform. I myself have said—and I ask pardon for this—that those who wish to begin with political structural reform had a diversionary purpose in mind. Gentlemen, they were the ones who were right. Contrary

[6] The date of the formation of the first Van Zeeland government, in which de Man participated as minister of public works and of the reabsorption of unemployment.

to me they understood the work of governing: if one wants to have success with economic structural reform, one must begin with political structural reform, one must give the government serviceable tools for political implementation."

The Parliamentary Report noted after this declaration: jeering laughter from the socialist benches. I believe that now, three months later, far fewer mockers would be found. And very soon, perhaps yet fewer and fewer. But in the meantime we are faced with the deplorable fact that to the question "which structural reforms?" we have no answer in our traditional party program, and in the *Plan du Travail* there can be found only a very incomplete answer.

What is worse: for four years there has been no programmatic effort in this area made in the Belgian Labor party at all. It appears that we still have a Commission for Political Reform within the Office of Social Research; but from the circumstance that the vice-president of the party[7] nevertheless has not succeeded in seeing a single communication about their proceedings or any results of their work, one can well conclude that it won't amount to anything. There are also, to be sure, a few party members— regrettably few, for that matter—who have taken part in the studies and reports of the so-called C.E.R.E.—the Study Center for the Reform of the State, which was founded in 1936 on the initiative of Van Zeeland, Ernest-John Solvay, and René Marcq.[8] But this work has nevertheless found no echo in our party, although it has made available a very attractive variety of published material that could at the very least serve as the starting point for discussion.

[7] I.e., de Man.

[8] Paul Van Zeeland, 1893-1973, former governor of the Banque Nationale, leader of the Catholic Social Christian party, and premier of Belgium in successive administrations between 1935 and 1937 (in which de Man was a minister); Ernest-John, comte Solvay de La Hulpe, 1895-1972, grandson and successor to the famous Belgian industrialist and philanthropist Ernest Solvay (information from the Institut Emile Vandervelde); and René Marcq, 1882-1947, lawyer and educator.

It thus seems urgently necessary to take up again the programmatic work concerning governmental reform at the point where, in March 1935, the volume *De Uitvoering van de Plan van den Arbeid*[9] stopped. And this time without the restriction that had to be accepted then, to give up those demands directly requiring revision of the constitution. This condition was simply the result of the initial doctrinal position that economic reforms must take precedence over political ones. If now this position is relinquished, as I think is indispensable, then constitutional reform must no longer be regarded as out of the question. Indeed, just as there are very many necessary political structural reforms possible within the confines of the existent constitution, so are there others that presuppose a revision of the constitution.

This last holds for one of the points that was proposed in the *Plan du Travail*: the abolition of the bicameral system. But there are, moreover, a number of further questions that should be investigated without feelings of inhibition stemming from the prior question of existing constitutional stipulations. I will identify a few here: national balloting or the referendum; the reform of the economically and administratively senseless system of annual budgets; the constitutional regulation of the more and more widespread system of the delegation of powers and of staffs; various aspects of administrative reform; and countless others!

But before going further into these matters, I regard it as desirable that there should be consensus about a few main goals, lest strength be lost in patchwork and details, in the absence of basic agreement and hence also of political momentum.

In order to provoke discussion I will sketch these

[9] Published simultaneously in Flemish and French, this volume (Brussels: De Sikkel, 1935), officially written by the Belgian Labor party's Office of Social Research under the direction of de Man, spelled out specific measures for the implementation of the *Plan du Travail* in Belgium.

goals—or rather, the most important of them—as I see the matter:

1. Governments should be made so stable that as a rule they will last in office as long as the composition of the electing Parliament remains the same.

2. The internal organization of the government should be reformed so that it will be impossible for party organs to disrupt the unity of authority and responsibility.

3. The internal organization of governmental departments should be set up so that the effective authority of ministers corresponds to their total constitutional responsibility.

4. The authority of Parliament, just like that of the executive, should be restored, so that an end will be made to the useless duplication of a bicameral system, to the futility of debate, to the largely unreal character of parliamentary supervision of the essential points of governmental policy and the administrative apparatus, to the ruinous intervention of irresponsible bodies and agencies.

5. For certain questions, such as those concerning the constitution and the institutions in which the Parliament itself has an interest, direct voting by the people should be made possible.

6. The consultation of private groups and representatives of special interests by the legislative and executive powers, which in the present circumstances means arbitrariness, disorder, and irresponsibility, should be regularized through appropriate corporative organization of a public-law character.

7. Legislation for the press should serve the free expression of opinion as against the corrupting influence of private interests and raise the standard of truth through effective responsibility in the case of misuse.

8. Particularly in the case of the economic responsibilities of the government, such as agencies concerned

with productive enterprise and public financial organs, special autonomous forms of administration should be devised, and business methods of implementation and of stability of leadership should be united with effective supervision by the state.

If we can agree about these goals, that would be a considerable step forward, putting the Belgian Labor party in a position to play an informed, leading, and decisive role in the strengthening of our public life, in the salvation of a democracy that is threatened by nothing so much as its own faults and shortcomings.

17

The Manifesto

The intellectual and political significance of de Man's reformulation of socialist ideology has been completely obscured by the sensational and impolitic "Manifesto to the Members of the Belgian Labor Party" that appeared in the public press shortly after the Nazi conquest of the Low Countries and France. It was followed by other, equally damaging wartime writings, in which he urged a policy of strict neutralism while expressing contempt for pluto-democratic regimes. But German policy, especially after the invasion of Russia, was not content with such a reserved stance, and gradually he became convinced of the hopelessness of his endeavor to maintain the disengagement of occupied Belgium, in the end retiring to an Alpine hut on Mont Blanc for the duration of the war, then at the very last moment making an escape to Switzerland, where he found refuge thanks to support among Swiss socialists.

Since that time, a conspiracy of silence has reigned about this enigmatic figure, convicted September 1944 in absentia of treason by a military court for conduct that was judged to be collaborationist. None wished henceforth to be tarred by the same brush, and where, as in the case of the Bad Godesberg program adopted by the German Social Democratic party in 1959, ideological innovation has substantiated the ideas he had so urgently advocated, his influence was entirely absent.

Two major considerations impelling his fateful ideological development—his refired pacifism, his renewed cynicism as to the operation of formal, bourgeois democracy—have already been presented in the last selections, but to make comprehensible the dynamics underlying his neutralist stand, it is necessary to bring out certain personality characteristics that infused all his writings and all his conduct, namely, that passionate, intense, and overriding dedication to the realization of a socialist world for which de Man had given his entire life. In a certain sense, one might say that his ideological innovations represented a surge growing out of successive bitter disappointments. The proletariat turned out not to be composed of heroic, selfless sufferers, but it was possible to foresee their transfiguration through the process of workers' education. This process was, however, a dream of uncertain and distant realization, and in the meantime de Man placed his hope in the participation in the movement of intellectuals and of other strata relatively untainted by embourgeoisement. But the socialist organizations were increasingly dominated, he discovered to his dismay, by professional careerists—practical politicians, petty administrators, union bosses—all earthly creatures of dubious metal for the building of the New Jerusalem. When their inert weight combined with the machinations of the capitalist enemy to block the realization of even the mildest approximation to the new society, de Man was placed in a situation where he would either have to reconcile himself to the preservation of the existing order, or have to abandon his subscription to the conventional political system—a dilemma rendered more acute by his conviction that with the growth of fascist totalitarianism the socialist movement had before it the possibility of eternal defeat. Faced with this dreadful prospect and freed by the German victory from the utter frustration of trying to activate the resistive elements of capitalist society, in any case unwilling to carry on a war that appeared to be already decided by force of arms, in simple desperation de Man attempted to escape through reinterpreting the Nazi movement into an instrument for the achievement of the socialist goal. Repelled by its brutality, appalled by many aspects of its doctrine, he nevertheless attempted to read into its activism the possibility for an escape from the miasma of philistine venality, and it may indeed be suggested that his very act of reluctant condoning of Nazism may be taken as an index of the passion of his devotion to socialism, defined in his terms as the repudiation of the bourgeoisie.

MANIFESTE AUX MEMBRES DU PARTI OUVRIER BELGE[1]

In the present circumstances, your president can consult only his conscience in order to reply when you ask him counsel. The leader, abandoned at his battle station, does not have the right to shelter himself behind the desertion of others; on the contrary, he has the right to take command, assuming himself the whole responsibility that this implies.

The role of a leader is not to follow his troops, but to lead them by showing them the way. Here is what I ask you to undertake:

Remain faithful to the interests that have been entrusted to you, see to the well-being of your members, the working of your associations, the execution of your administrative tasks.

Be among the first rank of those who struggle against poverty and demoralization, for the resumption of work and the return to normal life.

But do not believe that it is necessary to resist the occupying power; accept the fact of his victory and try rather to draw lessons therefrom so as to make of this the starting point for new social progress.

The war has led to the debacle of the parliamentary regime and of the capitalist plutocracy in the so-called democracies.

For the working classes and for socialism, this collapse of a decrepit world is, far from a disaster, a deliverance.

[1] *Gazette de Charleroi*, 3 July 1940.

Despite all that we have experienced of defeats, sufferings, and disillusions, the way is open for the two causes that sum up the aspirations of the people: European peace and social justice.

Peace has not been able to develop from the free understanding of sovereign nations and rival imperialisms; it will be able to emerge from a Europe united by arms, wherein the economic frontiers have been leveled.

Social justice has not been able to develop from a system calling itself democratic but in which the money powers and the professional politicians in fact predominate, one more and more incapable of any bold initiative, of any serious reform. It will be able to develop from a system in which the authority of the state is strong enough to undercut the privileges of the propertied classes and to replace unemployment by the universal obligation to work.

For years the double talk of the warmongers has concealed from you that this system, despite everything in it that strikes our mentality as alien, had lessened class differences much more efficaciously than the self-styled democracies, where capital continued to lay down the law.

Since then everyone has been able to see that the superior morale of the German army is due in large part to the greater social unity of the nation and to the resulting prestige of its authorities. In contrast, the pluto-democracies offer us the spectacle of authorities deserting their stations and the rich crossing the border by car without worrying about what happens to the masses.

By linking their fate to the victory of arms, the democratic governments have accepted in advance the verdict of the war. This verdict is clear. It condemns the systems where speeches take the place of actions, where responsibilities are dissipated in the babble of meetings, where the slogan of individual liberty serves as a cushion for conservative egoism. It calls for an era in which an elite—preferring a lively and dangerous life to a torpid and easy one, and seeking responsibility instead of fleeing it—will build a new world. In this world, a communal spirit will prevail over class egoism, and labor will be the only source of dignity and power. The socialist order will be thereby realized, not at all as the thing of one class or of one party, but as the good of all, in the name of a national solidarity that will soon be Continental, if not worldwide.

Carry on, then, the economic activity of our associations, but consider the political role of the Belgian Labor party as finished. This role has been fruitful and glorious, but henceforth another mission awaits you.

Prepare to enter into the ranks of a movement of national resurrection, which will include all the vital forces of the nation, its youth, its veterans, in a single party, that of the Belgian people, united by its fidelity to its king and by its will to realize the sovereignty of labor.

18

The Age of Doom

From his haven in Switzerland de Man contemplated the postwar world with rueful pessimism and profound chagrin. Just as the insupportable moral burden of his engagement in World War I had necessitated, first, recognition that different outcomes of the conflict would be historically significant, and, second, with the *grande désillusion* of Versailles, an adamant resolve never to be taken in again by such propaganda, so the burden of his disengagement in World War II prohibited acknowledgment that he had made a dreadful, culpable error of judgment. He fought bitterly and vainly against his conviction, and a pervasive dejection suffuses the pages of his major postwar publication, entitled in its first, English writing as "The Age of Doom."

The source of his deep pessimism lay not only in his personal circumstances and in the catastrophic devastation of World War II but also in the seeming destruction of any prospect for that realization of socialism to which he had devoted his entire life. Although he had acknowledged that some measure of the "embourgeoisement of the proletariat" was "sociologically conditioned (and therefore only in part ideologically produced),"[1] he had preserved the redeeming function of the movement by arguing that such embourgeoisement was epiphenomenal rather than integral, and he had advanced the thesis that by the very satiation of wants through prosperity the proletariat might be enabled to convert their remaining grievances into universalistic and morally motivated calls for action. Now, however, in the wreckage of all his hopes he

[1] See above, p. 231.

concluded that preaching "a renovation of motives . . .
could engage and encourage a handful of people, but
could not change the general orientation of the movement.
. . . In letting itself become 'absorbed' by its surroundings,
the movement found itself geared into the regressive evolution of the capitalist environment, the national state, the
parliamentary system, mechanized civilization, Balkanized
Europe. It participated in a general decadence."[2] To be
sure, a stoic fortitude demanded that the victimized proletariat still be supported in its struggle against the forces
of exploitation, but "the tragedy of all those at whom the
world laughs as do-gooders lies in the fact that they draw
their strength from the image of ideals that they cannot
realize. The more clearly the work to which they devote
themselves takes form the more clearly it becomes apparent how little that form resembles its original image. That
no perfect and just social order can exist they already knew
in ancient Athens. I have been driven to the same conclusion."[3]

From the vantage point of a quarter-century after de
Man's death—a period that, above all in comparison with
the convulsions of the interwar period, appears to mark a
regeneration of Western capitalism, and, if only by absence
of armed conflict among major, thermonuclear powers, an
opening of new and heartening opportunities for mankind—from this vantage point the deep pessimism of de
Man's last years may seem extravagant and even self-
indulgent. To be sure, no realist can ignore the precarious
nature of the conditions of peace, the dreadful impact of
the border conflicts that have taken place, the prospects of
fearful increase in human population together with the
potentialities for ecological catastrophe. No one could possibly be indifferent to the commercial exploitation of status
anxieties, the continued inequities in the distribution of income and wealth, the strangling crisis of the cities, racial

---

[2] "Lettre de 26 janvier 1949," *Ecrits de Paris: Revue Des Questions Ac-
tuelles*, no. 117, July-August 1954, p. 94.
[3] *Gegen den Strom*, Stuttgart: Deutsche Verlags-Anstalt, 1953, p. 286.

conflicts, the plight of the nonindustrialized world. But at the same time it would be equally unrealistic not to recognize the vastly increased portion of the population in industrialized societies enjoying participation in the affluent society; the relatively successful fulfillment of the commitment of the capitalist democracies to the program of full employment; the reluctant, uneven, but very substantial guarantee in various societies of universally available social, political, and economic rights; the relative decline in xenophobic nationalism; and the increasing popular recognition of mutual dependence in a finite world.[4]

To those who recognize the imperfectibility of man and his institutions; who acknowledge that the essential function of political institutions is to provide a legitimate means for the expression of ineluctable conflicts endemic to the body politic; who regard the disasters and squabbles of man as farce as well as tragedy; whose zeal for mankind is tempered by a knowledge of its failings—the intellectual heritage of Hendrik de Man may be rich. For in his persevering struggle to realize the rights of man in industrialized society he was brought to the enunciation of insights into the nature of social action, into the historical genesis of the socialist movement, and into the conditions of "socialization" that are of permanent relevance to the human condition. A victim of his own zeal, in his very fate he evinces the soundness of his insistence upon the importance of morality in human affairs.

THE LAW OF ACCELERATION—
DESTINY AND TASK[5]

The history of civilization is now being dominated by the theories of three men: the Frenchman Gobineau, the

---

[4] This paragraph has appeared in a slightly different form in the editor's "Le Socialisme: du mouvement social au groupement d'intérêt," *Revue européenne des sciences sociales et Cahiers Vilfredo Pareto,* vol. 12, no. 31, 1974, p. 65.

[5] Concluding chapter from "The Age of Doom."

German Oswald Spengler, and the Englishman Arnold Toynbee. These theories differ in many respects. They agree, however, on one crucial point. They all consider that civilizations are separate entities, which develop from birth to death according to analogous laws, like living organisms—compared with plants by Spengler and with individuals of a same zoological species by Toynbee.

It seems that there is something fundamentally wrong with this theory. The first doubts creep into one's mind on finding that its promoters disagree about the number and nomenclature of the civilizations it applies to. Gobineau counts ten, Spengler eight, Toynbee twenty-one, including ten doubtful cases, which "may possibly turn out not to be distinct and separate specimens,"[6] and not counting five "arrested" and four "abortive" ones.[7] On closer investigation, it appears that these discrepancies are due less to variations in the extent of our knowledge than to uncertainty about the criteria to be applied. Now this uncertainty would not exist if civilizations were like plants or human beings: cabbages in a row or people in a room can be counted easily enough if there are no more than a couple of dozen, unless visibility is so bad that they cannot even be identified as to their species.

More doubts are called forth by the recognition that of the uncertain number of ancient civilizations at issue, only four or five are sufficiently known to justify any theory about the laws which have ruled their inner development. The rarer the known facts, the easier they can be replaced by assumptions fitting into a general system, and the more conjectural and subjective this system becomes.

Moreover, it appears that the civilizations we know most about—or at least enough to form a general idea of their evolution—are interrelated in a way that differs essentially

[6] A. J. Toynbee, *A Study of History*, Oxford: Oxford University Press, 1934-[1959], vol. 1, p. 148. [N.B.: all footnotes henceforth are from the de Man manuscript.]

[7] Ibid., vol. 4, p. 1.

from the relationships (or lack of relationships) between the more remote and less-known representatives of the alleged species. The civilizations which developed around the Mediterranean basin, starting with the Egyptian and ending with the Western, are far more closely interrelated than any of the others. As to the latter, they might well comprise a larger proportion of connected cases than historians generally assume; yet there is little doubt about, say, Minoan and Mayan civilization being separate entities. The same cannot be said about Greece and Rome, nor about the relations between the Graeco-Roman world and ours. These relations are so close that the very historians who profess the doctrine of separate civilizations disagree about the way in which these "specimens" or "fields" should be kept apart, if at all.

According to the most recent classification, accepted by Toynbee, we have some knowledge of about six hundred and fifty "primitive societies" which, having failed to develop into "civilizations,"[8] have played no part in their "affiliation" or "apparentation." Toynbee also points out that no "unrelated" civilization "has emerged in the Old World within the last three, or in the New World (as far as we know) within the last two millennia."[9] On the other hand, it appears that of the ten civilizations Toynbee considers as being alive today (and which include three "arrested" and at least two doubtful cases), only one—the Western—is extending its geographical field, and does so with an effectiveness which threatens all the others with absorption.

These three sets of facts lead to the conclusion that the trend of cultural evolution until now points from diversity toward unity, through growing "apparentation" and "affiliation." One wonders, even, if the time has not come for the history of civilization to alter its course and to focus attention again, as our fathers and grandfathers did, on civilization as a whole, instead of cutting it up into a plurality of "specimens." There is such a thing as not seeing the

[8] Ibid., vol. 1, p. 148.   [9] Ibid., p. 185.

wood for trees. Perhaps, even, it would be better to stop using the word civilization in the plural, and to give the "specimens" a distinctive name, such as "cultural cycles."

Be that as it may, the fact is that the pluralistic theories, helpful though they have been in many ways, have too long diverted our attention from the cumulative process that justifies Pascal's image of "man learning ceaselessly." Six hundred and fifty primitive societies, and a couple of dozen civilizations, indeed make an interesting and instructive show; yet they should not make us forget that events such as the use of fire, the discovery of the bow and arrow, the domestication of animals, the melting of metals, the invention of pottery and weaving, etc., have no less universal importance than the steam engine or the internal combustion motor, and together make (to use the term somewhat arbitrarily applied by A. J. Toynbee to his "specimens" alone) an "intelligible field of study."

Viewed in that light, those rare ancient cultural cycles which are (at least presumably) unconnected, appear as the discarded sketches of an artist at work; whilst the connected cycles gain interest as their "interrelation" grows more marked, and lose their distinctive cyclic character in proportion.

This being so, there is little point in calculating (as some "pluralists" have done quite seriously) how many new civilizations would find time to develop before humanity must become extinct because of physical developments affecting our planet. If one accepts J. H. Jeans's estimate of 100 trillions (i.e., 100 millions of millions) of years as the probable duration of life on earth, and Spengler's (extreme) assessment of 1,000 years per cycle, this would give a chance to at least a hundred thousand million successors to Western civilization. Fortunately, we need not bother overmuch about the exactness of such calculations, nor about the nicety of the prospect as such; for it is clear from the outset that a very much smaller number of civilizations playing with the atom bomb, and who knows what else to follow after it, would suffice to deprive J. H. Jeans's trillionic figure of its character as a "constant."

The absurdity of this kind of reasoning is due to the erroneous assumption that we can foresee (at least as a probability) historical developments as exact science can calculate the probable effects of given physical causes. This is where the philosophy of history, as developed in the century of natural science, has made a fundamental mistake. Even the "spiritualist" Toynbee has fallen victim to the Spencerian delusion that history can use the same methods (and, incidentally, the same vocabulary) as physical and biological science. For one thing, physicists and biologists base their reasoning on the belief—justified by results in their sphere—that the more often an experiment can be repeated, the more it warrants general conclusions. But might it not be that this method is unfit to explain the adventure of mankind and civilization? History is not an experiment, but an experience, as essentially unique as mankind itself, and this probably explains why so many errors in the interpretation of history are due to the overstressing of similarities. Dissimilarities, on the contrary, because of the innovation they reveal, might well be the better key to the understanding of history as a creative, and therefore intrinsically nonrepetitive, process.

True, this way of looking at things does not tally with the spirit which has prevailed in Western science for the last two or three centuries. It is nevertheless Western in another, and possibly more fundamental sense, for it derives quite naturally from the Christian conception of the world in terms of creation, fulfillment, judgment, and redemption. That contemporary historians, whether they belong to a Christian church or not, have practically discarded this conception in favor of so-called positive science, merely shows that since the Middle Ages, the world has forgotten no less, perhaps, than it has learned. However that may be, the scientific explanation of history now seems to have reached a point where it is being menaced by *reductio ad absurdum*, unless we learn again to look for transcendent aims beyond the immanent causes, for unprecedented occurrences rather than for analogies between past events.

If we do that with regard to the present, we find, as a further reason to give up belief in "parallelism" and "repetition," that our own civilization is distinguished from all others by some essentially new features.

This implies a good deal more than is represented by such unprecedented Western achievements as the speed reached by our means of intercommunication, the population of our cities, the magnitude of our wars, etc. These are quantitative elements, and similar differences in size and number have existed between older civilizations—although on a much smaller scale—as a result of the cumulative effect of technical progress in "interrelated" civilizations. With regard to some of these things, though, it would not be unreasonable to ask if a limit has not been reached where, as Hegel put it, quantity turns into quality. It might be argued, for instance—on sound mathematical grounds—that instantaneous worldwide transmission of wireless messages is something essentially new as compared with the mere increase of speed represented by the introduction of optical telegraphy. But this is an academic question, which we need not solve to furnish proof of the qualitative novelty and uniqueness of some distinctively Western features.

One of them is that our civilization is the first to have used machinery set in motion by technically "produced" and not merely "borrowed" power. That this is an essentially new trait, with entirely unprecedented implications, is shown by the recent step from internal combustion power to atomic power; henceforth, mankind disposes of an instrument of such far-reaching potentiality that it might conceivably result in planetary and cosmic destruction.

Secondly, our civilization is the first to extend over the whole planet. Obviously, this does away with a number of

conditioning circumstances and possibilities which formerly faced civilizations, and replaces them by different
ones. To mention but one example: it is clear that a civilization with a worldwide radius of influence and power runs
no risk to be wiped out by war, unless it be internecine.
Hence all the problems of military power, colonial rule,
international relations, and national sovereignty itself,
[take on] an entirely novel aspect. The same is true of the
effects this new situation is bound to have on political and
social organization as a whole, including ideological scales
of values, moral standards, and codes of honor.

Regarding another consequence we may refer to this
passage from Toynbee's *Study of History*: "Under the conditions of our day, when the whole World has become en-
meshed in the net of our Western civilization, it is still quite
possible to imagine this Western Civilization itself breaking
down and disintegrating in its turn, but hardly possible any
longer to imagine new civilizations emerging without their
being related to the antecedent Western Civilization in
some degree. In other words, the possibility of 'unrelated'
civilizations ever emerging again seems now to be definitely
excluded by the accomplished fact of the world-wide expansion of our Western Civilization on the economic and
political planes."[10] This being so, it is clear that a stage may
soon be reached where the very species of distinct civilizations with parallel developments will have become extinct.

A third new fact is less easily discernible, but perhaps the
most important of all. Our civilization is the first to have
developed (in religion, science, and philosophy) a knowledge of itself implying a certain sense of shared responsibility, an awareness of a common task, and a longing for
collective self-determination. No civilization before ours
has been history conscious in this sense. The religious substructure of this new consciousness is the Christian belief in
redemption of mankind as a whole, and a consequence of

[10] Ibid.

the will of a unique God. Its political expression is the struggle for democracy, as the supreme form of social self-determination by conscious and enlightened volition. Its most striking modern intellectual manifestation is the "historicism" which, in one way or the other, has ruled philosophical thinking for more than a century. Hegel (whom Marx and the Marxians were not alone to follow) has laid its doctrinal foundation by assuming that societies and civilizations develop according to definite, cognizable laws, and that men fulfill their highest destinies in gaining consciousness of these laws and in carrying them out—true freedom being but the conscious acceptance of this necessity.

One cannot imagine Greeks or Romans—to mention our direct cultural ancestors only—bothering their heads about anything of the kind. To them, history was, at the utmost, a collection of stories fit to exalt patriotic feelings and promote virtuous behavior. The idea that it might represent destiny and duty rolled into one, and that its knowledge might assign its tasks or responsibilities to mankind, could not have occurred to people who believed that men were ruled either by the whims of a multiplicity of gods or by their individual reason. On the other hand, if we accept (again in agreement with Toynbee) that "progress towards self-determination and self-articulation" is the criterion of cultural growth,[11] then it is manifest that Western civilization represents a level of consciousness which has never been approached before.

If the sequel of events in time thus makes consciousness appear as the ultimate aim and achievement of life, full understanding of the process requires that this last stage be related to the preceding ones from which it developed, as far back as we know them. To make this relation intelligible, we must keep in mind certain conclusions reached by modern biophysics as to the origin of life itself. Lecomte Du Noüy has fitly epitomized them by saying that

[11] Ibid., vol. 3, p. 217.

life with its unforeseen properties, born of the dissymmetry of its structures, was less "probable" than the
simple inorganic evolution which had been going on
for a thousand millions of years, and which is still
going on right now. If one admits that the apparition
of life is due to an accident, to a fluctuation, how can
we explain that this accident should have been followed, during those thousand millions of years, by an
uninterrupted sequence of other accidents which
have, on the whole, increased the initial dissymmetry
and have finally carried it to the incredible extreme
represented by the human brain? We are therefore
forcibly put before this dilemma: either we are invariably dealing with accidents without any relevancy for
the boundless thermodynamic evolution of the universe, which is difficult to admit after all, in view of the
remarkable reoccurrence of the successive "accidents"
all of which follow the same direction—the "forbid-
den" direction; or else thermodynamic evolution, in
spite of its universality and crushing magnitude, has
merely been the preparatory stage to the occurrence
of biological evolution. In the latter case, this evolution
would appear as the principal phenomenon toward
which energetic evolution tended from the outset, although the laws ruling inert matter did not permit us
to foresee it. Thus, the improbability of life, and of its
progressive and polymorphous development, would
become intelligible, but at the cost of the acceptance of
a long-termed finalism.[12]

If history is to have any meaning at all, it is clear that—as
far as the evolution of life in its human stages is concerned—the second explanation, in terms of ends and
aims, is alone acceptable. In fact, it is being universally
accepted—explicitly by the telefinalists, implicitly by the
causalists, for after all, the latter go no further than to pro-

[12] Lecomte Du Noüy, *L'Avenir de l'Esprit*, Paris: Gallimard, 1941, p. 69.

fess that the aims of human endeavor are set by cognizable causes—which is merely another form of finalist motivation. It is indeed impossible for the human mind to conceive history otherwise than as a movement in time directed toward an end, whether that end be set by immanent causes or by a transcendent power, and whether that movement should be considered as a progression toward a desirable aim or as its contrary.

There is yet another, highly significant point, on which materialists and spiritualists, causalists and finalists must and do agree, because it finds its expression in objectively measurable quantities—time quantities in fact. To make its full significance obvious, it suffices to draw a list of the time periods elapsed since the chief events which mark the global evolution referred to above.

The first figures on this list, relating to prehistoric periods, are of course gross estimates. I have borrowed them from the most recent authoritative works I could lay hands on, and struck averages when I found extreme figures too wide apart. Of course, even if the margin of error were so big that some of those figures would have to be either multiplied or divided by ten (which is much more than the utmost difference between disagreeing expert estimates), the result would be practically irrelevant for our purposes, since they require no more than a comparison of orders of greatness.

Here are the (1948) averages in years:

Age of the earth	about	2,000,000,000
Age of life	about	600,000,000
Age of mammiferous life	about	150,000,000
Age of quadrumanes	about	45,000,000
Age of man	about	650,000
Age of Neanderthal man ("human" man)	about	100,000
Age of Cro-Magnon man ("artist" man)	about	40,000

Age of oldest known		
civilization	about	6,000
Age of Western civilization	about	950
Age of the steam engine	about	185
Age of railways	about	123
Age of automobiles		61
Age of air power		43
Age of atom power		4

I have jotted down only half a dozen landmarks to indicate the speed of technical and cultural progress in the Western world. The facts are widely known, and more detailed figures can be found anywhere. No matter which basis of comparison one chooses—be it the speed of traveling and intercommunication, the number of mechanical horsepower used, the amount of reading matter published, or any of the innumerable other "standards of progress"—one always reaches the same conclusion: things have developed faster in a century than they had for a millennium before, and faster in that last millennium than in the two or three dozen millennia which preceded. Changes which (rated by their importance) once required centuries now take years. This knowledge is now so widespread that it has become too commonplace for high school essays. What is not quite so generally known, though, is that this acceleration did not start with Western civilization, but has been going on, in what practically amounts to geometrical progression, since the earliest times of which we have any evidence.

The figures which, more or less approximately, relate to the first stages of the great adventure of life, man, and history, are so astronomic that their meaning can perhaps best be brought home by a comparison with familiar measures. Let us assume, for instance, that the highest figure on our list—2,000 millions of years, being the approximate age of the earth—represents a distance of 1,000 kilometers. Life, then, represents 300 kilometers. Savage mankind (starting with the Neanderthal man) has walked 50 meters; civilized mankind has had time to take three steps of 1 meter each; and man since the railway age could "cover" about 61.5 millimeters—2½ inches of a road as long as the air distance between New York and Chicago.

Acceleration also gives the clue to the understanding of a peculiar phenomenon which became apparent in our survey of cultural reversals. In every single instance examined by us, we have found that the first, upward section of the curves took much longer to develop than the later, downward sections. The downward movements, moreover, appeared to increase their speed on their way, from the apex to the present level. Verily, there seems to exist a law of acceleration no less important for the understanding of history than any law of analogy—rather more so, in fact.

Now let us put two and two together and see if we can find a representative curve with the two characteristics of the trends thus discovered: "pulsating" reversal of direction, and progressive acceleration. This curve exists, is simple and known to all. It is the spiral—the movement of a point moving in ever smaller circumvolutions toward a center.

The image has already been used by Goethe, though not exactly with the same implications. He was thinking of a "rising spiral," mainly to express the idea of progressive evolution (in biology) along a winding road. The spiral as a two-dimensional figure, of course, merely represents a movement, at an accelerated rhythm, toward a center. It all happens on the same plane. If we want to express another idea as well—namely that of a motion up or down—we must visualize our spiral against the background of a vertical plane. This is what we would see if we were looking sideways at a watch spring put flat, but the core of which is being pulled up or down by tongs. The spiral will then appear, if it expresses constant rise, as a series of points ascending the faster as the circumvolutions grow narrower;

if it expresses descent, the center of the spiral will accordingly be seen below the periphery.

As a matter of fact, we have found that the dialectical course of civilization, conceived as a movement toward the aims it sets itself, implies neither constant rise nor constant descent, but a succession of rising and descending phases. We have also found that these phases tend to grow shorter at accelerated speed. This again fits rather well into the image of the spiral, providing we visualize its end as moving up and down in phases as it advances toward its center.

This does not settle the question whether the point of arrival—by hypothesis the center—lies above or below the hypothetical point of departure (representing the beginning of civilization, or any other intervening landmark chosen as significant). Our grandparents would have answered confidently: above. They believed in progress, conceived as the prolongation of what happened before their eyes: the constant improvement of technique, the increase of wealth, the accumulation of knowledge. We have grown less sanguine since. We still hold that the cumulative element in civilization is a sign that it is moving toward an end, and we find it difficult to admit that this end might be situated on the same plane as the beginning. But we no longer believe in constant progression toward that end; we have, on the contrary, experienced phases of downfall so precipitous that we do not know whether we should not visualize the final outcome as the bottom of a maelstrom rather than as the top of a mountain. As long as we are traveling, we may hope for the best or fear for the worst, without being contradicted by facts—for until we know when the journey will stop, we cannot feel sure that our downward course (if we happen to be on one) will not be reversed into an upward one, or inversely.

Of one thing, though, we can feel certain, and this thing is of paramount importance. The circumvolutions of our spiral, whether they run up or down, are becoming narrower and narrower, and they have of late been getting so narrow that the center of the curve cannot be far away. The figures listed above speak a clear language in this respect. The whirling motion of the spiral which carries a curve toward a center has now reached the avalanchelike speed and power of a vortex. Where it will finally take us we do not know, but that we are nearing its end can hardly be doubted.

Mathematicians tell us that we can never be quite certain about the end of a curve of which we only know the beginning. To put it somewhat more precisely, though still in nontechnical language: if we follow a point which travels along a given curve to the limit of our field of vision there is no certainty as to where the next point will be. There is a probability, though, that it will be along the prolongation of the curve which corresponds to the algebraic formula (or to the general physiognomy) of its known section, and this probability will be all the greater as this known section is longer and its shape more characteristic.

We must therefore leave open the possibility that the curve which has thus far appeared to us as a spiral may, in its further course, develop into something quite different. However, the odds are against it. Our curve has the typical physiognomy of a development that points toward a near end—the end of a meaningful and partly intelligible process which started many millennia (or even thousands of millennia) ago.

It cannot be scientifically proved that this process covers the whole story of man, or of life itself, or of the earth, or—still more—of our whole universe, but it seems more than likely that it extends at least as far as the bounds of history. This would justify the feeling, which is getting hold of an increasing number of contemporary historians, that we are witnessing the "end of history," and possibly find ourselves already "out of history."[13] This may be partly due

[13] To my knowledge, the first to express this thought was the Frenchman Bertrand de Jouvenel.

to the sensation of the growing "unruliness" of events, even
in their immediate aspect as mere "material" for the historian, who feels overpowered by an unmanageable and
fast-growing mass of sources and can no longer make any
sense of them.

But there obviously is more to it than this purely subjective impression. The more we visualize our own time in the
frame of history as a whole (as we have tried to do in the
preceding chapters) the more the unruliness and sense-
lessness of contemporary happenings appear as an attribute of the events themselves. What we have come to consider as the "historical" relationship between causes and
purposes on the one hand, and occurrences on the other,
strikes us as being, like Hamlet's mad universe, "out of
joint." We feel bound to admit that we were mistaken in
identifying the "historical" with the "eternal." Whatever
seemed until then to make sense—and making sense out of
happenings is the essence of history—thus appears to have
got close to its limits in time and to be nearing its end.[14]

[14] The French mathematician A. A. Cournot (1801-1877) has invented
the term *post-histoire* to describe the condition which arises when some particular human creation has reached a stage where any further improvement would require a total innovation. It is then "perfected," morphologically "stabilized," an "archetype." This applies to institutions as well as to
implements. The wheelbarrow and the stagecoach, for example, have become posthistorical, because they could not be improved beyond a certain
point, so that further progress required the introduction of an altogether
new type. As an example of posthistorical stabilization in the institutional
field, Cournot mentions the bank note. One can imagine something quite
different taking its place, but one cannot imagine the bank note being
morphologically modified without becoming something functionally
different.

Something of the kind undoubtedly happens in the cultural field, and
this is one of the reasons why "progress" is not continuous. The love sonnet, for example, does not seem capable of further development; perhaps
not all has been said about love, but certainly all has been said that can be
put in a sonnet. In the same way, one can explain the fact that definite
arts, belonging to a given civilization, always seem to reach a stage of development where they become unable to express more; this can then be
done only by another art. So the European painters of the *Trecento* and
Quattrocento started where the sculptors of the thirteenth-century cathe-
drals had stopped; as an expression of the "world feeling" of the

I should not hesitate to call this end a catastrophe, if I could expect my readers to take this term in its strict original sense—not in the sloppy extended meaning it has acquired in ordinary language, where it is used to describe any kind of sudden disaster. In Greek tragedy, catastrophe means a "return," a denouement, a decisive event or turn which unties a dramatic knot. In this sense, at any rate, we may say that we are, to all appearances, moving fast toward a catastrophe.

Even with the prudent reservations implied by the terms "mere probability" and "decisive turn," I feel bound to admit that this conclusion has a wholly pessimistic sound. I must add that if I were pressed to reveal my inner feelings on the subject, I should further have to admit that the catastrophic outcome in the ordinary sense of the word—apocalyptic possibilities not being excluded—seems far more probable to me than the opposite. This, of course, is a mere personal impression, and it might not be worth mentioning but for the curious fact that I have always been considered by all my friends (whose judgment I could never refute by contrary evidence) as a congenital and incorrigible optimist.

After this confession, I feel more at ease to say that I should consider this book to have missed its purpose with anybody who would feel discouraged, despondent, or in any way depressed by its conclusions. There is, indeed, a solid line of defense to be held against pessimism—at least

---

eighteenth century, music took the place of baroque architecture as soon as the latter had produced its archetypes, which have been unsurpassed since; and a century later, symphonic music seems to have expressed all that can be expressed by its peculiar technique, so that musical "progress" either has become impossible or requires entirely new technical means—as most of its contemporary theoreticians indeed contend.

The term posthistorical seems adequate to describe what happens when an institution or a cultural achievement ceases to be historically active and productive of new qualities, and becomes purely receptive or eclectically imitative. Thus understood, Cournot's notion of the posthistorical would, in a more general way than intended by him, fit the cultural phase that, following a "fulfillment of sense," has become "devoid of sense." The alternative then is, in biological terms, either death or mutation.

against the passive kind of pessimism that breeds fear and despondency, as opposed to the "heroic pessimism"[15] that fights all the better as the chances are less auspicious.[16]

As a matter of fact, there are several lines of defense, drawn up in echelons.

First, we must remember once more that no amount of scientific analysis, based on facts past and present, can do more than show probabilities as to the future. Crystal gazing is not a scientific occupation. Even the physician who feels certain of his diagnosis is never allowed to forget that not every disease kills, and that it must be fought as long as there is life—and consequently hope.

Secondly, we must consider that even if the probability of our civilization being on its final downward course were a certainty, this perspective would not deprive anybody of his or her *raison de vivre*, nor justify any change in behavior amounting to renouncement or aloofness.

The only belief which this hypothesis would disprove is a false belief: the superstition of progress. Well, the sooner this be given up, the better for mankind. The worship of progress, which in the last century has served as a religion substitute, has been found since to be based on the worst kind of human self-idolatry. Besides being a fallacy, it is a danger, because it feeds a fanaticism no less intolerant and cruel than that of any religious wars. The Leninist phrase about the living generation being but "the manure of progress" can be made to serve as an excuse for the most con-

[15] The expression has been recently popularized by Denis de Rougemont, but I am not sure that it has not been employed before. I have myself used a near equivalent (in German) in my book *The Psychology of Socialism* (1926), and I had borrowed it from my friend Theodor Haubach (who was hanged as one of the conspirators of the twentieth of July, 1944, which had given him occasion to show that it does not need optimism to act heroically).

[16] Unfavorable odds even may imply a "sporting temptation," as jocularly expressed by the story of the London waiter who, just before the election of President Truman in 1948, had bet a large sum on him at twenty to one. When his friends later complimented him on having been so much wiser than the experts, he answered: "It wasn't that; I could not resist the odds."

tradictory, yet equally inhuman immolations; the massacre
of social adversaries by revolutionaries wearing red armlets
and the "genocide" of racial outcasts by political soldiers
wearing black lapels can alike be justified as human sacrifices demanded by the alleged divinity of progress. No
Moloch has ever been more insatiable nor more cruel than
this idol of our times.

And why should mankind be unable to live without this
faith in progress? Western civilization itself has done quite
well without it until two centuries ago, and for centuries
before that, it grew and developed under the sign of a faith
quite different—to wit, faith in salvation.

There is a good deal to be said in favor of the opinion
Bertrand de Jouvenel recently expressed as follows:

> Why should we be thus obsessed with the adventure
> of Civilization? Not that I do not treasure Civilization,
> but perhaps like happiness it is best achieved when you
> seek something else. It is not the business of Man to
> ponder ceaselessly on the future of Man, and to direct
> his actions in view of a collective and distant future. He
> is apt to miscalculate, and taking as his moral criterion
> that he must act in the manner most apt to further the
> envisaged future, he may act very immorally as judged
> by simpler criteria. . . . Now Civilization is something
> indeed very intricate but also very simple. It is felt in
> the simplest encounter between two men whose inter-
> ests are of course not identical: we are apt to say that
> they behave in a civilized manner or the reverse. This
> gives us a key. Civilization is nothing else than behav-
> ior. And behavior is nothing else than morality. The
> whole fabric of the philosophy of history collapses,
> confronted with the mother's insistent reminder to the
> small boy: "Do behave, John!" Civilization consists in a
> lot of Johns behaving, being not history-minded but
> morality-minded.

This is an acceptable way of putting the problem as it confronts everybody, but perhaps it does not quite settle the question that preoccupies a minority.

As to the overwhelming majority, it would be foolish to feel pangs about them which they do not experience themselves. The masses are nationality minded, race conscious, and sometimes religion conscious, but the notion of a civilization is so purely intellectual that most people cannot be expected to take great interest in its problems. The degree of their morality mindedness fortunately does not depend on their realization of a share of responsibility for the future of such an abstract historical entity.

Moreover, the experience of the white race thus far has been that dead civilizations always made room for new ones, and that the worst which could happen in the meantime was relapse into what Spengler has called historyless, zoological existence. This prospect can hardly be expected to frighten the masses, especially after a series of wars and revolutions such as have been inflicted on the present generation. Even people with a highly developed social sensitiveness then may come to feel like Jules Romains' "men of good will," who try to escape from the "zone of historical catastrophes" into that of the "eternal everyday."[17] In fact, far from being necessarily due to egoism, this attitude may—and often does—betray concern with the herds whose ignorance and credulity make them the eternal victims of bad shepherds. This is the message Voltaire intended to convey by letting his Candide conclude that "one must cultivate one's garden."[18] This is also, what the late J. Huizinga, one of the most "civilization conscious" men of this century, expressed thus: "We should not allow ourselves to be blinded by the disease symptoms of our civiliza-

[17] Jules Romains, *Les Hommes de Bonne Volunté*, Paris: Flammarion, 1932-1946, vol. 25, pp. 132, 147-150.
[18] The last words of Voltaire's *Candide* are in the original: "Cela est bien dit, répondit Candide; mais il faut cultiver notre jardin."

tion. They are painful and loud. But perhaps the healthy current of life runs through the big body of mankind with more power than we realize. . . . Undisturbed by foolishness and violence, a formidably big amount of life quietly goes on, through silent people of good will, everyone of whom builds a bit of the future as it is given to him to do."[19]

This is quite true; yet we cannot expect much of this building if the people of good will do not include men who make it their business to plan on a wider basis than the surface of Candide's garden. These men are to be found among the minority who feel their fate to be associated with that of "their" civilization, because they owe what they are to the culture of their minds, and this culture to the civilization they belong to. They can find little comfort in the thought of an assured zoological existence, outside of the zone of the catastrophes. They know, moreover, that no assurance of this kind (and not even much hope of it) can be found in the present condition of our society. But they also know that the critical, revolutionary, catastrophic epochs have hitherto been those where the thinking elite of mankind bore the largest responsibility and faced the most essential task in the history of civilization: to save the best part of the cultural heritage, to prepare its palingenesis after a new chrysalis stage, and to keep the Platonic torch burning until the time comes—if ever it comes—to hand it over.

"If it ever comes"—that we cannot refrain from making this reservation forces us to contemplate the third and last line of defense against despondency, fortunately the most formidable of all, the one which by itself suffices to make the position invincible. This line is defined by the thought that, whatever destiny may have in store for us, it will always to some extent be influenced by what we do or omit to do, so that, as we cannot judge accurately of this extent, which may be marginal, the only safe course is to do our

[19] J. Huizinga, *In de Schaduwen van Morgen*, Haarlem: H. D. Tjeenk Willink, 1935, pp. 208-209.

duty, regardless of chances of success. We can always choose between fighting and fleeing; and battles are decided, not by the odds as they appear at the beginning, but by the use commanders and soldiers make of such chances as are given to them.

The problem of determinism or freedom of the will is half solved as soon as one bows to the reality of such a common experience as finding that there are things one can do and others one has to take for granted. Everybody knows that our behavior is partly determined by heredity, physical constitution, and preexisting environment, and partly by our own efforts at choosing between good and evil, error and knowledge, appropriate and inappropriate attitudes. The beginning of all wisdom, in politics as well as in the little problems of everyday life, is to find where the limit between the two zones lies. If we underrate the zone of our freedom, we run the danger of being tossed about by outward circumstances, and of renouncing the chief privilege of man, which is to act upon his environment. If we are too sanguine about our power to do this, we risk to waste our strength on knocking our heads against various walls, besides suffering the pain which punishes such foolish ventures. There are things with regard to which we are absolutely powerless, and others that depend on us entirely; but there also are many of which we cannot know how far we can influence them until we have tried, and others of which we know that, as they depend on the behavior of a collectivity of which we are a tiny part, they can surely, but only infinitesimally (or marginally) be influenced by us.

These marginal cases are the most interesting of the lot, and they raise by far the most important problem of moral philosophy. This is, for example, the problem of the voter (asking himself if his vote might change the issue), of the soldier (can my fighting decide the battle?), of the philanthropist (how can my mite matter with regard to such misery?), of the rate payer (what difference can my bit of cheating make to the state?). Manifestly, these problems cannot be solved by pure reasoning. It is true that in cases like those of the voter or the soldier, the decision may depend on a very small marginal surplus, so that nobody knows for certain whether *this* small difference might not make *all* the difference as to the outcome. It is true, also, that these problems would assume a different aspect if all people tempted to shirk reasoned as Kant would like us to do, by thinking what would happen if everybody else acted the same way. But all this reasoning is bound to remain ineffective unless one puts some kind of common weal above one's individual comfort, safety, or interest. So ultimately, all boils down to a problem of moral duty, and this is what actually happens in all the cases where the sense of duty fights a battle—be it victorious or lost—with the forces that oppose it.

Behavior guided by moral motives has always and rightly been considered as the outstanding example of the freedom of choice between attitudes, which knocks the bottom out of the belief in man's behavior being determined by circumstances. The truth, the very simple truth, is that the environment to a large extent conditions men's behavior but that men, in turn, can (and do) cause their environment to change. As Goethe said, the deal of the cards given into our hands does not depend on us, yet very different games can be played with the same set of cards.

So it is with the freedom of man with regard to the common destiny represented by history. This destiny sets us tasks, and insofar we have to submit to determination; but it depends on us to recognize these tasks or not, to accept them or not, to accomplish them or not, and insofar we are free, and can contribute to give our destiny its future shape.

So much is certain at any rate: the first requisite for a recovery from our common ailment is that we should achieve full consciousness of its character and gravity.

As to the nature of the tasks which arise out of the present crisis of our civilization, there can be little doubt if one accepts the diagnosis made in the previous chapters of this book. We have found that the decay of civilizations is caused by the growing inadequacy of institutions to fulfill the functions originally assigned to them. This, then, is the "challenge" our society will have to respond to if it is to survive: to transform its institutions in such a way that they can solve the problems which, if unsolved, will cause a general breakdown.

These institutional problems come under the general heading of social and national disintegration. However, as they become more acute, they more and more concentrate into one: to make further war impossible by creating a world government, capable of assuring the use of atomic energy for purposes other than destruction. This being the previous condition to the success of all other endeavors, economic, social, and cultural, it is *the* challenge we must respond to, *the* task assigned to us by destiny, as we know it from past and present facts. Our future destiny we shall ignore until we have finished with that task or [have] broken down under it.

In the meantime, we should not allow ourselves to be frightened by the latter prospect. Fear paralyzes; on the contrary, to keep busy at a task is the best way not to be mesmerized by the Gorgon head of menacing doom. In one respect, though, it is good that we should remain aware of the menace, and of the accelerated speed at which we travel toward the end of the spiral: whatever we can do to influence its further course should be done without halfheartedness or postponement, for there seems to be little time left.

Selective Bibliography

A relatively exhaustive bibliography of both primary and secondary works relative to de Man up to 1966 is to be found in my biography, noted below; it in turn is largely based on J. and E. de Man, eds., *Hendrik de Man: Gesamt-Bibliographie* (Schwarzwald: Ring-Verlag, 1962). Material subsequent to that date is to be found in, or referred to by, the special issue of the *Revue européenne des sciences sociales et Cahiers Vilfredo Pareto* (also noted below), which published the reports to the International Colloquium of June 1973. An indispensable source of both current bibliography and of the publication of primary and secondary materials is the *Bulletin de l'Association pour l'Etude de l'Oeuvre d'Henri de Man*, 1974- , % Section de droit public, Faculté de droit, Place de l'Université 3, 1211 Geneva 4, Switzerland.

Primary Materials

AUTOBIOGRAPHICAL MATERIALS De Man wrote successive versions, differing significantly in content and emphasis, of his autobiography. As he himself indicated, his works of theory are also specimens of "spiritual autobiography."

The Remaking of a Mind: A Soldier's Thoughts on War and Re-construction. London: Allen & Unwin; New York: Scribner's, 1919.

Après Coup: Mémoires. Brussels-Paris: Toison d'Or, 1941.

Cahiers de ma Montagne. Brussels-Paris: Toison d'Or, 1944.

Cavalier seul: Quarante-cinq années de socialisme européen. Geneva: Cheval Ailé, 1948.

Gegen den Strom: Memoiren eines europäischen Sozialisten. Stuttgart: Deutsche Verlags-Anstalt, 1953.

MAJOR SUBSTANTIVE WORKS Preference is given to publication in English, then French, but in any case original publication is indicated as well. (It might be noted that Standaard Wetenschappelijke Uitgevereij of Antwerp and Amsterdam has republished six volumes of de Man's works in Dutch under the general title of *Hendrik de Man: Persoon en Ideën*, 1974-1976.)

The Psychology of Socialism. London: Allen & Unwin, 1928. Translated by Eden and Cedar Paul from *Zur Psychologie des Sozialismus*, first published in Jena by Diederichs in 1926.

Joy in Work. London: Allen & Urwin, 1929. Translated by Eden and Cedar Paul from *Der Kampf um die Arbeitsfreude*, first published in Jena by Diederichs in 1927.

Le Socialisme constructif. Paris: Alcan, 1933. Translated by L.-C. Herbert from various sources in German, 1928-1930.

Masses et chefs. Brussels: l'Eglantine, 1937. Translated by Henri Jourdan from *Massen und Führer*, first published in Potsdam by Alfred Protte, 1932.

L'Idée socialiste. Paris: Bernard Grasset, 1935. Geneva: Presses Universitaires Romandes, 1975 (second edition). Translated by H. Corbin and A. Kojevnikov from *Die sozialistische Idee*, first published in Jena by Diederichs in 1933 (and seized upon publication by the Nazis).

L'Exécution du Plan du Travail. Antwerp: De Sikkel, 1935. (Although this work is officially by the Bureau d'Etudes Sociales, the editorial hand of de Man, its director, is clearly visible.)

Leiding: Vlaamsch Socialistisch Maandschrift, January-August 1939. (A series of articles, in Flemish, on ideological and governmental reform.)

Réflections sur la paix. Brussels-Paris: Toison d'Or, 1942. (Seized upon publication by the occupying authorities.)

Au delá du Nationalisme. Geneva: Cheval Ailé, 1946. (An expanded version of *Réflections sur la paix.*)

Jacques Coeur: argentier du roy. Bourges: Tardy, 1952.

L'Ere des masses et le déclin de la civilisation. Paris: Au Portulan, chez Flammarion, 1954. Translated by M. F. Delmas from *Vermassung und Kulturverfall: Eine Diagnose unserer Zeit,* first published in Bern by A. Francke, 1951. The original version in English, "The Age of Doom," remains unpublished except for the last chapter included in the present volume.

Secondary Materials

Claeys-Van Haegendoren, Mieke. *Hendrik de Man: Een Biographie.* Antwerp-Utrecht: De Nederlandsche Boekhandel, 1972.

Colloque international organisé par la Faculté de droit de l'Université de Genève, les 18, 19 et 20 juin 1973, sous la présidence du professeur Ivo Rens. "Sur l'oeuvre d'Henri de Man." *Actes.* 3 vols. Mimeographed. Geneva: Faculté de droit de l'Université de Genève, 1974.

————. "Sur l'oeuvre d'Henri de Man." Rapports. *Revue européenne des sciences sociales et Cahiers Vilfredo Pareto,* vol. 12, no. 31, 1974, pp. 1-303.

Dodge, Peter. *Beyond Marxism: The Faith and Works of Hendrik de Man.* The Hague: Martinus Nijhoff, 1966.

Kähler, Otto Heinrich. *Determinismus und Voluntarismus in der 'Psychologie des Sozialismus' Henrik de Mans. Zur Kritik der psychologisch begründeten Sozialismus.* Inaugural dissertation, Rupprecht-Carola-Universität, Heidelberg. Dillingen a.D.: Schwäbische Verlags-druckerei, 1929.

van Peski, A. M. *Hendrik de Man.* Bruges-Utrecht: Desclée de Brouwer, 1969.

Index

LIBRARY OF CONGRESS CATALOGING IN PUBLICATION DATA

Man, Hendrik de, 1885-1953.
A documentary study of Hendrik de Man, socialist critic of Marxism.

Bibliography: p.
Includes index.
1. Socialism—Collected works.   I.   Dodge, Peter,
1926-
HX302.M244   1979   335'.0092'4   78-70288
ISBN 0-691-03123-1